Interpreting Israeli-Jewish national themes from postcolonial, ethnic and feminist perspectives, the book offers a dialectical "negation of the negation" of hierarchical Zionist tropes, rather than a simple negative negation.

— **Uri Ram**, *Professor of Sociology,*
Ben Gurion University of the Negev, Israel

Life in Citations

In her latest book, *Life in Citations: Biblical Narratives and Contemporary Hebrew Culture*, Ruth Tsoffar studies several key biblical narratives that figure prominently in Israeli culture. *Life in Citations* provides a close reading of these narratives, along with works by contemporary Hebrew Israeli artists that respond to them. Together they read as a modern commentary on life with text, or even life under the rule of its verses. It asks questions like: How can we explain the fascination and intense identification of Israelis with the Bible? What does it mean to live in such close proximity with the Bible? And What kind of story can such a life tell?

Ruth Tsoffar is an Associate Professor of Women's Studies, Comparative Literature, and Judaic Studies at the University of Michigan.

Routledge Studies in Comparative Literature

This series is our home for cutting-edge, upper-level scholarly studies and edited collections. Taking a comparative approach to literary studies, this series visits the relationship of literature and language alongside a variety of interdisciplinary and transnational topics. Titles are characterized by dynamic interventions into established subjects and innovative studies on emerging topics.

To learn more about this series, please visit https://www.routledge.com/literature/series/RSCOL

Life in Citations

Biblical Narratives and Contemporary Hebrew Culture

Ruth Tsoffar

Routledge
Taylor & Francis Group

NEW YORK AND LONDON

First published 2020
by Routledge
52 Vanderbilt Avenue, New York, NY 10017

and by Routledge
2 Park Square, Milton Park, Abingdon, Oxon, OX14 4RN

*Routledge is an imprint of the Taylor & Francis Group, an
informa business*

First issued in paperback 2020

Library of Congress Cataloging-in-Publication Data
A catalog record for this title has been requested

ISBN: 978-0-367-25654-8 (hbk)
ISBN: 978-1-03-208912-6 (pbk)
ISBN: 978-0-429-28888-3 (ebk)

Typeset in Sabon
by codeMantra

I dedicate this book to the memory of my parents, Juliet and Naji Saffar, who when they moved from Baghdad to Israel would have never imagined that one of their daughters would move further to the United States. Their courage, resilience, and deep wisdom have been my guidance.

Contents

Figures

Acknowledgments

I am grateful to many individuals, friends, colleagues, and students who have each contributed to the development of this work at different stages of its production. I especially thank Christi Merrill, Anton Shammas, Felicia McCarren, Elliot Ginsburg, Jennifer Robertson, Yopie Prins, Ramon Stern, and Uri Ram for their friendship, support, and enthusiasm about the project. Translating poems from Hebrew to English with my dear late friend Rachel Persico was always a sheer joy. Continuous conversations with Gil Anidjar were critical to the development of the project. Meetings with Peggy McCracken to discuss numerous early drafts were always refreshing and inspiring. The book also benefited from the editorial work of Genevieve Creedon, Kayoon Jung, and Shannon Dowd at different stages. I am especially grateful to Oriol, for his intellectual spark and joy in ideas, and for his indispensable help in the translation and editing of the manuscript. And as always, I am thankful to Francesc for sharing life together.

I benefited from my year as a fellow at the Frankel Center and the conversations I had with the members of the 2011 year. Just as important were several talks that I gave at conferences and events at the University of Michigan, Ben Gurion University, Tel Aviv University, Haifa University, and Neve Ilan (Israel), University of Indiana at Bloomingdale, University of Barcelona, Harvard University, Tulane University, and The Bellagio Center in Italy.

Several fellowships and grants supported the project at different times: the College of Literature, Science, and the Arts, LSA Associate Professor Support Fund, APSF, in 2012; a Fellow Award at The Frankel Institute for Judaic Studies, 2010–2011; and a Faculty Seed Grant from The Institute for Research on Women and Gender at the University of Michigan, 2010–2011. I also had the generous support of a summer grant from the Office of the Vice President for Research, LSA, in 2000, and 2005–2009, and the Hadassah-Brandeis Institute Research Award in December 2006.

Earlier and substantially different versions of portions of some chapters appeared as articles in the following publications: "The Trajectory of Hunger: Appropriation and Prophecy in the Book of Ruth", in Roberta Sabbath, ed. Sacred Tropes, Brill 2009, pp. 257–274; "The Trauma of Otherness and Hunger: Ruth and Lot's Daughters", in Women in Judaism: A Multidisciplinary Journal Vol. 5 (1), 2007: 1–13; and "'A Land that Devours its People:' Mizrahi Writing from the Gut", in Body & Society, Vol. 12 (2): 25–55, 2006. Thanks to their editors for their permission.

Introduction
Biblical Habitus

Michal Naaman's 1974 textual artwork "*Gdi be-chalav 'Imo—'Eretz 'Okhelet Yoshveha*" (A Kid in its Mother's Milk—A Land that Devours its People),[1] besides being an incisive statement in and of itself, is a good instance of the Israeli predicament of life in citations. With mere fragments of biblical verses and on an ordinary ruled notebook page, Naaman also pencils the scope of an alarming situation in Israeli society. The two items on one page with space between them conjure causal syntax, while the title of the piece is at odds; Hebrew reads right to left, but the title goes from left to right. She also rotates the page such that the faint, ruled lines run vertically. On the right, she inscribed in dense letters Moses's spies' grim prediction about "a land that devours its people", turning the biblical adjective "*'okhelet*" (consume, devour) into a dynamic verb. On the left, almost symmetrically, it reads, "a kid in its mother's milk", part of the dietary prohibition against mixing meat and dairy.[2] What is striking are the lines above the inscriptions, like musical notation, containing the letters from above with stoppers—short vertical lines—on each side, interrupting one logical arrangement with another. By amputating the first two words of the prohibition, "don't cook" (a kid in its mother's milk), she turns the imperative into a description. Whereas the prohibition has a major religious bearing for orthodox Jews, its secular, artistic rendition serves here as an abstraction of a violated ethical code of conduct. Michal Naaman has engaged with the theme of "a Kid in its Mother's Milk" in a series of paintings and installations since 1974 (Figure I.1).

By using the *daf*, the page, as a textual lesson, Naaman reminds us of the contemporary practices of proliferation that build on the reading of the Bible. The orthodox daily reading of the page of the Talmud is a gateway to Jewish texts, and it is part of a textual calendar of reading. Alone or in a small group, rain or shine, it brings one to the page as a site of active engagement; an ultimate source of interrogation, deliberation, and knowledge production, it is associated with the pleasure and wonder of having a conversation with the "greatest Jewish minds of all-time" in rabbinic texts.[3] As if to replace the daily page, *daf yomi*, of the Talmud, Naaman's page, too, is a site of reading that teaches. Here, she takes us back to the age of elementary school, to the raw space of handwriting

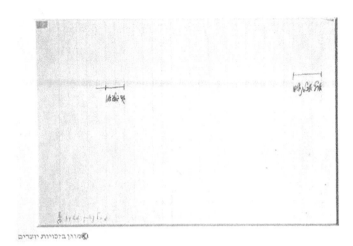

Figure I.1 Michal Naaman *"Gdi be-Chalav 'Imo—'Eretz 'Okhelet Yoshveha"*, Pencil on paper, 1974.

on yellowed, commonplace notebooks. Every Hebrew speaker is able to recognize the full narratives of these citations. In that sense, the artist builds on this familiarity. In fact, one does not need to be a religiously engaged orthodox Jew, major scholar, or intellectual; the school curriculum and the general public discourse, even when ostensibly liberal and secular, make such references an integral part of daily life and easy to decode. They are part of the rhetoric of modern Hebrew speaking and reading culture, frequently evoked in the press, the media, and the vernacular, so common that were it not for Naaman's slight variation and warning, most Israelis could string a hammock between the two quotes and reside comfortably in the uncritical space between.

It is significant that Naaman does not position the spies' narrative of "a land that devours its people" with its counter-narrative, "a land of milk and honey". Rather, she presents against and alongside the devouring land a fragment about the kid in its mother's milk. The proximity of the two expressions and their purported symmetry create a radical statement, foregrounded against the banality of children's notebooks. Indeed, the letters are scarcely visible, devoured, and saturated, like the kid, in the milk. Together the kid and the land render an atmosphere of indiscriminate devouring, a consumption that is utterly uninformed by ethics. Omitting "do not cook" from the prohibition "do not cook a kid in its mother's milk" alerts the Israeli spectator to the harsh reality, the loss of compassion for the young, and the consuming toll of the land of Israel. Naaman's novel temporality highlights the non-fictional meaning of her art, transposing her into a witness of reading whose quotes serve as visual evidence in her documentation of national culture. In its spatial syntax, on the page, she creates a new historical location of open time, where the milky blank page can hardly contain the epistemological notation of slaughtering. The kid is the sacrifice.[4] But Naaman's feminist statement also addresses the total lack of mercy towards the bereaved mother, (do not cook a kid in its mother's milk), and thus the path of destruction of both mother and child.

Naaman's sketch, indeed, suggests a cultural location through which to situate the force of the Bible, or to read, critique, and grapple with the enigmatic force of textual allusions. These two short inscriptions, rendered minimally and in the present tense, evoke the deep horror associated with their intertexts. They are pathetic, banal, and unfancy but nonetheless potent and injurious. Naaman's subsequent wall painting *"Gdi be-Chalav 'Imo"* (Gdi in its mother's) continues to interrogate the horror of the kid in its mother's milk. This work, in elongated vertical red text, is visible both in size and color. It fills the canvas in a way that escapes easy legibility. For now the signs are crowded; their meaning literally becomes dense as mother and son are mixed. Letters are curved, looped, and within the discourse of fluids, blood replaces milk. Here Naaman pushes the kid in its mother's milk a few steps further, creating an effect that recalls the fresh blood of mother and kid, but more alarmingly, she also engages in the banality that citation has produced and the way it normalizes violence. In a 1999 interview, Naaman describes the process of painterly composition as one of cooking, stating that "While I'm the one who knows nothing about cooking, I know how to take a verse from the Bible". Naaman cunningly refutes the idea of artistic talent, highlighting that she comes to the canvas wounded and lacking.[5]

My analysis of such ideas in this book leads the reader to the enormity of the predicament of collective and subjective life in relation to the biblical. When reading becomes a violent act, the question is how to read otherwise. How can we change the collective consciousness and undo reading conventions? And what is the role of teaching in changing deep-seated assumptions about reading?

The subject of this book is the increasingly widening scope of textuality among secular Israelis and the cultural fascination with the Bible. It is an internal critique of Zionism, focusing on several key biblical narratives that figure prominently in Israeli Jewish culture. I deconstruct these narratives along with works by contemporary Hebrew Israeli artists that respond to them. Together, they read as a modern commentary on life with the biblical text, or even life under the rule of its verses. This commentary also helps us understand how such modes of reading have embraced the appropriation and expropriation of heterogeneity and exclusion, continuously infusing textual reference with legitimacy.

While I am interested in interrogating these assumptions and the circumstances of their emergence, I am also deeply concerned with the threat, harm, and damage, both implicit and overt, that they exert. Critical to these concerns, therefore, is the subject of reading and the need to theorize specific modes of reading along with their attendant ideology, the degree of identification they inspire, and the attachment economy they demand. The project juxtaposes the central narratives with ethics of reading in contemporary culture, attentive to the multigenerational tradition of biblical engagement in Hebrew poems (some translated here for the first time), prose, film, and visual art. I examine this ideology at the intersection of feminist, class, ethnic, and post-Zionist perspectives and the immense discursive space that said ideology holds.

That textuality inhabits Jewish being, and that Jewish being inhabits Jewish textuality is indisputable.[6] Throughout Jewish history, the Bible has provided a strong foothold, strength of spirit to individuals and collectives, and a servile immunity from the future. The twentieth-century Israeli discourse of Hebrew modernity has consistently relied on Jewish intertextuality as a site of legitimacy and legitimization, an unfathomable source of knowledge and power that has played a crucial role in the interpretation of Jewish (diasporic) history, collective memory, calendars, and life cycles. This discourse informs many sites of nostalgia and longing for the creation of a native national culture. Hebrew intertextuality is based on a long tradition of the dialogic reading of texts, and on the debate of their meaning at different moments and locations in Jewish history. The practice is evident in the creation of a Jewish body of works that provides a domestic archive of linguistic, legal, and ethical references and principles. Over time, Jewish textual sources have come to embody an institution of knowledge for the people of the book, even within a secular framework, endorsing particular narratives, models, and codes.

What does it mean to live in such close proximity with the Bible, and what kind of story can such a life tell? How can we explain the fascination and intense identification of secular Israelis with the Bible? This practice is not limited to orthodox Jews today or to religious settlers in the West Bank, but includes secular Israelis, those who would most likely define themselves as liberal, modern, and non-observant Jews. Founding narratives have been a fixture of Jewish collective consciousness. In the Zionist enterprise, the Bible wields immense constitutive power as the primal script, giving birth to selfhood, nation, and ontology, and presenting home and sustenance with the utmost guarantee. With time, these narratives have come to inhabit a vast and highly protected site of culture, blurring the distinction between story and history, myth and national biography. They have interred Jewish Israeli consciousness beneath layers of morality, legitimacy, righteousness, and banality, enforced from within by privileged cultural authorities, institutions, and myriad models and practices of identification. Along with the life thesis that they have mobilized, they have also constructed deep-seated, taken-for-granted cultural assumptions about the universality of the Bible and its ultimate value in generating the "literate" subject—knowledgeable, humane, and benevolent.

The Israeli discourse of Hebrew modernity builds on the already privileged authority of Jewish textuality, turning it into an ever-dynamic and productive site of legitimacy. Everyday life and language (or "doing language") are performative acts (Butler 1990), saturated with allusions and references to textual realities operating as part of the same cultural continuum. Drawing so heavily on the written word, on a long tradition of textual debates, commentaries, and interpretations, has constituted a bibliophilic culture. Narratives are coded in the naming system—people's names, the names of cities and streets, the life cycle of the individual, the communal calendar and holy days—together, they map and further mobilize a multi-referential construct with layers upon layers of meaning. They have potentially provided a political claim of historical ownership, territorial gain, and lasting presence. They have also led to the emergence of an embodied, textually situated mindset. They have produced the *Hebrew reading subject.*

The Bible industry, as I argue here, refers to the increasing commodification of the Bible and the different emerging objects and appropriation of Biblical narratives, predicated upon the identification of the Hebrew reading subject both *with* and *as* its protagonists, landscape, or language, and in the service of nationalist and capitalist interests. After becoming fluent in the Hebrew language, along with the process of 'Ivrut, Hebraization, it has become a national habitus, easily consumable, providing a shared logic and system of signs through which to generate meaning and respond to life. In this Bible culture, individuals' cultural context has been embodied in their comportment as doxa, a taken-for-granted "second nature" space.

When Identification Generates Identity: "Click Here to Get Biblical!"

Among secular Israelis, the Bible has gained prominence over the post-biblical texts. "Tanakh 929", for example, is an online endeavor that seeks to further invest Hebrew readers in the biblical reading experience, named after the number of the chapters in the books of the Hebrew Bible (December 2014). It frames the undertaking as a "challenge" for daily self-improvement, akin to dieting or exercise. Following a daily schedule, participants read one chapter, discussing it online or in person with friends or colleagues. "Why Tanakh?" the website asks.

> It is a foundational text, a common denominator on an international level, whose stories and ideas reach out and echo within our own lives, to this very day. As a book, Tanakh is amazingly rich: enjoyable, adventurous, and moving – but also thought-provoking and controversial.

"Tanakh 929" is thus a project that smuggles biblical content into a secular framework. They simultaneously presents the Bible as *only a book* and *the only book*, encapsulating the raptures of all of literature (romance! intrigue!).

In approaching the Bible in purely literary terms, 929 is complicit in a false neutering of the text. The project makes proto-nationalist fervor and spectacle accessible to those for whom spirituality would otherwise be a barrier. Gurevitch argues that the Book's "focusing on that 'primary' story does not necessarily mean it had a determinist power of a 'mental gene' that permeated the Judaic mind. Rather...the power of the story lies in its readoption by the various Zionist movements" (1997, 204). Thanks to rabid decontextualization, the text, and its habitus can now be freely applied to any fact or sphere of life. The invitation to *Torah-ba-salon* (Torah in the salon) builds on the imagined community of the Bible. 929 therefore represents not a singular mode of secularization of the religious so much as an insidious/uncanny injection of religious content into the secular. The website's winking subtext is clear; now, even atheists, leftists, intellectuals, and queers can be a part of the discussion, provided they follow the general indigenous Zionist scripts. And indeed, participants find themselves unwittingly duped into Zionism, as the culmination of the current reading "cycle" coincides with the seventieth anniversary of Israel.

The Bible industry has continued to bloom through endeavors both big and small, collective and personal. On more broadly national terms, Prime Minister Benjamin Netanyahu launched the Jerusalem Bible Operation on April 13, 2012, and was its first participant, having selected the verse that most thoroughly represented him. The objective is to engage individuals in claiming "ownership" of one verse as a way to promote the world's "best-selling book" as a global treasure of the shared "origin story of all humanity". As critically, this marketing campaign assumes that one can be reduced to a biblical citation, as if to say: tell me your verse and I will tell you who you are. It carries a promise of being "included" in the reading community of the Bible, an I.D., attaching names to verses (in different colors!) within the planned House of the Bible, in Jerusalem. Another of the website's intentions is to expand the translation project of the Bible beyond the 2035 languages and dialects that already exist to languages such as Korean and Georgian.[7]

For Israel's fiftieth jubilee celebration, the Ministries of Education and Culture initiated an international competition of painting Bible scenes. The best of the 800,000 submissions were included in the book *Children of the World Illustrate the Bible*. Anyone who purchases fifty or more verses (as gifts for friends or relatives) receives a copy of the book. In addition to producing citations intended to communicate representation, a simultaneous economy emerges around the Bible itself as capital.[8] The incentive behind such an operation is tied back to the biblical and emblematic Zionist vision of Israel as *Or La-Goyim*, "light unto the nations", the key metaphor from the prophet Isaiah as a spiritual and moral beacon to the entire world. Present-day Zionism capitalizes on this notion as a modern version of state- and city-centered ideology. The number of examples is indeed overwhelming, but I will add a few more to further develop the scope of the condition of citationality.

Obviously, electronic communication and internet data have contributed immensely to the mushrooming of biblical sites. The site *Textologia* includes a vast number of citations, articles, and films on different subjects.[9] *Mikranet* (Bible-net) is a huge secular search engine for everything biblical, mostly for educational purposes, with a specific section, "Israelis speak Tanakh". It includes texts, class material, news, articles, films, and videos; it also makes links to other subjects and disciplines, like biblical interpretation, linguistics, archaeology, literature, and art. *Mikranet* links to other sites, currently introducing the 929 website and its specific films and content.[10] Another such large undertaking is the Bible Marathon: an international race in October of 2019. The forty-two-kilometer run reenacts a biblical antecedent of a messenger from the tribe of Benjamin bringing news of defeat in the battle against the Philistines (1 Samuel 4: 12).[11]

Critical perspectives on Israeli history among artists and filmmakers are also coded through biblical narratives translated into contemporary frameworks. The satirical show "This is Sodom" (2010), by *Eretz Nehederet*, is a comedy about the last three days before the destruction of the city[12]; *Ha-Yehudim Ba'im* (2014) "The Jews are Coming", by Natalie Marcus and Asaf Beiser, is a controversial satirical show that reclaims ownership over the stories from religious people, as one of the producers argues: "This is our heritage and there is no reason we can't deal with and dig into the material of what made us, our DNA" (http://www.jewishhumorcentral.com/2018/03/the-jews-are-coming-controversial.html).

Personal projects have followed. Letters and citations play an important visual role in a park portraying biblical stories that opened on Sep. 23, 2018, in Northern Israel.[13] *Mikhmanim* is an ecological biblical village in Galilee that makes nature accessible to Israelis "through the Bible" and through the experience of returning to the past.[14] Dr. Hagai Ben Artzi guides tours in biblical sites as a way to teach the Bible on foot. The bookshelf of biblical stories for children is another problematic place: children are exposed from young ages to abridged versions of these narratives in many formats—textual, visual, and audible—and these materials take precedence in their imagination (Shalev 1985, 1994; Semel 2015).[15] In 1985, Meir Shalev published his satiric work, *Bible Now* (1985); between 2003 and 2009, Ephraim Sidon wrote *The Bible in Rhymes*, a five-volume satirical series of biblical narratives, illustrated and in verse. It was later produced by Israeli Educational Television

(Sidon 2003–2009). Surely, such works bring refreshing innovations to the narratives, challenging rigid religious and heteronormative modes of interpretation. As Yael Zerubavel argues, they contribute to turning the past into a dynamic site of collective memory and to the general contemporization and popularization of the Bible among secular Israelis.[16] But often, like in the case of Nava Semel, a feminist who attempts to introduce less patriarchal meanings by writing a modern secular commentary to the Bible, an even more intensified degree of identification can be enacted. While she subversively "corrects" several narratives, she also strongly claims: "I want to enter the Bible... my self's face is so reflected there" (Semel 2015).[17]

Doing Reading, Doing Bible

Edmond Jabes, the Egyptian Jewish poet, asserts that "Judaism is an extended lesson in reading", a position that has been approximated traditionally through the practice of the daily page of Talmud and Gmara'. Jabes's books tend to announce themselves *as* books, with titles like *The Book of Questions* or *The Book of Resemblances*, about the book, situating "the book" as the condition/substance of Jewish practice. But Jabes's poetry tells us that even beyond ritualized, structured engagement with Jewish texts, the Modern ethos of Judaism is still a figurative extension, a lesson of a lesson on reading within a long discursive process of interrogation, not only about *what* is being read, but also about how to read, and where, when, with whom, and with what, all possible extended questions that together constitute the act of reading. In other words, reading is never a given but rather an act that continues to generate possibilities.

Jabes's idea of an "extended lesson" can teach us about the difference between being a reader and *doing* reading, a process of becoming the *reading subject* of Judaism. Naaman, like Jabes, comes to the page not as a scheduled reader. She comes from within the Zionist reading habitus of liberalism and modernity. Her piece utilizes the full tension of that which Nakassis attributes to the act of citation, "a play of sameness and difference, identity and alterity, an interdiscursive calibration of an event of citing and a cited event, [which] is reflexive about that very fact" (Nakassis 2013). I wish to situate this phenomenon of Israeli citationality and elaborate on its unique features within the Zionist and the neo-Zionist climate.

Citation has been theorized preliminarily, not within textual traditions, but rather within the broader framework of the philosophy of language, communication, and speech acts. A representation of representation, it is a performance that Butler sums up as that "which constructs the social fiction of its own psychological interiority" (Butler 1988, 528). I will develop this further here. Prior to Butler, both J. L. Austin and Jacques

Derrida had approach the subject of citation as a critical aspect of communication and speech acts. Austin develops the notion of the speech act and performance within linguistic rules. He introduces the performative utterance, different from the constative, descriptive utterance in that it is able "to accomplish something through speech itself" (Cf. Derrida 1988, 13). The pronouncing of actions (to declare, promise, order, and vow) results, under "ordinary" circumstances, in performing them within the conventions of language and genre.[18] An utterance is an act, an illocutionary act that highlights the capacity of language to act and do things. Literary performative utterances hover between language and event; they perform acts. As such, citation is genetic, natural, arbitrary, and derivative (Austin 1962; Derrida 1988; see also Culler 1997).

Derrida elaborates that every language is communicative, performative, and ritualistic, and that different performative acts, ordinary or not, are all part of "general iterability", which together establish discursive practices. Language is performative in the sense that it doesn't just transmit information but performs acts by its repetition of established discursive practices or ways of doing things. Such possibilities, versions, and quotations of ritual are constituted and constitutive through repetition and iterability, moving from communication to performance. In other words, "for something to be a sign it must be able to be cited and repeated in all sorts of circumstances" (Culler 1997). Reading practices signify and have an important role in the formation of the subject. *Citational reading, therefore, similar to writing, builds on a reiterative structure of signification* (Disch and Hawkesworth 2016, 45). The structure of repetition and iterability is critical to making the sign into a homogeneous space of communication. Such a structure enables the sign to be the same but also to differ and defer. For Nakassis, this is a critical aspect of citationality, defined as "… a meta/semiotic of citation… one powerful means through which language acts, through which repetition begets difference, through which newness comes into the world" (Nakassis 2013, 54).

Butler further expands the definition of citation to the realm of identity and its formation. Building on Derrida's thesis that performativity of language is not a linguistic category but a social-political one built on the mechanical economy of citation, she focuses on gender, body, and sexuality. Citation, for Butler, means that "the practice by which gendering occurs, the embodying of norms, is a compulsory practice, a forcible production and a continuous one" (Butler 1993, 231). Butler demonstrates that performativity is not just about speech acts, but also about bodily acts. Language and performative language along with the force of power, constraints, and authority establish discursive practices, embodied epistemologies, and categories of identity. "This iterability implies that 'performance' is not a singular 'act' or event, but a ritualized production, and chained ritual reiterated under and through constraint…"

(Butler 1993, 95). She is concerned with the attempt to denaturalize citation in the "lab of norm" (Ibid. 10).

The study of citationality in Israeli culture provides us the opportunity to ask questions about the theory of subjectivity and the making of the Hebrew reader. The process of the construction of the reading subject along with the intentional and unintentional doing and undoing of the Bible is at the unique intersection of religion, modernity, and nationalism. Using Simone de Beauvoir's thesis that a woman is not born a woman but becomes a woman, one can analogously claim that one is not born a reader of Jewish text, but becomes a reader, and that to read as an Israeli Jew not only constitutes identity, but also differentiates and refines for us the idea of "reading difference" not only among different literate, textual cultures, but also between different moments in Jewish history. Regardless of the halachic question of who is a Jew, the category of Jewish consciousness and mindset in the modern context is highly relevant. Belonging and the cohesive boundaries of the community are being defined along different parameters.

In this work, therefore, I am engaged in the study of not only what the Bible says but also what it does. Ritualistic, citational reading of the Bible—the word, the verse, *daf*, the page, *parashat hashavua*, or the weekly portion of the Torah—does not tell us about the historical development of reading and the different meanings of rituals, but it does help us understand the *reiterative structure of signification* (Disch and Hawkesworth 2016). Reading acts, like gender, derive from reading discourses. They are reactualized and reproduced following an invented cultural script. The ritualized, disciplined process of performing is perceived as the natural process of forming the uniquely Jewish/Israeli self.

This may be similar to the Hebrew, Israeli cultural performance of textual citation and intertextuality, what one might call "doing Bible", a style and method of textual, biblical engagement that follows, as with gender, endless performative acts of reading and signification. Insofar as they substantiate the meaning of a text, these acts also adapt it to contemporary systems of power. Reading is a phenomenon that is continuously produced and producing. It is a compulsory, forcible production but also provides limited space for agency and freedom. It is possible to claim that the Israeli performance of "doing Bible" plays a constitutive role in the production of the subject. Along with its historiography, gaps in memory and history, intertextuality, translation, and literacy and oral storytelling, it has evolved into a discursive logic and solid model/structure of cultural meaning-making. In the fundamental structure that undergirds subjection in Israeli Jewish culture, citationality gains its power from the historicity and intertextuality of reading. Reading citationally, similar to what Butler (1990) claims about gender, is that which qualifies the subject for life within the matrix of Israeli cultural intelligibility.

The protagonist of Udi Sharabani's short story "Those who need to enter, enter" (2009) features a man walking. He is an ageless man walking with pockets loaded with notes, texts, and letters that threaten to explode.[19] The bowed position of his head adds to the acuteness of the total subservience of the walking body, total resignation to a harsh verdict of "doing textuality".

> Someone who once was someone passed me in the street. He wore a coat and all this came out of his pockets. Everything came out of his pockets. His thoughts fell out like papers that went through the laundry, that were kept forgotten in the pocket, crumpled, crumbling, letters that spread on the paper, letters that now came out of the lines of the page even if he did not want that, even if he made efforts to write between the lines. He passed me on the street, and it fell out of his pockets. Spilled out like the confetti of thoughts mourning. ...
>
> Udi Sharabani, "Those who need to enter, enter", 2009

Sharabani's body has become the emblematic archive, which by now houses an embodied cosmogony: he is a walking Kolboink, all-containing vessel, a person who indiscriminately keeps everything (see Chapter 2). Coming in and coming out, a gushing of life's confetti which has lost its meaning, he is anxious to keep it all, preserve it, protect it, make it part of his body, if only he could.

The Hebrew term "*tsatetet*" more closely manifests the condition of citationality in Israeli culture and emerges from within the textual practices of reading and writing. It also conveys more closely my idea of citation as a life condition of this habitus. The root *tstt* means to cite, to quote, and to allude. Already in the Bible, the form of *pa'elet* follows morphologically the semantic pattern of names of diseases, disorders, or syndromes, such as *baheret*, bright spots, a skin disorder, or *tsara'at*, and leprosy (Leviticus 14, 56). Modern Hebrew substantiated this form with terms such as *kalevet* for rabies, *tsahevet*, for hepatitis, *sakeret*, for diabetes, or *gazezet*, for ringworm.[20] Other terms were added, conveying excessive, exaggerated conditions or acts. Rubik Rosenthal describes the historical development of the *pa'elet* pattern, distinguishing between the vocabulary of diseases, and that of speech (*daberat*, for example, for excessive speaking or *Chatsefet*, the outbreak of *chutspa*), and a third of office and bureaucracy (*sachevet*, a more recent term, the red tape and procrastination). "*Tsatetet*" hovers extensively between a condition and a disease, one of citing, reciting, quoting, reiterating, and re-using a phrase, and is at the heart of language and communication.[21] It alerts us, like Sharabani's story, to the economy of excess that moves from simply generative and rote to progressively clinical and even pathological.[22]

As a disease, *tsatetet* continually places the Bible as the obvious reference of daily, secular life, reinforcing it as a law of nature. In order to understand the extent of this attachment, it is important to comprehend the general role of Zionism and especially of the Bible in the Israeli Zionist imagination. For that, it is also important to draw the contours of Jewish life after Auschwitz and the massive displacement of waves of immigrants from Eastern Europe to Israel, shifting the imagined community of the Jewish people against Europe an communism, anti-Semitism, British colonialism, and increasing pan-Arabism. Zionism came to heal the Jewish problem, to restore sanity after the insanity of those accelerated years of the first half of the twentieth century. The Bible, the mother's gift of all gifts of the imagined "becoming", grounds language, calendar, history, time, and territory. It effectively provides, as Naaman's art suggests, a conceptual page on which to dwell.

Such a place of dwelling is the principal locus for the embodiment of social categories. Pierre Bourdieu's analysis of the habitus helps us think about the Bible as a unique book habitus. It is, as he tells us, a "structured structure that generates principles of practices of everyday life, while at the same time, it is structuring a structure of appropriation and incorporation" (Bourdieu 1995, 17). Bourdieu's thesis explains the transition of lived experience from a physical space to a mental structure in the way it has been appropriated as a privileged category of perception and appreciation. In the Israeli context, the book is the objective category that has provided a cognitive schema and principle/s of socio-cultural order, of perception, thought, and action. Canonic and sealed, the Bible asserts the origin story along with the history of the people, providing, Yerushalmi suggests, "a constantly renewable lease of life" (Yerushalmi 1989, 12). He develops this idea:

> Read through from Genesis through Chronicles it offered not only a repository of law, wisdom, and faith, but a coherent narrative that claimed to embrace the whole of history from the creation of the world to the fifth century B.C.E., and, in the prophetic books, a profound interpretation of that history as well.
>
> (Ibid. 1989, 14)

For Yerushalmi, the transmission or reiteration of history within the sacred texts, as sacred texts, is "a capsule history at its best" (Ibid. 12). Accordingly, not only is it the case that "the history of the biblical period is present in the Bible itself" (Ibid. 17), but also that the Bible links and equates the meaning of history, memory of the past, and the writing of history, whereby "they are held together in a web of delicate and reciprocal relationships" (Ibid.). Yerushalmi highlights reading practices as a mechanism of continuous transmission of Jewish learning and memory that replace history. For us, it explicates the phantasmagoric quality of the Bible in grounding one in time and place, chronological and divine.

The textual order that the Bible provides is rooted in the consistency of the history of reading and the shared acquired system of meaning it has produced. Analogous to the home, the biblical habitus makes moral, relevant distinctions between good versus bad, and us versus them and thus marks social and national boundaries (Bourdieu 1995). With its authority, it further regulates and organizes bodies, gestures, and ways of thinking about life. This doxa, the taken-for-granted belief in the order of things, as Bourdieu theorizes, is perceived as natural and non-arbitrary, giving legitimacy to the prevailing understanding of the world.

In the same way that the habitus of the body is engendering, the habitus of the Book is generative and producing. To what extent can we claim that gender construction is similar to the construction of a readership? They are obviously different: dichotomies and hierarchies of gender work in different ways, mapping different social arrangements and degrees of obligation, and yet, some aspects of their productive mechanisms and formation are similar. In both, the chain of iterations constitutes the power of the discourse. Reading, like femininity, is "not the product of a choice, but the forcible citation of a norm, one whose complex historicity is inassociable from relations of discipline, regulation, punishment" (Butler 232). As we will see, incorporating the reading of the Bible into the school curriculum disciplines the production of the norms of citation and its performance. To an extent, like with gender, we achieve subjectivity through it, helping both to recreate it and to reinforce textual codes, norms, and conventions. Moving from the body to the Book still gives centrality to similar patriarchal ideologies that center around issues of reproduction, genealogy, and kinship. Categories of sex and gender are conflated and understood as laws of nature and the Law of the Bible. The normalization of the practice is invisible.

Note that Judaism is a religion that is based in orthopraxy, in ritualistic and liturgical conduct rather than in orthodoxy in faith and grace, like in Christianity. Practice is immanent to the very principles of the religion. One is implicated in it through acts rather than through belief. Although to be Jewish entails more than reading the Bible, in the Zionist mindset, the constituted subjectivity that the Bible offers to its reader is the foundation on which one is made to feel implicated in the culture, the history, and the tradition. Even among purportedly secular Israelis, the Bible creates a fluid space where orthodox knowledge becomes secular and further naturalized as part of the vernacular.

And indeed, engagement with and close reading of biblical narratives has proven a highly productive locus through which to understand contemporary Israeli culture, especially the volatile hybrid of religious and nationalist discourses. Nonetheless, one of the challenges of this work is how to assess the impact of repeated reanimation of biblical allusions

on subjectivity, gender, and minorities and how to account for its violence. Moreover, it is to assess how issues such as the transition from
the so-called collective nationality, melting pot, and homogeneity, to a
diverse, heterogeneous, society have altered the meaning of these narratives. What other efforts have been made to diversify reading beyond
canonical, institutional, and patriarchal practices, and how? And how
can we read the subtle codes that distinguish between religious and secular reading?

In my earlier book, *The Stains of Culture: An Ethno-Reading of
Karaite Jewish Women,* (Tsoffar 2006), I discuss how, since the eighth
century, Karaite Jews, followers of a branch of Judaism, have negotiated
cultural differences through their distinctive approach to reading and
interpreting the Bible. During a time of schism and the emergence of new
sects in Judaism, one could argue that ideological differences of religious
correctness, class, ethnicity, and sexuality, were all articulated through
the politics of reading and halakhic exegesis. Living in such proximity
to the text, disagreements between reading communities are reified as
differences in textual meaning. Somewhat similarly, in the early years
of the twentieth century, cultural differences were negotiated through
passionately written arguments, with a unique emphasis on nationalism
and secularism. Within the intensified national debates of Israeli/Jewish
society, literature was not only one of the primary media through which
people participated in the negotiation of Jewish identity and the future of
the Jewish state, but also an instrument for creating a radical shift in collective consciousness. Hebrew literature regarded itself as the "true and
legitimate custodian of national literary creativity" (Miron 1984, 49).
"It appointed itself a watchman unto the House of Israel, an institution
responsible for the moral and cultural well-being of the nation" (Ibid.
49–50).[23] It sought to become the nation's frame of reference, a political
guide with programmatic and didactic functions.

In the next section, I will provide a brief historical account of the
debate around the place of Jewish religion and the Bible within Israeli
culture.

A Nationality Debate: *"The War for Religion and a War against Religion"*

The configuration of nationality and religion is unique to Israel and to
the way Israeli citizenship is being constructed. The question was how
to translate religion into political and civil society. At the core of the Zionist enterprise was, and still is, the debate concerning this relationship
between the people and its religion. Although the Zionist movement did
not seek to continue the Jewish tradition, it obviously aspired to build on
its foundations. Most active members of the Zionist movement were not
only socialist and secular, but rejected the religious halakhic tradition.

Theodor Herzl was adamant about the total separation of religion and state, envisioning a democratic and modern state modeled after Western countries like Germany. In *The Jewish State*, he famously pronounced,

> Faith unites us, knowledge gives us freedom. We shall therefore prevent any theocratic tendencies from coming to the fore on the part of our priesthood. We shall keep our priests within the confines of their temples in the same way as we shall keep our professional army within the confines of their barracks.
>
> (1896)

Nevertheless, in his opening speech of the first congress, Herzl said, "Zionism is our return to Judaism even before there is a return to the Jewish State" (Ibid.).

Half a century later, David Ben Gurion, in his sixth year as prime minister of the established State of Israel, revealed,

> The religious debate in Israel has been further complicated by the very specific nature of the Jewish religion....The existing arrangement is a compromise, which obviously, like any compromise, cannot be satisfying. This compromise was established in order to prevent a religious war. Both *the war for religion and a war against religion*, which could deeply harm the ingathering of the peoples, which is a top priority of the State.
>
> (1954 c/f Tevet 1997, my emphasis)

The "arrangement" refers to the inclusion of the religious parties in the Knesset, an act that has since redefined the unique texture of Israeli democracy.

Indeed, with increasingly massive waves of immigration, Ben Gurion was under acute pressure to find a pragmatic solution to the secular/religious schism. He was looking for a pragmatic solution, according to Durkheim's sociology, for the glue or cohesive force that would replace religion and still unify the fragments of the nation (Durkheim 1995).[24] In his despair, he initiated in October 1951 a private, yet highly sensational, visit to the "Chazon Ish" (Rabbi Avrohom Yeshaya Karelitz), the leading orthodox authority at the time. His urgent question to him was, "How will religious and non-religious Jews live together in this land without exploding from within? How will we live together?" (Melamed 2013; Cohen 2015).[25] Chazon Ish's answer was a talmudic teaching about an encounter between two camels, one with a heavy load (of commitments and commandments) and one with no load, and there being room for only one camel on the road. He concluded that the right-of-way belonged to the one with the heavy load. Chazon Ish reinforced implicitly the common perception that unlike the fullness of religion, secularism is an empty wagon, a self-centered, narcissistic, and hollow way of life. Thus, religious Orthodox Zionism advocated *medinat halakha*, that the people of Israel were created for the sake of the Torah, following the slogan, after Rabbi Mohilever: "The Land of Israel, for the people of Israel, according to the Torah of Israel". On the other side, the idea spearheaded by Ehad Haam was that Judaism had evolved out of the Jewish spirit and its national culture. The essence of his secular Judaism was that the Torah served the people.

This process reduced the political discourse to a binary model of religious/secular, and as is often the case, failed to acknowledge the existence of other groups.[26] Critically, the *masortim*, traditionists, belong to an ethno-national identity of Jews, mostly of Middle Eastern and North African origins, who represent a diverse approach to Judaism along a more relaxed scale of orthodoxy. In 2006, it was estimated that 39% of Israelis identify as masortim. They strongly espouse their Jewish identity as part of the values of the Jewish family and community, with a deep, loyal sense of belonging to its history and faith. Whereas in the past sociologists included *masortim* within the religious group, most now consider them a cohesive group of their own, at the forefront of modern changes and even a post-secular perspective in Israel (Liebman and Yadgar 2009; Yadgar 2010). Yadgar asserts that *masortim* articulate a critique against Israeli secularism as white, imported, neutral, and dependent on the state to define Jewishness (Yadgar 2011).

As early as 1950, Uzzi Ornan, an active supporter of the separation of church and state, founded the League against Religious Coercion in Israel. Ornan was a prominent leader of the Canaanites, an ideological movement that was founded in 1939 and in spite of its small size had a major impact among intellectuals of the period. It advocated a Hebrew rather than a Jewish nation, not to the exclusion of Jews, but to the inclusion of all people of Canaanite origins. It highlighted the Canaanite antiquity of the Bible within the ancient Near East rather than its Jewish actuality. Ornan's book, "*'Tsipornav shel ashmadai' Shmonah Prakim be-Chiloniyut*", The Claws of Asmodai: Eight Chapters in Secularism (1999), is an important manifesto about the deterioration of Israeli democracy. Ornan seeks to educate his reader, providing ways to identify the camouflaged power of religion and giving very specific instructions as to how to push against anti-democratic legislation (Ornan 1999).

And yet, the definition of secularism still needs elaboration. Talal Asad's critique of the model that relies on a Western definition that positions secularism at the center of the project of modernity as a linear, neutral process tightly responding to religion or emerging from it. As such, it is universal and hegemonic, responsible for the emergence of other institutions and systems of thought such as "constitutionalism, moral autonomy, democracy, human rights, civil equality, industry, consumption, and freedom of the market—and secularism" (Asad 2003, 13). Asad proposes to situate secularism in particular historical contexts, as a dynamic, heterogeneous category, and to be attentive to hybrid, often competing and oppositional principles that presuppose its discourse (Asad 2003). Indeed, Israeli historians, sociologists, political scientists, and anthropologists have taken into consideration Asad's critique in different ways, seeking to redefine Jewish secularism, writing its historiography, periodization, and denaturalizing its meaning (Sorotzkin 2014; Ohana 2017). Sorotzkin, following Asad, suggests that secularism initially represents a discourse with a unique grammatical system that draws on mythical and sacred dimensions. It is this discourse that has mobilized the basic categories of "secularism" as a liberal, political doctrine that uses violence in order to justify its "universal rational foundations" (Sorotzkin 2014, 297). Sorotzkin concludes, therefore, that Jewish modernity and Jewish secularism are a product of invasive modernization that took place in the sites and centers of Jewish existence (Ibid. 309). Nonetheless, in Asad's analysis, Israelis do not comprise an obvious case of secularism for they do not recognize the collective mythological origin of biblical narratives and belief systems (Asad 2003).

The practice of citation and the illusion of secularism provide Israelis a misleading sense of autonomy and individuality, assumed to be free of religious coercion and ideology. In her recent article, "Here is our Torah: The Six Commandments to the Proud Secular", Eva Illouz, a sociologist at the Hebrew University, attempts to show that the secular wagon of secularism is not only unempty, but that it is an "expansive, moralistic, intellectual and existential option, that has nothing for which to apologize" (Illouz 2014, 8). Acknowledging that the contemporary individual crisis of identity is intensified by the increasing zeal of religion, she argues that crises and the chaotic challenges that they pose foster a rewarding way of life. The doubts, restlessness, and critical perspective, the desire to know and to even accept the fragility of this knowledge, render one able to "walk through crisis". This unconditional empathy and the ability for total identification, she asserts, enable one to become the Other. Illouz's postmodern analysis of the secular, however romantic and optimistic, gives us an idea about the way the secular is imagined in the perplexing reality of Israeli culture.

Ben Gurion, following Durkheim, was looking for a means to bind individuals together in the secular, modern democratic nation, effectively generating social solidarity, altruism, and religious ethics. The Bible presented an ideal solution. It first had to be reintroduced and reinvented within a secular and national framework. Indeed, recovering the roots and reconstructing the past were critical for the creation of the new "imagined community". For that, as Zerubavel asserts, "The Zionist collective memory elevated the period of antiquity as the Hebrew nation's heroic past and enhanced its commemorative density" (Zerubavel 1995, 215). The fact that the people of Israel were sovereign during the time of the Bible (unlike during times of exile, in the Talmud, for example) was significant in making the Bible into a native, etiological master-narrative.

The Bible was Ben Gurion's mandate, and along with nationhood, formed the two pillars of the Jewish ethos.[27] Motivated by the deep fear that secular Israelis would carry "an empty wagon", he made critical decisions regarding the character of the public and political spheres. He also legislated the study of Bible lessons in the national curriculum of secular education, starting in the second grade, which, in 2002, was changed to the first grade.[28] The Bible Study Group in Ben Gurion's residence during the Fifties and Sixties consisted of the leading biblical scholars of the time. They studied strategies for Israeli wars and settlements through the wars of Joshua Bin Nun (in Ben Gurion's Diaries Cf. Ram 2006, 43). This tradition of Bible Study Group has been repeated by numerous politicians and is continued by Netanyahu.

From its early formation, Zionism advocated a modern and democratic state. And yet, Zionism encapsulated a broad range of positions and political diversity. Scholars propose several periods in Zionist development towards religion and democracy. Sociologist Uri Ram identifies three different periods in Zionist sociology, arguing that classical Zionism was replaced in large part with two competing alternatives: the democratic post-Zionism and the ethno-national neo-Zionism, which is partly religious and is driven to contest globalization. Both classical and ethno-national Zionism draw heavily on the Bible.

The special Israeli formula of religion/democracy has since redefined Israeli secularism, democracy, and citizenship: it has created fierce debates that are frequently exacerbated at different political moments. For example, Shafir and Peled in their 2002 analysis suggest that the huge wave of secular Russian immigration in the nineties would lead to a process of liberalization, and even to the possibility of a creating a private, individual religion (Ibid. 2002). Yet, with the new 2018 nationality bill that the Israeli Knesset has adopted, Israel has restated that it is a Nation-State for the Jewish people, excluding all national minorities through a motion that came to block any possible vision of liberalization and democratization. The law fails to acknowledge equality, minority rights, and democracy.

Mobilized by the emancipating and liberating frenzy of the Zionist revolution, Hebrew writers came to writing with many imperatives and moral obligations. They painted it in rhetorical colors with flourishes of pathos. As many literary scholars have noted, it was Hebrew literature that gave birth to Modern Jewish nationalism (Miron 1984; Brinker 1989; Harshav 1993; Shaked 1993; Hever 2002). "It is important to remember that Hebrew literature was the precursor of Zionism", Zivah Shamir reminds us. "Even today, it is almost the only glue that can unite, in an immigration country, people who have no common background,

and turn them into one people" (Sheleg 2015).[29] Menachem Brinker
goes so far as to claim that it is the involvement in Hebrew literature
that has driven immigrating Jews of the Second and Third Aliyah to Palestine and not to America. "Who were the peoples of Second Aliyah?"
he is asking as a matter of fact, declaring that they are "all readers of
(Hebrew) literature" (Brinker 1989).

Indeed, Hebrew literature was part of the Zionist solution. It was, as
Ahad Ha'am proclaimed, the prerequisite for achieving the "normalcy"
of life as a nation (Miron Ibid.). Writing in Hebrew has had its own
phantasmagoric dimension—a sacred, sublime, and passionate act of
inscribing the protocol of the revolution. Now, it was is written down
in an ancient language, its undertaking articulated and grounded in the
broader context of Jewish history. Hebrew literature had a major impact
on drawing the demographic map of the Jewish people. Writers and literary scholars played key roles in secularizing the theological revolution,
using literature to provide an engaged platform for the normalization
of the Jewish collective and the articulation of socialism, modernity,
and nationalism in Judaism. In the transition from religious to secular,
Hebrew literature and its textual production of books, magazines, and
daily press helped to constitute the cohesive force that unified the people
and replaced the authority of the religious institution. In the realm of
cinema, the notion of national homogeneity was developed through Zionist narratives that were widely disseminated (Shohat 1989).

The Hebrew Bible and its narratives laid the foundations of this language revolution. But even more so, Uri Ram, a sociologist, emphasizes
the uses of the Bible within a historical framework, asserting that Zionist historiography relies primarily on the role of historians, especially
the so-called "Jerusalem branch" headed by the historian and former
minister of education, Ben-Zion Dinur. They were the "captains" of the
pragmatic, narrative shift in their conceptualization of the Jewish past
(Ram 2006, 28). Intersecting his thesis with the politics of knowledge
and the sociology of politics, Ram historicizes the unique Zionist invented tradition, arguing:

> Modernity did not emancipate Jewish nationalism from its con-
> straints of two thousands years ... Jewish nationalism did not
> emerge out of Jewish identity, but rather was cast to it as a life saver,
> lest it be swept away by the turbulence of its time.

(Ibid. 31)

Moving from inventing tradition to promoting it, the educational system, Ram shows, implemented a civil program for the creation of a new
national Jewish subject (Ibid.).

The Sabra kid was to bear the brunt of this history, a preconceived
blank slate who merely awaited the revered teachers of the nation to

burden her with meaning. The education of the first generation was carried out as a mission of the civilizing process with a redemptive horizon. It sought to blend the national dimension with the religious in the holiday calendar, life calendar, and overall school curriculum. It advocated the melting pot ideology as a supreme righteous model that complemented cultural socialism, collectivity, and equality. The State Education Law was instituted in June, 1953 by Dinur. The study of the Bible, along with the subject of *moledet*, cultural Israeli geography, and Israeli Jewish history, distinguished from world history and geography, were sanctified to fit the national and civic ethos. The historical, geographical, and biblical concepts were translated into a national language, saturated with love and passion and with an explicit emphasis on extreme "affective economies". For Sara Ahmed, emotions or affects are cultural products in an external, horizontal space of communication. The impact of relationships between the ordinary and the fantastic are formed through attachments, objects, and bodies. Her economic model works on a "metonymic slide" (Ahmed 2004, 119), that unlike the Freudian model, which is developmental and vertical (conscious-unconscious), is horizontal, contagious, and contiguous. It is based on the attachment of bodies in space (Ahmed 2004). Forging love of country and unambiguous loyalty to the land were staples of the educational system, where the personal body became part of the national official body, owned by the state, as national property. The education system made the school into a resourceful institution that disseminates authority, knowledge, and paradigms of being in the world, relegating from the school to the home and to the streets and public spaces. With the compulsory 1949 Israeli Security Service Law requiring service at age eighteen, the trajectory of a child became highly scripted and staged for the unique performance of "being Israeli".[30] In his Knesset speech in June 1953, Dinur articulated the purpose of the educational system, saying: "...that each and every one of its citizens will see the state as part of the self of his personal being" (In Ram 2006, 51).

The Bible also provided the historic, mythical epos, bridging the gap of 4,000 years to the present (Ram 2006, 42). Historically, textuality was tied to Zionism's meta-narrative of homecoming, Kibbutz Galuyot, which not only conveyed the physical ingathering of Jews from all over the world, but also became a new metaphor for the immense enterprise of converting diasporic Jews—their experiences, histories, languages, and appearances—into a single homogeneous society.[31] The melting pot ideology assimilates difference. Numerous tactics were employed to engender collectivity, community, and an ethos of belonging and nativeness. Reading Hebrew and other textual practices are critical among them. Zionism, initially the discourse of a European minority, gradually came to function as a totalizing scheme within discriminatory hierarchical systems. These systems effectively managed to exclude minorities—women,

Middle Eastern and North African Jews, and Palestinians—from positions of power and from access to resources. With its sweeping creed of fulfilling the nostalgic dream of a Jewish homeland and its boundless appetite to settle the account of 2,000 years of wandering and oppression in the Jewish Diaspora, Zionism has become an immense ideological apparatus that not only produced its own system of giants and grasshoppers (to borrow from the account of Moses's spies in Numbers) but also, more alarmingly, has produced a deepening amnesia around the mythological fête of milk and honey, creating the conditions for the devouring and silencing of its own subjects.

My methodology consists in large part of a close reading of texts, going into the details of language roots and translation. This is especially relevant to the subject of the crisis of reference and the critique of culturally disciplined reading. At its best, it continues a Jewish tradition of engaging with texts, following the steps of post-structuralism and deconstruction. As a scholar of literature, I have come to understand that close reading of texts is the most effective, responsible, and accurate way to generate meaning, helping to best constitute a critical position. Earlier, through my concept of Ethno-reading, I developed the commitment to step aside, "speak with", "speak nearby", and speak from below to redefine the process of interpretation as a political and ethical endeavor, as by now have others who have worked on minorities, trauma studies, silence, and intersectional persona, whether in literature, ethnography, film, or other disciplines.[32] Questions such as how to listen, represent, and cite, how to do and undo, read, unread, and reread are all at the core of this process, keeping one on the edge of one's reading wit.

In addition to the analysis of biblical narratives, I provide ample readings of literary texts, films, and artworks, some of which reflect the phenomena of *tsatetet*, and many others which have made efforts to temper its wounding effects, or to challenge it. Attempting to diversify the position of those artists, I strive to expand the range of authors, their cultural positions, and cultural locations, while still reflecting the broad extent of their engagement with the Bible. My choices are based on thematic argument, often resulting in a fragmented approach, highlighting specific aspects of narratives and specific works by these authors. Also critical, as I have already pointed out, it would be a mistake to consider Zionists, Orthodox Jews, or secular Israelis as monolithic groups representing similar investments in and identifications with their Israeli identity. To the extent that it is possible to engage so many fields of knowledge—cultural history, critical literary critique, and historiography—my project draws on different contributions to cultural and feminist theory to draw internal connections between literary artistic production and the reproduction of textuality. In that sense, it is not an exhaustive study, and I hope it will inspire other scholars to engage with this subject.

Again, my intention here is not to underplay the astounding value and contribution of Hebrew and Jewish sources, nor to present a deep engagement with writing and reading. The rich tradition of Jewish intertextual interpretation was a lifeline anchor for Jewish diasporas across millennia, and occasioned the intellectual trajectory of discourses and disciplines throughout history. It is critical to acknowledge its magnitude, wisdom, and impact. And yet, this project points to the "disorder of reading" (Derrida 1998) within a process of accelerated and excessive neo-national, neo-Zionist ideology. A violent process in itself, that ideology also instructs a violent, oppressive reading.

In Chapter 1, "Moses's Tragedy of Binarism and the Discourse of the Udder", I explore the sublime space of milk and honey in the Bible and the way it has been mythologized in Israeli discourse. Milk and honey have been privileged in the Zionist imagination and the narrative of return. I trace the historical development of their vicissitudes, along with those of "a land that devours its people", from the Bible to various Zionist manifestations, from socialist to capitalist economies, and from local to global markets. Nowhere was it given that milk has the ability to drown its drinkers in an overflowing, intoxicating river of obliviousness.

I begin my survey by interrogating the utterance of "A land of milk and honey", within its performance for Moses through the burning bush in Exodus and the narrative of the twelve spies in Numbers. God's spectacle is communicated through the most performative language. Does that explain how the image of milk and honey has snowballed into a monolith that is only taken literally or at face value within the public imagination? I explore numerous artistic and literary works that draw on the abundance of this citational cosmology, from Shai Agnon's miraculous goat, through Shlonsky's physical-theological ecology of the "human udder", to Dan Pagis's grammar drills in "Exercise in Practical Hebrew". I follow with Shoshana Shababo's parodic sticky honey and its lacquered reality, and I interrogate the history of Tnuva, Israel's largest food company, the mobilizer of the discourse of milk as the ultimate elixir of the nation, promoting its global neo-capitalist economy. The devouring of the self has been articulated in different ways; I conclude with a poem by Sami Chetrit that laments the Mizrahi mental injury that forces on its subject not only the loss of his accent, but along with it the silence of the inheritance of the past and its melodies.

Chapter 2, "Gifts of Wounds: Ishmael, Isaac, and the Legacies of Abuse", positions the narratives of Isaac and Ishmael within a contemporary understanding of child torture and abuse, exploring the mechanisms of othering and violence in Genesis. The textual assumptions about their pliability condition the boys' trajectories. My thesis shifts the axis from one that divides Abraham's sons to one that divides father from sons. The paradigm of Abraham's actions moves from an obedient hand to an invasive hand, abuse that is governed by the hand, and like any abuse, it reifies the paradigmatic asymmetry of power relations.

My close reading of the narrative of the Binding of Isaac asserts that the demands of ideology and its ethical expectations are articulated around Abraham's slaughtering knife, the *ma'akhelet*, and the Hebrew root, *'akhal* (to eat). Drawing on the ramifications of such a reading, I engage numerous poems that directly address the *ma'akhelet* and challenge the reader's receptiveness from generational, ethnic, gendered, and sexual positions. My analysis of David Grossman's books, *Be My Knife* and *To the End of the Land*, highlights the tragic cultural performance of the knife. Shelly Elkayam and her gendered poem, "Whereto Do You Love Me", engages the *ma'akhelet* as the ultimate site of incisive interrogation of God's tyrannical love in Israeli culture.

My close reading of Genesis 16 examines the scandalous interaction between Hagar and Sarai. It shows how they have introduced not only the first cries and laughter, but also the two extreme categories of inclusion and exclusion, foreshadowing the total rejection of Ishmael's otherness. How is this otherness depicted and what is its internal logic? Following the thesis of the male gaze, I conceptualize the "pregnancy gaze" as the ultimate patriarchal desire for pregnant bodies, articulating both the extent of Hagar's withering gaze and that of Sarai's internalized insult. Who is the authority that makes torture permissible? A series of citations—Sarai cites Abraham who cites God; Sarai's torture of Hagar unleashes a series of ruptures, bodily as well as mental and discursive, all collapsing categories of self, body, and culture. Ishmael's depiction represents this utter collapse. "His hand is against/inside everyone, and everyone's hand is against/inside him (kol-bo)" (Gen. 16: 12) encodes a thesis of this violated category. It explains the paradoxical construction of the *kolbo*, the all-containing container that is a priori unable to contain. I further reflect on the cultural space that Genesis opens up with the desire "to be built" through children at the core of Jewish narration and its history. The kolbo signals an aberration, the condition of an accelerated and manic hand, and a testimony of the violated integrity of the son. It speaks through "hands dialogue" of the invasion and occupation of other bodies, cultures, and categories.

I develop the modern Hebrew *kolbo* and its overflowing possibilities. I discuss the physical abuse and the production of children's otherness in three modern Hebrew works by David Shahar, Yehudit Katzir, and Albert Suisa. Together, these works unfold a story of the liminal and homeless condition of the Hebrew child at home. Read in tandem, attentive to the specificities of ethnicity, religion, gender, and class, they depict the profound tragedy of the abandoned child with different degrees of injury and trauma. For example, Suisa's *Akud*, Bound, ties back into the Sacrifice, Isaac, and Ishmael more explicitly, telling us what it means to be bound by the force of textuality. Suisa's three protagonists in a working-class neighborhood of North African immigrants are trapped within their imagined Bible and its grid of textuality, in their street "yeshiva". Suisa's harsh critique of textuality intersects the gender, class, ethnicity, and sexuality of his protagonists, who have full agency as readers. Yet, their mindset overflows with a web of fragmented narratives: infinite allusions to texts, teaching, and the voice of the Fathers.

Chapter 3, "Ruth's Homecoming: Meta-Bread, Transformation, and Offspring", takes a novel position regarding The Book of Ruth as a continuation of the story of Moab and its historical conception. I pay special attention to the total destruction of Sodom and Gomorrah and the Moabite trauma of death and hunger in Genesis. Once read together, the crises around death and scarcity of both semen and seed (in Hebrew *zera'*) fully expose the insidiousness of Ruth's *traum*. Will the Bible be able to resolve the deep-seated trauma of generations? What kind of shift in consciousness is needed in order to overcome it? The domestication of Ruth's otherness into Judea and Judaism, I contend, is predicated not simply on her graceful desire to follow Naomi, her mother-in-law, God, and people, but also on her ability to allow Boaz's bread to speak its fullness through its performance of measure: he gives her *pat shlemah*, a perfect, whole bread. The reiteration of the signifying process of bread is a signature that marks the citational performance of God, male, land, and language in the perfect economy. Seed and sperm are equally generative, like a literary sign, they all produce and reproduce. They not only survive but manage to rekindle a new burst of possibilities: literary and allegorical. Ruth adds immense meaning to this process of signification, and it is not surprising that the narrative was used for national purposes.

I rethink the symbolic space of bread through my concept of the "Breadscape". The Breadscape, I theorize, is a multilayered site; both real and imagined, it covers a huge cultural space full of social, ecological, religious, and national properties and potentialities, and is coded with desires, hopes, anxieties, crises, and pathologies. Inasmuch as it has a crucial role in mobilizing a discourse of feeding, it also draws the contours of collective ontology and consciousness. This space, therefore, does not stop at the mouth; it opens multiple sites of demanding cultural cavities, a broad spectrum of scarcities and desires for land and offspring, belonging and possession. The Israeli Breadscape is a unique, dynamic site of inquiry. It draws on a synthesis of meaning that embodies more than bread and texts as food, and that allegorizes the Book (and God) within a secular framework of literary provision. The Breadscape has become an important archive of citations.[33]

I augment this discussion with Yehuda Amichai's poems on names, naming, and otherness within Jewish genealogy. For Amichai, they comprise an indispensable aspect of Hebrew intertextuality, epistemes of its broken narratives and wounded history. Names are citations. The meta-narratives that are inscribed in names such as "Ruth" and "Yehuda" comprise the "meta-bread", the predicament of change, knowledge, and otherness. I demonstrate the scope of artists' engagement with the book of Ruth by introducing the works of Amos Gitai, in film; Adi Nes, in photography; and Michal Ben Naftali, in fictional philosophy. Fictional works by David Grossman and Benny Barbash focus on the way children carry the burden of culture through storytelling and textual production. Will they ever survive reality with this hunger in the story, for the story?

Within mythologies of hunger and satiation, the Breadscape can conceptualize their signification and their multiple constitutional manifestations through language, objects, symbols, and images. The Epilogue, "Ruptured Breadscape: Palestinian Narratives of Departure", provides an initial comparison between the Hebrew-Jewish Breadscape and the Palestinian one through works that address the trauma of the Nakba at the intersection of nations, war, poverty, memory, and literary production. I suggest that through the tropes of food, specifically bread and pita, Mahmoud Sayf al-Irani, Anton Shammas, and Elias Khoury depict a Palestinian Breadscape as a place where the story has lost its mouth, as well as its body, memory, and consciousness. The story of Jewish return has mobilized, transformed, and uplifted (from *'aliyah*, ascending) newcomers into natives, while the story of Palestinian departure alternately has paralyzed, made invisible, and starved the Palestinian natives.

Notes

1 In a later version of this work, Naaman renders the latter phrase in English as "a land that eateth up the inhabitants thereof", using the American Standard Version of the Bible, Numbers 13:32.

2 The prohibition, "Do not cook (seethe) a kid (goat) in its' mother's milk" (Exodus 23:19 and 34:26 and Deuteronomy 14:21), is responsible for the production of the Jewish dietary law, referred to as "Kashrut", a systematic, metaphoric model where eating demands a consciousness of marked distinction, with attention to time and space. One must separate meat from dairy products (in eating, cooking, and relishing), which also usually means waiting half an hour after eating dairy and six hours after eating meat. The conscious mouth, by this system, becomes a site of halachic control over what one eats and when. The principle that explains this prohibition is the concern for the mother, a measure of mercy to avoid the immersion of the offspring in its biological mother's milk.

3 Aryeh Markmen, "How learning Talmud every day, rain or shine, indelibly altered my view of reality". February 26, 2005, www.aish.com/jw/s/48894407.html

4 The work's inclusion in the Educational Technological Center's database of art on the Akedah speaks to its reception, making accessible Naaman's critical perspective in contemporary Israeli public discourse. It appears along with

the works of other canonical Israeli artists—Yigal Tumarkin, Yoram Rozov, Menashe Kadishman, and Moshe Gershuni—who have all, in their respective idioms, protested the national myth of the sacrifice by engaging directly with the Genesis story of the Akedah. Orna Silverman suggests, "[Naaman] moves from the Kashrut of the biblical, religious law to the secular national reality, presenting the kid as a tragic victim of cynicism and inhumanity. The kid is the ram, that which has been 'eaten,' that which was sacrificed to the Molech of wars". *Molech* is an Ammonite deity associated with passing the sons "over fire" (II Kings 23: 10) or with human sacrifice. See: www.myjewishlearning. com/article/9-things-to-know-about-the-daf-yomi-daily-page-of-talmud/

5 See Karpel (1999).
6 Textual culture is defined here differently from "textual culture" or "textual studies" as a field or discipline in the Humanities.
7 www.facebook.com/pg/TheJerusalemBibleInitiative/about/?ref=page_internal. And also: www.mybible.org.il/media/23216-pm-netanyahu-launches-inscribing-the-tanakh-website.html
8 www.mybible.org.il/bible-paintings.htm
9 www.textologia.net/?page_id=2
10 www.cet.ac.il/mikranet/new.asp
11 www.biblemarathon.co.il
12 sites.google.com/site/aviavi600/direct-movie/sdom
13 www.facebook.com/teamcoco/videos/1813981828660691/
14 www.michmanim.co.il/copy-of-7
15 www.facebook.com/miri.regev.il/videos/
16 Zerubavel (2013).
17 www.ynet.co.il/articles/0,7340,L-4719885,00.html
18 Austin clarifies: "I must not be joking, for example, or writing a poem. Our performative utterances, felicitous or not, are to be understood as issued in ordinary circumstances" (Austin 1962, 21–22).
19 Sharabani defines himself, rather than as a writer, as a "person who writes". He is the author of three novels as well as a poet, journalist, screenwriter, and producer. He lives in Tel Aviv and is a second-generation Mizrahi of Iraqi origins.
20 The term is closely associated with the "*yaldei ha-gazezet*" scandal (in English, "the children of the ringworm)", or "the ringworm affair", referring to the harsh, traumatic medical treatment that was provided to immigrant children in Israel, especially from North Africa, in the 1950s. Scalp ringworm was treated with excessive amounts of radiation.
21 A political stance towards citationality can be seen in the work of Ortal Ben Dayan, a scholar and celebrity who approaches citations as political testimonies. Her website, *Hatsatetet*, focuses on the Zionist leadership, where she exposes obvious, explicitly discriminatory, racist statements from the Zionist archives about women, Mizrahim and Palestinians. https://hazatetet. wordpress.com/about/
22 Hebrew authors amusingly invented new diseases: Bialik referred to *na'emet*, speech giving, and Shlonsky rhymes to an inquisitive child, "there is no end to your *sha'elet*, questioning". The Hebrew speaker has no difficulty comprehending the pattern. It is frequently used, built into the language. https:// blog.ravmilim.co.il/2011/06/23/simulated-disease/
23 Discussing Modern Eastern European Jewish authors, Dan Miron emphasizes, "During the last 200 years…a Jew's committing himself to literature was inextricably bound up in an ideology; a secular Hebrew literature, a secular Yiddish literature, hasidic Hebrew-Yiddish literature, a Jewish literary

expression in a non-Jewish language, etc. Even the total assimilationist made a similar commitment in a negative fashion. By his very choice of language and context, every Jewish writer expressed loyalty to a certain conception of the national culture and indicated his faith in its further development towards specific national-cultural goals" (Miron 1984, 50).

24 In Illouz, 2014.

25 Ben Gurion was also burdened by the question of the mandatory army service of religious women. For more on the visit, the conversation, and its impact see Melamed, 2013; "Which wagon is Fuller: the Secular or the Haredi one?" www.makorrishon.co.il/nrg/online/11/ART2/502/494.html

26 See Fiener's recent work on the roots of secularism (2010) and Ruderman's work on the formation of secularism as part of liberal Judaism (2010).

27 http://mailstar.net/bengur-recollections.html

28 The idea was to start right in the advent before the *Shavuot* holiday (late spring) once the children learned to read.

29 https://musaf-shabbat.com/2015/05/31/הספרות-הפכה-לקולב-פוליטי-יאיר-שלג/
  Ha-sifrut hafckah l-kolav politi" (Literature Turned into a Political Hanger)

30 Also the title of Shafir and Peled book (2002); see also Almog (1997); Almog (1999).

31 For an elaborate critique of the nationalist discourse of homogenization in Jewish histories and cultures, see Shohat (1989 and 2001).

32 Tsoffar (2006); Chen (1992); Caruth (1995); Felman and Laub (1992).

33 As it operates, it can leave its subject unaware of its mechanism.

1   Moses's Tragedy of Binarism and the Discourse of the Udder

Long before I read about "A land flowing with milk and honey" (Exodus 3: 8), I had sung those very words. At the tender ages of four and five, our soft kindergarten voices filled the air, intensified by our clapping hands and stomping feet as we repeated the mantra.[1] "*Eretz zavat halav, halv u-dvash...*" with special sweetness we imagined the flowing white rivers and waterfalls. It was indeed a delicious song, and for many years the melody was highly popular, ever-present on the tip of every tongue—in schools, on the radio—a constant companion to the *Hora*, the Israeli folk circle dance,[2] and campfires, along with other Hebrew songs. A few years later, I learned to read it, fascinated by the biblical story, the Promised Land, and Moses and the Twelve Spies.[3]

In the national revolution that was Zionism, close proximity to the Hebrew language entailed more than relying on written culture; it involved an all-encompassing site of active engagement that is imagined, informed, and situated by the written word. Zionist discourse has come to embody an institution of knowledge that imbues Jewish narratives, models, and codes with vitality that is specifically attuned to a secular framework. The Bible has provided Modern Hebrew literature with the most prolific signifying scenes through which to think through contemporary Israeli culture. Such scenes have not only undergone a process of Israelization and naturalization, but they have also been presented as the embodiment of the nation's biography within a specific timeline and collective, and necessarily selective, memory.

Crucial to articulating this new ontology of the Jewish state is, therefore, the Hebrew language, which was steeped in Zionist discourse with a mystical dimension and revolutionary momentum of its own (Kimmerling 2001). Throughout history, Jews read the Bible in Hebrew, and since the late 1800s, the story of the Hebrew language has been entwined with the historical chapter of Zionism; to write in Hebrew became a redemptive act that not only helped to inscribe the Israeli master-narrative and its native subject, the Sabra, but was also instrumental, as I mentioned earlier, in inventing the 'new Jewish man' of modernity (Almog 1997, 127–132; Peled 2002, 28–30). Hebrew became an ideology in and of itself, simultaneously articulating the project of Israeli nationalism while building on old semiotics and structures

(Zerubavel 1995). The invention of the Sabra was just as much the creation of a new Hebrew-speaking Jewish native as it was of a trained reader of Hebrew texts. Benjamin Harshav puts it in a different order, describing Israel as 'an ideology that created a language that forged a society that became a State' (Harshav 1993, viii).

As it concerns milk and honey, the story of the burning bush is but one such moment that has been made available for symbolic consumption. The imaginary spectacle that accompanies this narrative was notably loaded with an *a priori* sense of victory in the song *Mul Har Sinai* ("In Front of Mount Sinai"). Written two days before the Sinai Campaign in 1956, *Mul Har Sinai* became the unofficial anthem for this war. It was performed by the renowned army troupe Lahakat Hanachal, and was written and composed by the two canonic contributors, Moshe Vilensky and Yechi'el Mohar, respectively. Building on the burning bush's total inconsumability—the song was composed before the operation began, before they knew the results—further militarizes and nationalizes it as a transcendent revelatory event not only awaiting the arrival of the soldiers of the State of Israel, but also preserving the people's flame for eternity.[4] The song charts a cycle of return from the burning bush and Moses's Mount Sinai to the return of Israelis to Sinai in the present. "Oh flame of God / in the eyes of the youth / oh flame of God / in the roars of engines / this day will yet be retold / my brothers / of the nation's return to [Sinai]".[5]

The song had immediate ramifications on the reception of this war in the public imagination. The location of the "flame of God" both in the eyes and speech of Israeli soldiers and in the roars of its engines (tanks and bulldozers alike) deifies state violence and ontologizes the Israeli Defense Forces (IDF) as an instrument of divine will. What is more, the song sets a dangerous precedent by asserting Jewish ownership or "right of return" over, not just Sinai, but any site of biblical importance. The crescendo of the song reintroduces the singular event of the burning bush with a heroic masculinist loudness of war and victory, as an eruption, penetrating both the physical geographical territory of Egyptian Sinai and, more mentally, the biblical myth of Moses. That "the day will yet be retold" is a taken-for-granted admission that it is the victor who controls the historical narrative, especially given that the War of Independence in 1948 was perceived as a war of the few against the many. The prolonging of the literary-historical throughline from biblical wars to the present conflict evokes a sense of absolute belonging within a centuries-long narrative of adversity and survival.

The Divine Project of Imagining

The performance for Moses through the burning bush is the ultimate spectacle of God's appearance in Exodus, especially given the rarity of seeing any aspect of God. It is a scene of heightened affect communicated through language, sight, sound, and even smell and heat. By virtue of its divinity, it amplifies the scale of communication and the volume of meaning that the event can hold. In God's project of imagining, language is coextensive with the visual, at the same time tying together language, land, and food. Whereas scholars have written substantially about this encounter, the focus on the connection between language and ideologies of provision remained neglected.

Before engaging concretely with the above, I wish to further contextualize the language within the narrative, highlighting its performativity with the speech act of feeding. Moses has just fled from Pharaoh, who sought to kill him upon hearing that he, Moses, killed an Egyptian man. The gender transitions in Moses's life from the threatening, male space to protective, female space are indeed striking: Pharaoh's decree to throw the male sons into the Nile had informed his rescue by his mother, Yocheved, his sister, Miriam, and Pharaoh's daughter, who also adopted him and raised him, while his mother, Yocheved, nursed him. Once in the desert, after helping Jethro's daughters water their flock around the well—a vital public site in the Bible for social encounters and exchanges (Scarry 1985, 189)—he married Ziporah, Jethro's eldest, and made his temporary home in Median. Thus, in spite of being a *ger*, a foreigner, and against the Egyptian space of enslavement and increasing violence, Moses is thriving; he fathers his first son, and also shepherds the flock of his father-in-law (Exodus 3: 1).

It is in such a moment, in the spacious desert of seclusion, that God summons Moses, the shepherd, to this miracle of words and objects, a performance of awakening. The encounter with the divine opens a huge paradigmatic space at the intersection of sight, voice, memory, and knowledge. The revelation marks the zone of divine performative intimacy, a category of sacredness in *Har Ha-'Elohim*, God's Mountain in *Chorevah*. In addition to the awe-striking fear, *yir'ah*, that God's presence inspires in Moses, it will also have to move him, to urgently mobilize him to go to Pharaoh and become the leader he cannot yet see in himself. The force of the event presupposes that Moses will undergo this major transformation: from the rescued individual, he will become the agent of rescuing, and he will be made from a leader of tribes into the historical leader of the Israelite nation.[6]

> And I have come down to rescue it (my people) from the hand of Egypt, to bring it up from that land to a goodly and spacious land, to a land flowing with milk and honey, to the place of the Canaanite, and the Hittite, and the Amorite, and the Perizzite, and the Hivite, and the Jebusite.
>
> (Exodus 3: 8)

The pattern of repeating the target place with three attributions, "to a goodly and spacious land", "to a land flowing with milk and honey", and "to the place of the Canaanite", helps to constitute unequivocally a referentiality of the land of Canaan that is deceptively literal.

> "*eretz zavat chalav u-dvash*"[7]
> A land flowing with milk and honey

Eretz, land in Hebrew, is feminine. The literal translation of the Hebrew is "a land oozing with milk and honey", an allegorical allusion to the secretions of the female human body, which in turn is reinvested with positive, eroticized value (see Song of Songs 4: 11). The femininity, or rather, feminization of the *land—zavah*, in feminine—is further signified by the oozing fluidity of the milk and honey, both as female fluids and as part of a female bodily discourse (Irigary 1985). In Leviticus, a *zivah*, a female "oozer", alludes to the status during the period of confinement or abstinence—from sex, for example—mandated by a woman's ritually polluted state (Leviticus 15: 28). The word is usually associated with pollution, sexually transmitted diseases, and foul discharges. In "a land oozing with milk and honey", the context of oozing is utterly brimming with nurturing potential. This positive investment of the female body with such erotic/nurturing potential is only accomplished via the same body's linguistic proximity to the land and its nourishing secretions. Later, when God spells out to Moses what to tell the elders of Israel, he reiterates the expression word for word (Exodus 16–17). The concern with re-establishing the reference, as God does, in terms of the land's "goodness", inhabitants, and land products, is tied to the need to substantiate the project of imagining and Moses's assignment as leader. It mediates the abstract idea of Canaan into a vivid, concrete reality, while all along making the departure from Egypt a certainty of memory.

The project of imagining, thus, starts with Moses, as a new beginning, complementing the spectacle of the burning bush. In this speech act, God establishes the performativity of the land as it "[flows] with milk and honey". In such a system of distribution, the language is loaded with communicative responsibilities. Moses must surmount a huge obstacle of representation: how can these Israelites in the desert, who know only the hardship of Egypt, come to grips with such an abstract promise? God's performance informs the very performance of the land when he tells Moses, who is stuck in the desert, how to start the project of imagining, how to communicate with slaves the fact that they are on the road to freedom, and to "a land flowing with milk and honey". The text engages several temporalities: speaking to Moses, to the people, and to the eternal God of History.

But as much as the project of imagining is an abstract one, it relies heavily on the materiality of language. "Language never gives mere signs", Walter Benjamin tells us (Benjamin 1996, 69). And the language of materiality specifically distinguishes between linguistic communication and mental communication. Objects communicate their materiality into human language beyond their immediate meaning. Benjamin uses the example of "toy", saying that the word communicates to the player a "rhythm of play". It is founded on the magic of language, on the notion that the word "...points to something else: its infiniteness" (Benjamin 1996, 62–63). The language of revelation, as Benjamin theorizes, is predicated on its ability

> to make the relation between mind and language thoroughly unambiguous, so that the expression that is linguistically most existent (that is, most fixed) is linguistically the most rounded and definitive; in a word, the most expressed is at the same time the purely mental.
> (Benjamin 1996, 66–67)

Taking "the inviolability of the word as the only and sufficient condition and characteristic of the divinity of the mental being that is expressed in it", is what is meant by the concept of revelation (Ibid. 1996, 66–67). Although subjectivity plays a large part in differentiating these associations from person to person, Benjamin is more interested in the collective production of meaning in mental communication—in our case, the shared foundation of associations that the phrase "a land flowing with milk and honey" conjures up. In the world of food, such objects have an even more magical effect, alerting several registers of language, body, and imagination. Milk and honey, similarly, activate a new restoring conversation between 'adam and 'adamah, man and land, whereby "eating well"—good, plenty, and enough—is its staple. And it is precisely what the land is intended to represent: "eating well".

God provides Moses, in addition to the visual magical signs—the transformation of the rod into a serpent, and of the hand into a leprous, white hand—with a language that acts, models, and continuously signifies. This coextensive speech act is sensual and provocative, intended to result in unconditional trust and mobilize Moses beyond his self-doubt and lack of enthusiasm and beyond his claim of speech impairment. Moreover, to speak to Moses in the language of milk can be captivating, if not highly constructive; he, who in Pharaoh's daughter's search for a "nurse of the Hebrew women" (Exodus 2: 7), has been brought back home to his biological mother, Yocheved, can best understand the phenomenal, constituting power of milk and its political bearing.

Canaan's abundance of constant provision helps to sanctify its image; this abundance is strongly predicated on the fact that the land is "spacious" and "good", attributes that speak to the absolute intrinsic moral value of the land within an ontological account of the covenant. This "goodness" is especially noteworthy because the text itself reserves such positive absolutes for reminding us that the "good" of the creation story, is all that is good, beyond "good" and "bad", a divine content that concludes God's work and blessing in Genesis. And this mighty goodness, uttered in four words, is unfolding its new logic, tying milk and honey in the poetic episteme of enduring action that competes with the mother's milk and displaces her breast, the limited good of her body, with the infinity of God's breast (see also Ofrat 2010). The verb *zavat* signals a productive act, compounding in a special syntax the adjective and the verb, turning the two godly substances into a timeless provision that supersedes seasons, histories, or politics. Insofar as they are visual, they always keep close to the lips and the palate, preserving a humming of nurturing flow.

> Go, Gather the elders of Israel and say to them: YHWH, the God of your fathers, has been seen by me, the God of Avraham, of Yitzhak, and of Yaakov saying: I have taken account, yes, account of you and what is being done to you in Egypt, and I have declared: I will bring you up from the affliction of Egypt, to the land of the Canaanite and of the Hittite, of the Amorite and of the Perizzite, of the Hivvite, and the Yevusite, to a land flowing with milk and honey.
>
> (Exodus 3: 16–17)

Indeed, one possible intended reading interprets the expression "a land flowing with milk and honey" as continuously flowing from the burning bush, never consumed, always performing, lasting, and occurring. The bush and the divine utterance of milk and honey work forever hand-in-hand via the text to reify a set of concrete expectations of God and man, and of land and language cohering as event. While this land is infused with agency, actively producing both milk and honey, it is the language of superlatives and absolute provision that keeps generating not only the two substances but also the very environmental conditions of their flow. For the hungry generation of Egypt, the expression is a continuous affirmation of belonging.

God's project of imagining, therefore, is a project that hovers between the unfathomable burning bush and the immeasurable milk and honey, materializing both magical events. The code of the godly land, at this early stage, is neither presented in the metaphoric framework of idyllic Paradise, as Northrop Frye conveys, nor as a figure of speech that articulates universal mythology. It is rather presented as a concrete metonymy of the blessed land within the overall project of a new reality. Indeed, later, when Moses asks the twelve messengers to bring the fruit of the land with them, he places trust in the fact that God's words translate literally and not metaphorically.

Biblical commentators and Jewish scholars have read the expression with the raw, bio-agricultural reality of Israel in mind, looking for concrete evidence of milk and honey's existence in the land, as "two synecdoches... for agriculture and animal husbandry" (Alter 2004, 320). Most tend to think that the honey is not clover honey, as bee farming was not yet practiced, suggesting instead that it refers to a sweet syrup extracted from dates, closer to what is common in Iraqi culture and is nowadays available in the Israeli market as "*silan*". Scholars are also divided as to the exact meaning of "milk". While some raise the possibility that the source of the milk was the fluid oozing from figs and dates and other fruits, arguing that herding and *chalav*, animal milk, were not that common in Canaan, Rabbi Akiva and other Talmudic authorities suggest that "milk" most likely refers to animal milk, although it is obvious that the milk could not be of cows, but of goats and sheep. In fact, the very fact of such debates signals the incredible generative potential of the expression—it calls forth the phantasmagoric property of the land, its nurturing power to the extent that it aspires to locate God within the Land. Linguistically, this genetic connection to the land through milk transforms the land into the motherland and homeland, tightening the Hebrew semantic relationship between yeled, *moledet*, and *toldot*, "a child", "homeland", and "history", from the root, *yld*, which means to give birth. The very field of conception and birthing is now appropriated, replacing mother's milk and any other milk, with a metaphoric fluid that informs the new genealogy of nativity and the desire for national return. From now on, to imagine the land means to develop a taste for it.

Contributing further to this biblical spectacle is the narrative of the twelve spies (Numbers 13). Here, in the desert, closer to the Land, Moses, in response to his people's misgivings, has sent the leaders of the twelve tribes to tour the Land of Canaan; they have to return with answers to the questions "what is the land?" and "what are the people?" God's project of imagining has gone astray, and the language has faded. Indeed, in the scene of the Spies' splendid return, they carry a branch on their shoulders that bears the fruits of the land: grapes, figs, and pomegranates. Certainly, this branch has since carried more than the weight of fruits; it has also borne the paradigmatic weight of historical Jewish longing and the specter of redemptive return. For modern Zionism, the embrace of the master-narrative of national homecoming hinged on the visual representation of the spies bearing grapes that was highly popular in the media of the time, in postcards, stamps, artwork, and textbooks. It would become one of the foremost material objects that would intrinsically tie the landscape to biblical language and imagery, while remodeling the symbol of the land and its infinite potential (Figures 1.1–1.3).

The sanctified *sneh* (burning bush) has constituted a site of promise, desire, and longing, moving away from any trace of conflict and violence. Milk and honey as part of the imagined land will flow in the so-called story of the twelve spies. But as I mentioned, this story has a grave cost. To begin with, life in the desert slowly takes its toll:, for how can an

Figure 1.1 A Children's Bible Illustration, *HaShomenr HaTsair*, the leftist youth movement, links the story of the weekly portion of biblical reading (6.15.2011) to political debate on democracy and occupation.

Figure 1.2 Sergio Ratescu, Petach Tikva Center, 2007 (Attribution: Dr. Avishai Teicher).

Figure 1.3 The award-winning designer George Hamori addressed the theme of the twelve spies in the Israeli national postage stamp for the High Holidays of 1954. The quote from Numbers 14: 8, "A land that flows with milk and honey", appears on the tab.[8]

Figure 1.4 The logo of the Israeli Ministry of Tourism.

imagined promise compare to the still-palpable memory of Egypt, the plate of fish, meat, squash, and alliums? "Our gullets are shriveled; there is nothing at all, nothing but this manna to look to" (Numbers 11: 6). The nostalgic gaze of the slaves demands an unambiguous, active real-ization, not only of immediate food, but also of a way to reset the scale of hunger and appetite within the context of the future land (Figure 1.4).

Alas, the messengers' testimony is accompanied by particularly con-tradictory outcomes; ten of the messengers recognized that "yes, the land is of milk and honey" (Number 13: 27), but they claim that it is also a place of fortified and powerful cities, populated by *nephilim*, gi-ants (13: 32). Caleb, who rushes to restore order, repeats the expression as a shared foundational knowledge: "It is a land flowing with milk and honey", whose inhabitants can be easily defeated (Numbers 13: 7). Nonetheless, the dispute gets heated when the ten spies insist that the land is not only densely populated, naming its different nations, but also overwhelmingly stronger, and that the land is "a land that eats its inhabitants" (Number 13: 32). They even add that these giants made them feel tiny, like grasshoppers, and that that is how the giants saw them. The panic this generates is evident in the Israelites' response. They break into tears, repeating twice that they would rather have died in Egypt, expressing a desire to return to Egypt, and even threaten-ing to stone Caleb and Joshua when they attempt to calm them down (Numbers 14: 7–8).

They will all be punished. The journey of the desert generation will take on a different route and will last forty years, a harsh span of time that will inform every aspect of their body, memory, and history. The ten messengers, who have already been introduced as liars, will perish. It is exactly at the end of the forty years that Moses recounts another version of the spies' account to his people (Deuteronomy 1–2). In that sense, the two narratives are important; they bookend the forty years, providing closure at another critical moment. A few mere paces from the border of Canaan, Moses, who will not enter the land, is giving his testimony with his last breath. Joshua will lead the Israelites, who are finally entering the Land and will become the new occupiers and settlers of the land.[9]

In the broader narrative of Exodus, these chapters are indispens-able because they convey how the Bible prepares Moses, and then the Israelites, to transition from the land of slavery to the magical land of infinite abundance, and from a tribal society to national unity (Fredman 1981; Pardes 1994). They also tell us about the anxieties of the desert generation, articulating the Promised Land in terms of a dialectic of extremes, a land of abundance in a time of crisis, in terms of food and feeding, hunger, and devouring, and their constitutive differences. Their impact, my close reading shows, goes beyond their binary construction, to the ability of language to produce a saturated, consuming mindset within an affective economy of provision, in which the milk-drunk subject ends up being devoured. It is this transition from the gushing mouth of provision to the starving mouth of cannibalization that has gone entirely unnoticed by those contemporary Israelis who take refuge in biblical verse and its fantastic pull.

Walking the Distance of Bipedalism

> "Why is God taking us to that land to fall by the sword?...
> And the earth opened its mouth and swallowed them up...
> the earth closed over them and they vanished."
>
> (Numbers 14: 3)

From the grand narrative and language that function as engines of movement, we turn to the body, the legs, and the feet, focusing on the mechanics of a new movement and ways of observing the other. Indeed, at the center of the mission is the attempt to collect knowledge about otherness, of the land, of the people, and of their cities. These three sites of otherness are observed by former slaves, mediated by the experience of the desert, and conceptualized through the language of God and Moses.

When God tells Moses to send the leaders of each of the twelve tribes to Canaan, in Numbers 13, he uses the verb "*la-tur*" the land, which can be translated as "to scout", "to observe", "to search", or "to explore". Moses instructs them to "see the land, what it is" (Number 13: 18). The version in Deuteronomy uses the verb "*le-ragel*", which derived from the noun regel (foot or leg).[10] It is translated "to spy" although not in the contemporary sense. The emphasis on legs and feet in the story of their journey shifts the focus to knowledge that comes from below and through the experience of the lower part of the body and its contact with the land. Note that walking is physically taxing; during their days of touring on foot, the messengers covered, according to some commentaries, 800 kilometers, and in the late-summer heat.[11] The imagined language of revelation of God and Moses is being complemented by bipedal language and its pragmatic realism:

> When Moses sent them to scout out the land of Canaan, he said to them: Go up this (way) through the Negev/Parched-Land, and (then) you are to go up into the hill-country.
>   And see the land—what is it (like), and the population that is settled in it: are they strong or weak, are they few or many;
>   and what the land is (like), where they are settled: is it good ("*to-vah*") or ill ("*ra'ah*"), and what the towns are (like), where they are settled therein: are (they) encampments or fortified-places;
>   and what the land is (like): is it fat or lean, are there in it trees, or not?
>   Exert yourselves, And take (some) of the fruit of the land—now these days (are) the days of the first ripe-grapes.
>
> (Numbers 13: 17–20)

Moses's instructions to the spies prior to their departure are explicit questions that are structured along six sets of opposite parameters: what is the land, is it good or bad, fat or lean, with trees or without; what are the cities, are they constructed in camps or in fortresses; and what (how) are the people, are they strong or weak, few or many. His "ethnographic" method of inquiry provides the script for the whole narrative. It constitutes a thesis about how to gather knowledge on the new place and people. Insofar as the whole operation was intended to strengthen the people's trust in God (as some commentators claim, relying on the account in Deuteronomy), Moses's instructions are specific and coded. He poses only three questions that are closed, limited each to two dichotomous answers. There is neither in-between options nor any regard for context or history. While the names of the different nations that populate the land of Canaan are mentioned, there is no desire to gather information about them and their differentiated identities. Rather, the whole style reminds us of a clear-cut military operation and one that intends to help design strategy for focused action. Simply put, these are poorly issued orders, biasing the spies' reconnaissance.

It is possible, therefore, to approach the scandal of the spies as a methodological one, namely, the tragedy of binarism. The foundational patriarchy of Genesis is continually (re)produced into a structure that has since arranged Western human philosophy and knowledge along reductive dichotomies of day and night, Heaven and Earth, or male and female. Here, Moses introduces several axioms that will eventually undermine his perception, revealing the inherent "violent hierarchy" (Derrida 1982) of such a paradigm. Moses's questions directly determine not only what the messengers impart, but also the reception of their words. In the broad framework of faith and trust, then, the exchange and its language expose the responsibility of the listeners with regard to what they hear and how they are able to read it.

The critical question is to what extent the testimony of the messengers can challenge the divine code of the land as it was intended. The first ten start by introducing a fantastic visual testimony. Following Moses's request, they display their gift, a cluster of grapes, pomegranates, and figs, in front of the entire community, pointing to it and stating bluntly, "We came to the Land that you sent us to, and yes, it is flowing with milk and honey, and this is its fruit" (Number 13: 27). The visual is indeed a heavenly spectacle, incongruous with the landscape of the desert: seductive fruits that reveal the taste of future, concretely reifying the language of abstraction. But then the report shifts radically, moving from the description of the land to that of its people, and from a language of plenty to *'efes*, literally "zero", which, as a conjunction means "but", "only", "however", saying the nation is *'am' az*, a fierce, furious and mighty one. Their delivery is packed with information and is further intensified by their description of the exceedingly large, fortified cities. It is assumed that the "children of Anak" are the "Anakites, primeval giants, from whom the tall-seeming Canaanites were reputed to be descended" (Fox 1997, 723); *Anak* literally means giant, highly threatening indeed.

The messengers, then, strategically map the different nations settled in the land, alluding to the Amalekite, the Hittite, the Jebusite, and the Canaanite peoples. They emphasize, as Ofrat comments, that the land is not empty, but rather populated (Ofrat 2014).[12] When Caleb silences the messengers and argues against them, saying that the Israelites are able to possess and inherit the land, the ten insist that "We are not able to go up against the people; for they are stronger than we" (Numbers 13: 31). The narrator, then, continues, interfering with the flow of the narrative, and defines their speech as *dibbah*, a false account, libel and defamation, or as it is often translated, "an evil report". *Dibbah* is a total, forceful speech; it relies on the validity of testimonial proof to continually produce sensation and horror.

> So they gave-out a (false) report (*dibbah*) of the land
> that they had scouted out
> to the Children of Israel, saying:
> The land that we crossed through to scout it out:
> It is a land that devours its inhabitants;
> All the people that we saw in its midst are men of (great)
>   stature,
> (for) there we saw the giants—the children of *Anak* (come)
>   from the giants—
> we were in our (own) eyes like grasshoppers,
> and thus were we in their eyes!
>
> (Number 13: 32–33)

Size leaves an incredible impression on the ten messengers. The testimony wherein they saw the giants, not only imagining themselves as tiny as grasshoppers but being seen or looked at by the giants as small, further sensationalizes and dramatizes the encounter and adds staged force to the rhetorical allegory of power, lack of power, self, and otherness.

Grasshoppers are tiny, light, and almost invisible. In Chapter 3, I discuss how Hagar's way of looking at Sarai, the power of the pregnant woman's gaze, effectively belittles Sarai, putting an end to her master plan to conceive, for her, a son to Abraham through her servant-girl Hagar. Such a sensation of smallness, within the politics of seeing and being looked at, entrenches the power hierarchy and brings the Israelites to a still further level of affective helplessness. Nonetheless, the giants introduce size as a law of nature, within an ecological hierarchy of power: the smaller will be threatened by the bigger. This, of course, predates the account of David's victory over Goliath. This experience of encountering the giants radically distorts the spies' sense of self and body and leads to the hyperbolic depiction of the land. The grotesque sight of insects facing giants could represent an antecedent of their horror of being eaten, as grasshoppers are the only insects that are kosher, according to

Leviticus. Ironically, the grasshopper is another biped of the desert; its hind legs are powerful, important for its leaping ability, and thus for its survival.

Commentators have traditionally stumbled in their attempt to understand the severity of the punishment of the spies, asserting that the problem is not that Moses expected them to not speak the truth but rather that the messengers added to the truth their own opinion and thus turned their report into interpretation and personal judgment. Nahmanides (1194–1270), for example, focused his explanation on their use of the term *'efes*, "zero", and "but". Alluding to its loaded semantics, he asserts that it was used to distill in the audience the conviction that the price of occupying the land was too high (1961). Isaac ben Moses Arama (c. 1420–1494) follows, suggesting that it is this very term that turns their position from spies to advisors (cf. Liebes 1997, 130). More recently, Tamar Liebes, for whom the saga is a political argument between the dissident majority of the ten messengers and the pro-institutional supporters Caleb and Joshua, concludes that indeed, the sin of the spies is their divergence from objective reporting (Ibid. 1997, 120–133). Indeed, the ten spies have abandoned Moses's requirement for a testimony of the land, shifting to impart their interpretation of it.

In doing so, the ten messengers have shifted the subject of their discussion from the strong people/nation to the land. How and why has the attribute of strength been transposed onto the land, and how can one explain the land's newly acquired agency of hunger? It is possible that reacting to the poetics of a "land of milk and honey", they provide a contrasting parallelism in line with the original subject. The transition speaks to a new kind of hunger, for the narrative swiftly moves to the narrator. To the extent the Israelites are able to start imagining their Canaan as a land flowing with milk and honey, here, in front of the ironic testimonial fruits of the land, the speech act of a "land that eats its people" turns the magical land into an imagined new mouth, where bodies disappear before divine truth, violating the code and its reference in the name of telling the truth. Such a language of utter horror makes no exception for milk and honey. Languishing still in the binary axiom, it erases any trace of the positive magic of the land.

A land that eats its inhabitants, *yoshveha*, exaggerates the irony of the grammatical possession. The verb, *'okhelet*, eating, tells us that the Bible distinguishes between eating, *'okhelet*, and devouring, *bola'at*, as it will appear in the later story of Korach (Numbers 16). This narrative provides us with a rare example that makes vivid, to the horrified people around Moses, as well as to Bible readers, that the expression "a land that eats her inhabitants" is not a mere abstraction. Korach, Datan, and Aviran, who want to join the priestly tribe, demand to know why Moses led them out of the nourishing "land of milk and honey", now referring to Egypt. For their transgressive doubts and scorn for God, they are punished with the "mother of all punishments"; they, and all their kin and property, are not eaten by the land, but devoured by it (Numbers 16: 32). Here the Bible uses the verb *bala'*, to devour, swallow up, gobble, and consume.

The Bible tells us that the land's hunger is ravenous; it ends up snatching not only the grammatical subject, but also the confidence of listeners, turning them into terrified wailers who proclaim their desire to die in Egypt. For now, *eretz*, land, is slowly drawing the national discursive borders of the nation between mythological measures and the hyper real. The three words "*'eretz 'okhelet yoshveha*", radically shutter any subtext of godly code. They violate any illusion of an organic genetic bond, not only between the people and the land, but also between the people and their God. Nonetheless, an eating land, *eretz 'okhelet*, in feminine, points to the fact that the subject has undergone an oxymoronic change whereby the land that feeds people is turned into a land that feeds on people. The verb reintroduces the land as violently starving, a paradigmatic shift for the hungry, complaining Israelites, who are dependent on the land (and on Moses and God), but will now have to defend themselves from it. Moses's project of imagination has communicated in a magical language the satiated body that was nurtured with/by milk and honey. The economy of provision has produced a landscape as a new place of a "purely mental being" where the relation between the mind and language is blissfully unambiguous (Benjamin 67). Rather than "exact food" or "enough food", there will be plenty. And yet, this same land now opens an abyssal ontology where body and language are its very consumption. A land that devours its people signifies an abstraction of a second expulsion, an alternative paradise, where man is not only abandoned but also disappeared. "If we only had died in Egypt. If we only had died in the desert" (Numbers 14: 2) is already erasing its imagined bliss. Indeed, the terror of the description is thus evident in the response of the community of the Israelites who break into tears and even question, in the words of the epigraph, the whole point of coming out of Egypt. Language is critical here. Caleb, who at first silences the community and insists that they can overcome any difficulty (13: 30), responds later with Joshua more forcefully; they "ripped their garments, They said to the entire community of the Children of Israel, saying: the land that we crossed through, to scout it out good is that land, exceedingly, exceedingly!" (Numbers 14: 7). Could Caleb's words and his attempt to restore the "goodness" of the land (more literally, "very, very good is the land") hold up against the severity of the *dibbah*? The divine gift of "a land flowing with milk and honey" was scripting the matter of the Hebrew imaginary as concrete sustenance, normalizing settlers' life in the land of return. God's reaction to the people's response is also extreme, wanting to utterly destroy the Israelites. And it is Moses who begs him to save them. That is when God determines that the generation of the desert will never set foot in the land of Canaan. The forty days of the spies' excursion were translated in to forty years of wandering in the desert.

Nonetheless, the grave result of this encounter reveals the depth of the meaning of the intervention of the ten messengers. The timeless language of a land that devours its people makes this expression an axiomatic truth within an accumulative historical reading. The state of emergency that the spies introduce undermines any hope of security for sustainable food, cities, land, and God, all those categories that Moses has carefully constituted. The transformation of the eating mouth to the eaten mouth and body articulates a new threshold of the lost body, where *'efes*, the grammatical conjunctive, marks discursive flows with horrific terror, a potential sum of nothingness, (also zero), and total emptiness. Indeed, an eating land leaves no trace!

As we see within Zionist discourse, consuming milk in excess is intoxicating, resulting in a drunken subject. It operates narcotically on the level of language, narratives, images, and rhetoric. More alarmingly, it performs through its practices of consumption, for the milk is both being consumed and consuming. To the extent that God's project has been engaged in establishing a clear referent to the Promised Land, "a land of milk and honey" seeks to contain a concrete truth of material reality. The more the land is metaphorized, the further away it moves from this referentiality. Zali Gurevitch approached this dilemma through the concept of the "double site" of the mythical/historical story of the place, *Makom* (a place but also the name of God), a singular non-site that is always resisted, and can never be owned. Rather than a healing place to mend the tear of exile, the land continually hovers between the dialectics of voice and place (see Gurevitch 1997, 203–216).[13]

In the following section, I elaborate on the ways in which milk and honey have been privileged in the Zionist imagination and the narrative of return. I trace their vicissitudes in various Zionist manifestations, from socialist to capitalist economies and from local to global markets. Milk as milk—the white liquid from lactating mothers, whether humans, cows, or goats—has been deployed metaphorically to invoke purity, virginity, wellness, and the land of Israel itself, igniting its meaning, turning its serene economy of "flowing" to overflowing and flooding. Honey, the golden innocence of raw nature, turns into the sticky signifier of Heaven's sweetness and its glazed reality.

"Human Udders" and the Other of the Nation

> Oh clodded fields of Jezrael!
> Nurse! Suckle!
> …
> Because for you are the nipples of my breasts.
> > Avraham Shlonsky, "Yizrael"

Zionism built its connection to the land precisely by amplifying the magical properties of the textual milk and honey. In the collective system of signification, milk, like fire and sword, becomes a discursive event that revitalizes and engenders the relationship between Adam and *Adamah*, man and land (Katz 1996, 85–105). Within the context of exile and the Jewish diaspora, milk is a synonym for house and home, security, productivity, protection, and innocent, if procreative, sexuality. The land of milk and honey is an expression uttered as a promise or speech act, a promise that could only be fulfilled in the act of returning to the land. Zionism made that return possible.[14]

In the master-narrative of Zionism, the image of a land flowing with milk and honey is invoked to underscore the promise of plentiful or even infinite bounties. In other words, as a promise in response to historical, territorial, genealogical, psychological, and physical hunger and thirst, the "land flowing with milk and honey" substantiated the ideological economy of abundance in a visceral, visual, and sensual way.[15] Moreover, culture was perceived as colluding with nature to (re)produce and magnify the land's abundance, thereby creating tenacious associations between manual labor and prosperity (in the socialist sense). Hard work was the mode in which "milk and honey" could be extracted from the earth, a mode often articulated through the agricultural and sexual metaphors of plowing, sowing, or seeding the soil; Adam, the male, fertilizes *adamah*, the feminized land.

Nowhere is this allegory elaborated more fully than in Avraham Shlonsky's poem, "Yizrael" or "Jezrael". The poem is an invitation to the breast, as if the condition of becoming a native—a Sabra or Israeli-born Jew or native—was contingent upon drinking milk (in Shlonsky, Poetry 1958, 4). Avraham Shlonsky (1900–1973) was "the father of Hebrew neo-symbolism" (Gur 2002) and a pioneer of the Israeli avant-garde: an important poet, editor, and translator who had a major impact on the development of Modern Hebrew literature and language. Initially, Shlonsky locates "milk" in the mountains of the Gilbo'a that are like "a caravan of nursing camels with humps in the sky", and later in rivers: "Flow, flow, milk of rivers, flowing over the banks". The poem that begins as a zoomorphic description of the big breast of nature shifts in a crescendo to the speaking "I" calling: "But here also my udders fill with milk – The human udders! And my flesh – overflowing breast – protruding high from the earth". The anthropomorphic description of the landscape invites she-camels, horses, humans, and God to nurse and suckle at "man's udders". These human udders, "*'atiney 'adam*", introduce a new epic body, duplicating the pair of women's nipples, "*pitmot*", but also increasing the vigor of the milk's flow. Shlonsky's poem constitutes an *udderance*, a speech act accomplished through the phantasmagoric udder that defines the parameters of national nourishment.

For Shlonsky, it is through breast and milk that native identity is acquired. He maximizes the semantic space of the breast, drawing a broad link between the vocabulary *shad*, breast, and *shdemah*, a field, or vineyard, like in *shadmot* Jesrael and Shadai, like in *Saddai*, one of the attributions of God.[16] And indeed, once the distinctions between the land, the poet's body, and God are eliminated, they draw a figurative economy of excess where the omnipotent poet's milk is both "flowing", and "flowing... flowing over the banks", or overflowing. This collective orgy of milk speaks in a language of transformation; it blurs other distinctions and differences. Gideon Ofrat suggests that the desire to turn the body into the land serves to make the land real and concrete, a part of the godly, omnipotent vision of eternal union. The speech act is uttered by the praising son in a new alternative religion, a new testament (Ofrat 2010). Such a resurrection can take place through the ritualistic clothing and labor as a way to acquire a new skin and a new identity. Shlonsky asks:

> Who is great here, who is small
> In the kingdom of work and very flesh?
> The earth is unrolled here, the scroll of a new testament.
> And we –we are twelve.

(172)

Indeed, the passion for the land was authenticated on the premise of its physical, theological ecology, as Boaz Neumann shows us (2009, 2011 English translation). "The Jewish sweat and blood transformed the Land of Israel into a meaningful place; they strike a border zone, defining the land as Jewish". Neumann theorizes that the pioneers of the First and Second Aliyah presupposed that the land demanded to be fed and therefore they must feed her before they can feed on her. This perception had produced what he terms, "Hebrew ecology" in which they "performed" intimate acts with the land where "eroticism was not a metaphor". In this existential history of those who had transcribed the Zionist myth in their body, the land gave birth to the New Jew, while his fusion with the land was continuously enacted through different rituals throughout life and death, when he ultimately "returned his body" to the land, reunited with her and perhaps was even reborn again (Neumann 2009, 43). The theme of uniting with the land is common in the discourse; it imagines the land as feminine, while the male pioneer, the new Jew, inseminates the land. Seeking to realize the oft-cited famous affirmation in Hosea's vision, he declares the famous speech act, "I betroth you to me forever" (Hosea 2: 19). With his own flesh, sweat, blood, and hard work, he unites with the land to the point of embodying, "*ve-'reastich li le-'olam*", "I betroth you to me in blood" (Ofrat 2010).

The overflowing nature of the milk is tied to the grandiosity of the speaker and the abundance, not only of the land but also of his speech. Humans are treated to feminine hospitality in an act that emphasizes and idealizes the land, with its eroticized "nipples" (mountains), as female. But the speaking "I" of the poem, as Shlonsky identifies in the last section, titled "Toil", is a manual laborer, a road paver: "your son, Abraham, poet-road paver in Israel" (Shlonsky 1966, 172–173).[17]

Shlonsky recognizes that according to the new ideology and ethos of the pre-statehood pioneers, the natural and hospitable attributes of the female land oozing milk and honey must be subordinated to the actual working of the land—as a new theology—which also makes possible the beginning of a new genealogical relationship between humans and the land. Like Abraham, the first Jewish patriarch, Avraham Shlonsky also provides, through his poetry, a singular narrative of sacred religion that revives the old intertext and infuses new blood—milk—into its veins. His poem thereby becomes a newly inscribed canonical text.

Words are, for Shlonsky, the very building block with which he builds his roads. "Stanza" in Hebrew is *bayit*, both "house" and "home". Linear roads are also paved with intertexts of biblical, Jewish allusions, of narratives and objects. The leather strips of the Tefillin, the phylactery of male ritual, "stream down" the stanzas of his poem like the very trajectory of his new roads. Indeed, elaborating on the Hebrew language, and the tight connection between *'adamah*, *'adam* and *dam*, land, man, and blood, or *moledet* and *holadah*, homeland and birthing, between *har* and *herayon*, mountain and pregnancy, and between *zera'*, seed, and *zera'*, sperm, Gideon Ofrat critically asserted that these complex, erotic relationships of the pioneer to the land are more pathological in nature, referring to the making of the perverted, impotent, and infantile pioneer, who never grew up under the protection of the motherland. For him, being bound to the land, with the compulsive need for the mother, desiring her milk and having to feed her, infantilized the male pioneer, especially during the period between 1920 and 1942, a condition that is at the root of the early Jewish-Zionist Oedipal complex (Ofrat 2010).[18]

A feminist reading of this redemptive substitute for the mother and wife recalls that the language of the Bible has eliminated the female subject from the narrative. This elimination occupies a huge cultural space substantiated by patriarchal codes and benefits from further support through the colonial male gaze. They inseminated the land with the prototypical voice of male figures, with metonymic bodies; fathers, prophets, and poets have ecstasized an entire Hebrew discursive tradition (see also Neumann 2009).

The Zionist Reader of the Sacrifice, a Milk-Drunk Sabra

> When we Israeli Jews of today gaze at the Land of Israel, we see it
> largely through the eyes of the *halutzim* (Zionist pioneers). When we
> feel it with our bodies and souls, we sense it largely through their
> sensibilities. We are tied to the land and have difficulty giving it up
> because they were attached to it. The Land of Israel time by which
> we live is to a great extent the mythic time the pioneers defined
> by their actions. When we speak Hebrew, we speak their language.
> When we love the land, we love it largely through their love. And
> when we are willing to lay down our lives for it, we are prepared to
> die the "beautiful death," for which they, too, were prepared.
>   Boaz Neumann, Land and Desire in Early Zionism

(2011, 7)

I belong to the Sabra generation, children of the Zionist revolution. I was
one of the youth of this crowded generation of native-born and countless
newcomers from the huge Jewish diaspora. My formative years were
an accelerated process of appropriation in the whirlpool of the Zionist
melting pot that turned us all into *'Ivrim* (Hebrews and Israelis). Songs
like "*Eretz zavat chalav udvash*" (a land flowing with milk and honey)
were seductive and infectious/irresistible. They articulated in a few
words a whole future of wellbeing, along with the land, the language,
the body, and the dream. The focus was on our geo- and theopolitical
immersion in the land, making the eternal wandering Jews, *unheimlich*,
unhomely, and non-native, into *bne-bayit* (children of the home), and
nothing else. Milk and honey were not only flowing in the land, or in
posters and other visual imagery; they also flowed through our veins as
we absorbed the songs and stories like sponges. We grew up within the
narrative as we learned from a young age to possess it. Over time, the
narrative became us, our most valuable inheritance of both past and future. It provided us with the very meaning of life and survival.

   Several decades later, the song is an anachronism. Other songs, singing styles, and melodies found their way. Nonetheless, milk and honey
still flow deeply in the Israeli children's imagination; a recent multime-
dia site "Tech Architects" is an enrichment program that caters to Elementary and Middle School education in hundreds of Israeli schools. It
promotes, as its statement asserts, "attentive learning [that] unites and
makes it available to those who love learning" with an array of links,
search engines, activities, and archives. One specific sixth-grade class
assignment from December 2007 used a 1904 cover of a German Zionist journal as part of the interactive class project that marks the sixtieth
anniversary of Israei Independence Day, "Architects—Visual Images of
Zionism". The material for this activity was taken from Rachel Arbel's
book, "One Hundred Years of Zionism".[19] The visual image, "*Chalav*

Figure 1.5 A 1904 cover of a German Zionist Journal.

u-dvash", Milk and Honey, is a depiction of "the ideal Zionist land" (see above), a blue ink drawing of two cows on the lower right side of the page, and bees over a beehive on the lower left. The Hebrew captions *chalav* ("milk") and *dvash* ("honey") are marked above each image. In the middle of the page lies an elliptic bouquet of flowers that frames three male pioneers bending down and working the land, facing the far horizon. The page is symmetrically centered and balanced. The inscription of the word Tsiyon (Zion) inside the Star of David decorates the top between branches of palm trees (Figure 1.5).

As early as 1904, while still articulating the Zionist ethos, hard labor and incessant working of the land were not only inscribed as conditions for its plentiful bounty; they also defined it in aesthetics and symbols that codified the whole experience, using biblical language as the absolute axioms for immediate practical claims. The story of the twentieth-century arrival to Zion was conflated with the story of Exodus out of slavery and into the Promised Land. The pioneers in the image sit romantically alongside cows and bees in the harmonious productive re-demption of the land.

In the class assignment, both ethos and aesthetics play an important role; the instructions to the students specify:

> *Eretz Yisrael*, (The land of Israel), has been described in the Bible as a land flowing with milk and honey. The sweet flavor of raisins and almonds, and the fascination of Rabbinic tales that tell of a land of figs and dates, goats and sheep, have created an ideal image of the Land of Israel.
>
> (Tech Architect website)

Alluding to the causal, linear connection between the pioneers' hard labor and the production of milk and honey, the activity asks students to respond in the forum:

> How do you perceive the Land of Israel? How do you see her image? Is it a land of technology? The land of research? The land of development? The land of agriculture? The land of silence? The land of the Bible? Create a picture, stamp, or a sticker about the subject that you choose, and give it a title.
>
> (Ibid.)[20]

The questions, notwithstanding the difference, could remind us of Moses's questions to the twelve spies. But if we thought that his questions were closed and limiting, offering two oppositional answers within a strict binary system, the class assignment was even narrower, engaging one monolithic line of thought even while offering six questions/answers.

Evidently, the assignment was intended to be thought-provoking, creative, and highly engaging. It invited the students to rethink in their own terms the biblical image of "a land flowing with milk and honey", and its connection to contemporary Israel, bridging over a hundred years of Zionism. I was eager to read the students' responses. Overall, the comments were troublingly short; concentrating squarely on the expression, they described the artwork in minimal terms. Counter to the intention of the assignment, the image failed to inspire imaginative thinking or innovative artworks. With little elaboration on the subject, the responses were repetitive, narrow, and banal. Many reiterated the expression, taking its assumed meaning for granted. Many students proposed to make the milk and honey visible through drawing and lettering: one student, suggested a poster with the instructions: "to write a title, 'a land flowing with milk and honey,' and to make (draw) a beehive of honey and children eating honey". Another student proposed to show the picture of the Israelites coming out of Egypt arriving at the Red Sea which splits open, showing a big sign, "A land flowing with milk and honey".

The expression, biblical and Zionist, textual and visual, has been literally internalized through concrete taste and image, reflected most palpably in one of the students' enthusiastic suggestion to institute in the calendar "the day of honey", so "that everyone will bring honey (to school)" (Tech Architect website). Although "a day of honey" is not yet instituted in the Israeli calendar, in the celebrations of both the New Year and the holiday of Shavu'ot (Feast of Pentecost), honey and milk, including dates, apples, honey, and all dairy products, respectively, are the focus of the ritual meals.[21]

The meta-awareness of the students signifies, to some extent, an implicit consciousness of the trope as a trope, even if in less critical or salient terms. The students are able to acknowledge the repetitions in the tropic deployment of "milk and honey", taking the terms for granted.

A Loud Note in Goat's Ear

Even from the remote Jewish villages and shtetls, fairytales and other legends and folktales nourished the Jewish imagination, conspicuously weaving mysterious ties to the land of Israel as the land of sublime sustenance. These narratives played a significant role in solidifying the ideological network of travel back to the Promised Land. In 1925, Shai Agnon put one of these storytelling traditions into writing, preparing it for his daughter's birthday. The popular Polish tale "The Fable of the Goat" tells the story of the impoverished and sick old man whose doctors recommend that he drink goat's milk. The goat that he bought disappears for a few nights at a time and returns "with udders full of milk, sweet like honey and of the taste of Eden". The curious son decides to follow the goat in order to find out where she goes. Holding a cord that he ties to its tail, he goes into a miraculous cave that transports him to the city of Tsfat, in northern Israel, the historical center of the Kabbalah. The son writes a note to his father, hastening him to follow the goat as he did and come to Israel. He places the note in the goat's ear. Alas, the father, so horrified not to see his son back, fails to notice the note, and in his despair and mourning ends up slaughtering the goat, only to then find the note, crying out,

> Vay! Vay! Woe to the man who robs himself of his own good fortune, and woe to the man who requites good with evil! Woe to me, I could have gone up (*la-'alot*) to the Land of Israel in one bound and now I must suffer out my days in this exile.

No longer does divine intervention offer redemption. The story's tragic ending highlights the redemptive reward of life in Zion: the opening of the cave has since been sealed, as Agnon tells us, "and that youth, if he has not died, shall bear fruit in his old age, full of sap and richness, calm and peaceful in the country of life" (Agnon 1966, 93–96, Barney Rubin's translation).[22]

For many, the tale is an allegory "that touches the very essence of the Jewish people" (Zur-Glozman 2013). For Zivah Shamir, a scholar of Agnon, this tale unfolds the core history of Zionism prior to Agnon's immigration to Israel, responding to the early Zionist debates that wrestled with the question of "Where to" (Shamir 2011, 230–245). Indeed, Agnon's text elevates the language, turning it into a beautiful narrative highly saturated with biblical allusions, especially to the Song of Songs, as well as allusions to rabbinic sources. Since its publication in 1923, it has become a classic staple in school curriculums: it has been published both for children, with illustrations, and for adults, was translated into English, and has been performed on radio shows and theater productions (Pausa and Mar'ah Theaters, in 2007). It inspired comics and animations, such as Max Cohen's prize-winning Yiddish short animation, Di Mayse fun di Tsig (2004), and more recently, a version with illustrations by *Shay Charka* (Zur-Glozman 2013).[23] Numerous readings and dramatizations of the tale, including several performances by students in Middle School, are available on YouTube; both professional and amateur, they closely follow Agnon's text. In one such production, presumably a class assignment, which was posted by a group of young women, the granddaughter replaces the son.[24] In almost all of them, though, the description of *Eretz Israel* is articulated as 'a land of milk and honey", although Agnon does not use the exact expression.[25] These adaptations, along with the one by young rappers Yonatan Zehavi and Yarin Gan El (2015), reveal a premature attempt to interrogate the discursive foundations of "'*Eretz zavat halav u-dvash*".[26]

The note has never reached the father, remaining silent; nonetheless, it resonates in the ears of the Israeli Sabra, who continuously read the story with a singular desire to always get closer to the land of Israel and its milk, even while living there.

Pathological Synonyms: A Practical Project in Nationalism

The Sabra's classrooms were the ideological frontline in the project of shaping Zionist consciousness. Nevertheless, for Dan Pagis (1930–1986) to enter the classroom means to impart an acutely different lesson about milk and honey, something he accomplishes through his eleven-stanza poem "Exercises in Practical Hebrew", *Targilim be-'Ivrit shimushit*. Pagis, a Holocaust survivor, was an established scholar of Medieval Hebrew literature as well as a Hebrew poet and translator, most widely cited for his short poem, "Written in Pencil in the Sealed Railway Car". The first three short stanzas of the eleven in "Practical Hebrew" comprise the opening page of his collection "*Milim nirdafot*", "Double exposure", literally "Synonyms" (1991 [1982]). As we will see, it is precisely the *shimushiyut* of the Hebrew, its practicality and instrumentality that he seeks to address within the wider "lexical" phenomenon of synonyms and synonym-making. Since its publication, the poem has gained considerable popularity. It is an excellent choice for a close reading that can reveal its multilayered depth and complex relationship to our biblical allusions.

Once again we find ourselves in the Hebrew classroom, loaded with mimicry and potentially transformative epiphanies. And Pagis enters the poetic classroom as a grammatical wizard, playfully conjuring the material for his grammar drills, as if the philological acquisition of language can make meaning secondary to morphology, form, and syntax, as if it is possible to separate them from their biblical semantics. His dynamic speech adds to the effectiveness of the lesson. Its text renders salient the space between language and speech, literature and pedagogy. It is not that surprising for Pagis to return to the classroom; the Hebrew classroom has been one of the most saturated frontiers of cultural appropriation, especially the notorious, *shi'ur moledet*, the course on our local, native homeland, which was an introductory assortment of history, geography, biology, and literature, all centered around the national map of *Eretz Yisrael* (Almog 1999; Azoulay and Ophir 2002; Gur-Ze'ev 2004). These were the moments during which the Sabra culture had been drilled into our minds through vivid and tangible symbols, images, and tunes, naturalizing the subject with an emphasis on differentiating Israel from the rest of the world, and "us" Israelis, from "them", the others. These were the moments in which we, the Sabra kids, were continually born and reborn into an accelerated space of becoming Hebrew.

Pagis's epigraph is alerting; it frames his "Synonyms" with rhetorical allusions, both in the second person, singular, masculine, speaking to "you", including the reader: ha-shalom *lekha*, "Are you at peace?" (2 Kings 4), a sarcastic concern, followed by a second question, *ha-ratsachta ve-gam yarashta?*" "Have you murdered and also taken possession?" (I Kings 25: 19), an admonition (also repeated in stanza #10).[27] Pagis's first question, *"ha-shalom lakh?"* ("are you [feminine] at peace?"), alludes to the story of the Shunamite woman when she approaches the prophet Elisha. Rewarding the Shunamite woman for her gracious hospitality— she provides room and board when he passes through the town; Elisha miraculously brings about the birth of a son after proclaiming "you will have a son". She insists that such an act cannot be possible given the age of her husband, but the prophet reassures her that it is an act of God. Years later, her son dies, and when she hurries to the prophet, the first question Elisha instructs his helper to ask is "are you at peace, is your man at peace? Is the child at peace?" She ironically replies with "We are at peace", even though she came to rebuke him in light of her son's death. In the end, Elisha revives the son.

Pagis's second question, also an idiom, takes us back to the words of the prophet Elijah, denouncing King Ahab about the double crime he committed against Naboth the Jezreelite, a humble man in his kingdom, whose vineyard he confiscated and whom he murdered (1 Kings 21: 19). The phrase has been used to convey one of the harshest moral lessons within the codes of ethics in Jewish law. Although in the Bible, the phrase precedes Elijah's prophecy of doom, in contemporary politics it leaves a void of shamelessness that in a way enables such acts. Pagis insists on framing the whole lesson within the synonymous shame; for, who is the murderer now? Whose land is being confiscated? And how shameful is it that these acts are practiced shamelessly? And Elijah's speech is proclamatory, it is shaming the king, but the semantics of the shaming act are tied to the doomed prophesy of Ahab's death, aiming to erase not only him and his lineage, but also all that is human in him. Although his death is iconic and radically memorable: "All of Ahab's line who die in the town shall be devoured by dogs, and all who die in the open country shall be devoured by the birds of the sky" (1 Kings 21: 24).

Insofar as these two questions inform the eleven poems, the sentence in parentheses "(an example of interrogative sentences in a grammar book)" shifts the semantics into a grammatical register. The literal meaning of "Synonyms", in Hebrew, is revelatory: *Milim nirdafot*, "persecuted words", in the passive tense, also refers to a consecutive meaning, that which follows, or succeeds, semantically. Pagis will soon make clear that the poem's predicament and its prediction should read as a charge against both content and linguistic forms; "what" is said and "how" it is said are inherently connected. In a wider sense, Hebrew culture and Hebrew language conflate with one another. Have we, readers of the poems, all murdered and taken possession? Aren't we all complicit in the act of taking possession of the land? Pagis turns it into the ultimate, timely example of interrogation. But rather than simply a lesson of synonyms in the dictionary, he is talking about synonymization as a method of life.

Other poets and songwriters allude to these narratives with different degrees of urgency. Ten years earlier, Natan Yonatan (1923–2004), wracked with grief after the death of his eldest son during the Yom Kippur War, wrote a poem in which he lamented the land and its part in his son's death. In *"Shir Eretz"* ("Song of the (Home)land"), Yonatan intersects the two biblical narratives, saying: "A land that devours its people, / milk, honey and blue, / sometimes it even itself plunders / the ewe-lamb of the poor neighbor".[28] Milk and honey are tied together with a devouring land that robs its neighbors in a causal relationship that Pagis further develops, augmenting a multilayered conversation on the lasting reality of these allusions and their synonymization.[29]

"Shalom, shalom", at the beginning of the poem and in its end, always as a pair, welcoming and cheerful, obscures behind its "hello" greeting the more complex homonymic one, shalom as "peace" and shalom as absence of peace. As it appears in the poem, "Shalom, shalom" highlights the emphatic greeting and the significative abyss between one shalom and the non-shalom. This vagueness leads to his comment on temporality in Hebrew; it has past and future, referring also to the perfect and imperfect tenses, but has no present tense, only *benoni*, a middle voice, an inherently transitive event with no reference to the subject, or agent. What does this *benoni*, the liminal zone, mean grammatically, and how is it translated ontologically? Implicit here is the loss of the present tense when verbs are transformed into adjectives, describing a permanent situation, and even becoming a noun. A verb like *'okhel*, for example, could designate the action of eating in the third-person singular, "he eats" or "he is eating", but as an adjective, and a noun, especially with the definite article, they become "the eating person", "eater", and "diner". In the context of intertextuality, the loss of present tense adds to a void, one that is thickened by texts and intertexts, fluctuated between the loaded past and the empty promise of future and hope.

Pagis's intertextuality culminates with the use of the two other fragments as pedagogical props, "a land flowing with milk and honey" and "a land that devours its people", relying bluntly on their readymade availability, and on the way that they are circulating in contemporary culture.

> A land that eats/devours her inhabitants.
> Her lovers devour her lovers.
> Change it all to future tense.
>
> (Pagis 1991, 211)

He will take the idea of a devouring land one step further, when the lovers of the land eat and are being eaten in an endless, vicious cycle of eaters and lovers. He will also grammatically exaggerate the mythological excess of milk and honey in stanza 10, by using the plural, "Lands flowing with milk and honey. This is declarative. If you happen to see them, send regards, That is imperative". Later he warns dryly "don't be sweet, lest they devour you" (1991, 213), highlighting that devouring is an extended act of adoration, where the eaters and lovers, *'okhelim* and *'ohevim*—both in active participle of *pa'al*—devour each other, making "devouring" a synonym of "love" and "lovemaking".[30] Together, they imply the utter falsity both of love and land, but also of the language that is blinded to their real meaning. He thus concludes, "If you happen to see them, send regards" (*d'ash* is an acronym of *drishat* shalom, literally "a message of peace), "What's new?"

Nothing is actually new. And yet, if we were to think that Pagis has brought to the classroom sharp knives and explosives, we soon realize that their banality in culture turns them into decorative, pedagogical toys. To the extent that they have pointed to trauma, loss, or any crisis, they are no longer able to articulate their edge and horror; belonging to the interior archive of culture, they appear to be overly "domesticated", reliable, trustworthy, and risk-free.[31] Here, the poet himself models and mimics the practicality of the Hebrew language. Attentive to the question of how to be mischievously subversive, he never offends "his students", i.e., his readers, a position that has likely contributed to the canonicity and popularity of his work.[32] Rather, he presents the semantic charge of his biblical citations in a simple and unthreatening (albeit cunning) manner of teaching. True, he nonchalantly moves from time-less present to future and from singular to plural, reducing the register of biblical allusions to a casual register of spoken grammar, but the implicit question still remains: how easy is it to deconstruct the poetic figurative meaning from this plain syntactic, tense system? How far can he reach through parodic "conjugation" of the disturbing expressions? Seeking to alert us to their reduced semantics and meaning-making by showing us the predicament of synonyms, his lesson instructs a poetic grammar as a new textbook manual of spoken language, as the very principle of language, constituting the grammar of life.[33]

Using the biblical expressions as common, shared references builds on their function in collective memory. They have become, what Amos Funkenstein calls "topocentric", in the cultural vocabulary: fragments of narratives, institutions, and historical events that have been reducing rather than producing historical-critical consciousness; selectively historicized biblical allusions that have become the "prototypical principles of narratives" (Funkenstien 1993, 8; also Zerubavel 1995; Chetrit 2010). The reductive, decontextualized meaning of the topocentric is a critical aspect of synonymization. Pagis's "*Milim Nirdafot*", (Synonyms), like his treatment of similes (in the Introduction), provides poetic configurations from which to examine the very predicament of meaning-making and the signifying process of contemporary Hebrew, responding to the process of "selective memory" (Zerubavel 1995) and elimination of meaning. In the seven lines of the ninth stanza, for example, Pagis compiles an impressive, comprehensive list of twenty-four references to the word "shame", reminding the reader of the rich, diverse lexical scale of the phenomenon, culminating in the last gesture, which scolds the reader: "shame on you!" With this chain of the twenty-four idle synonyms of shame together with homonyms like, "shalom, shalom", Pagis draws the contours of the ironic, dull signifying space of language. It helps to convey the extent of the drama both in language and even more so in the cultural politics of daily life, invoking the affect of the epigraph—with the double charge of murdering and confiscating—imparting along with the shameful void a hollow, meaningless language. At the same time, the reverberating rhetoric of "Have you murdered and also taken possession?" keeps the historical charge of David and Uria.

An unreliable system that takes on itself to signify too much of the burden of culture, Hebrew has become the answer and solution to a long list of cultural predicaments so much so that it serves as their ideological alibi; it appears functional, instrumental, and harmless. Pagis's virtual walk through the Hebrew grammar leads to one cemetery on the right and another cemetery on the left (stanza x); exemplifying the potential of the Hebrew to manipulate meaning and hide differences of registers, class, gender, ethnicity as much as of life and death, the living dead and the dead who are alive. Sacred and casual, euphemistic and literal—it ironically exposes not only violence but also the ability of language to camouflage the truth and perform under different covers. It implicitly explains the numbing effect of citations and how it has become possible to live within and among them.

Shoshana Shababo's "Honey Moon" and the Beehive

> That which I loved, they withheld from me, and that which I hated, they shoved into my soul.
>
> Shoshanna Shababo, *Love in the Town of Safed*[34]

Although it is ostensibly a fictional account, Shoshana Shababo chooses to call her work "Honeymoon" (1932), an essay. It is a rather short story about Golda, the heroine, her "dumb" only son Zalman, who has just married Mazal, a young Yemenite, and the "sweet" transition from hopeless, burdened widowhood to supreme happiness. In fact, two honeymoons frame the story: first Golda's, and later, her son's. It presents a rather critical gendered, ethnic reading of a honeymoon drenched in honey. In fact, the wedding tunes are parodically replaced by the buzzing and humming of the bees in Golda's farm. Her affection for the beehives exceeds her affection for French culture or reading and literature; the former affinity is "mental, profound, and struck in her heart and personality..." (Shababo 1996, 219). In fact, Golda loves the bees in a way that cannot be articulated, so she exalted all that love, labor, thrill, and cheerfulness in one sacred word: "Honeymoon", as a code that says it all (Ibid.). Shababo builds on the feminine production of the bee, *dvorah*, which the Hebrew marks both morphologically and grammatically as feminine. This highly saturated site employs the very making of honey in and for the double honeymoon not only as a code of commencing the sweet, happy, erotic life of the newlyweds, but as a framing device and prerequisite to the sublime utopia. Honey's sweetness leads to an all-encompassing sweetness. After all, would Zalman, the schlimazel son of Golda, "a born loser", literally, in Yiddish, "rotten luck", find a woman like Mazal (whose name means "luck"), if not for his mother's passion for the land, for the bees, for their buzzing and for the nectar of their flowers? This beauty stands in striking contrast to the lowly way the narrator introduces the three characters.

Shababo's subversive narration reverses the paradigmatic image of the diaspora as a long lasting disease or crisis: "The first days of her honeymoon" thus opens the essay, describing Golda's mindset in the morning, engulfed with the sudden burst of memories that take her twenty-five years back, to the *galut*, the time of divine, paradisiac happiness, "there she was, a gentle young woman, married to a rich merchant; she lived lavishly, gave birth to a son, she saw happiness..." Under the happy clouds of the memories of her own honeymoon, Golda's present seems bleak indeed as she reflects on her life:

> Golda recalls her arrival to Israel, her deceased husband, her little Zalman...here, her husband died and the child grew up, grew up, he remained disabled... his head is small in comparison to his body. His brain is underdeveloped and not that normal, Zalman is enfeeble ... later, with her own force and money, she bought this piece of land, planted an orchard, built up a big farm, built a house, a house in Israel.
>
> She is a farmer... fat, thick, a big-bellied balky piece of meat... her face is swollen, her eyes small, her forehead narrow, her nostrils are wide open and her voice is thick and coarse... She gained all this in Israel, during twenty years of labor.
>
> (Ibid. 219)

Golda's twenty years of Zionism result in a grotesque caricature, in a constant sigh of despair at her son's lack of luck in finding a bride. Zalman—the *metumtam* (the dumb one) as she refers to him (Ibid. 220)—comes back from his trip to the city (to find a wife) beaming with happiness and joy; he enthusiastically utters "honeymoon" as a secret code word between them, so the neighbors will not catch on. What is more, when he describes to his mother how he met Mazal, she stereotypically presupposes that he met a servant, although Mazal works in a café as a waitress. Shababo describes her as "A Yemenite woman, with colored lips, black skin, thick flesh, a steady gait and confident voice".

Shababo's first novel, Maria, which was published in 1932, the same year as "Honeymoon", was critical and provocative. It was followed by the second novel, *'Ahavah be-Tsfat* (Love in the Town of Safed), which represented anything but the national socialist-Zionist literary ethos of her time, especially after the inflammatory Arab-Jewish conflict of 1929. Maria, the story of a young Arab-Christian woman who escapes to a convent in Haifa, opened forbidden sites of women's desire, and elaborated on the psycho-social, local, cross-cultural and intimate interaction between Jews and Arabs, Muslims and Christians. It was received as a literary scandal and a major disappointment. Shababo was accused of mocking her teachers' high expectations, especially those of her mentor Yehuda Burla, and of writing vulgar, sensational, melodramatic novels, and was soon placed outside of the purview of the Hebrew literary establishment (Halevi 1996, 10–12). She died relatively unknown in 1992.

Shababo (1910–1992), along with a long list of women authors of the pre-State period (1882–1948)—including, to name a few, Devorah Baron, Batya Kahana, Nehamah Pukhachewsky, and Rivka Alper—refused to engage with the ideal new Jew of Modernity that dominated the literature of male authors (Berlovitz 2009, Zakai 2011). Their short story collections, novels, poetry, and literary works in Hebrew periodicals and literary supplements have been marginalized, ignored, and trivialized, denying their significant role in the promotion and formation of Hebrew literature and the literary community (see also Berlovitz 2009). Shababo, who was born in Zikhron Yakov to a Sephardic family from Zfat on her father's side, and Iranian on her mother's, was subject to even harsher exclusion. Her unique voice among the women authors and her intent to diversify the Hebrew Ashkenazi discourse with her focuses on the local life of the New Middle Eastern, Sephardic women were violently silenced. In that sense, it is important to contextualize "Honeymoon" within a critical perspective. Even the choice to title it "an Essay" reveals an attempt to de-fictionalize the account of Golda.

Shababo's critical approach is manifested in her liberal gestures about love, desire, and freedom in marriage. Against Golda's assertion that her son's disability will limit his chance of getting any *shidduck* (he is dependent on his mother), Shababo constructs a reality that exceeds the mother's dreams: a marriage of mutual love with a double buzzing, in which the "Z" sounds in their names—counter-hegemonic prototypes—add to the concert of the bees. This is especially poignant against the background of Golda's admiration for the bees and for the order in the beehive as an institution of honey. Now, with the three productive females around him, his mother, his wife, and the bee, Zalman, the good-for-nothing, emerges as the mensch of the land; he performs his masculinity according to gendered and Zionist assignments. Golda's farm of golden honey becomes a utopian paradise whose intoxicating smell not only attracts bees for more honey, but also literally drenches Golda with the sweet, sticky aroma of honeymoon memories.

Within the mist of honeymoon nostalgia that Golda experiences that morning, and from within the cloud of sticky burning reality of the Zionist gaze of honey and bees, Shababo manages to present us with an ironic, exaggerated account that maximizes the symbolic site of honey as a local carnival of actualization whereby Zalman can proclaim his emotional independence from his mother.[35]

Tnuva

The Zionist entity that best epitomizes the new work ethic associated with tapping into and multiplying the abundance of the land is Tnuva. Tnuva is Israel's largest food company, although it is primarily associated with cow's milk and dairy products, including an infant formula called

Figure 1.6 Distribution of Milk in Schools between the years 1936 and 1945 (Tnuva Archive).

Yammi.[36] Tnuva usurps the mother's breast; they are representing themselves as synonymous with the mother of Israel. Tnuva as such is the arbiter of milk consumption, of Israeli belonging and becoming. Founded in 1926 as an independent, non-profit cooperative agricultural organization, Tnuva is now a capitalist enterprise that in recent years has absorbed small companies and manufacturers and markets brands along with specific commodities.[37] The company dominates the Israeli market and has entered into the global market and beyond, to the Milky Way; they were the first company in the world to post an advertisement in outer space. (https://www.tnuva.co.il)

In Figure 1.6, the nurse is administering milk to schoolchildren during a snack break. True, nurses were a central part of the schools and each school had a nurse who was in charge of students' health and hygiene. Here, she sits in the first row as the representative of the medical system, not only supervising milk during the morning food break, but also overseeing the children. (Mass immigration called for heightened attention to children's hygiene as part of the civilizing process of Europeanization on the national premises.) As the ultimate authority on health and hygiene, Tnuva and the associated/complicit medical institutions had a major role in determining the standards of aesthetics and decorum that defined the healthy, able-bodied Sabra.

The seating order of the girls in the front row is also revealing; centered in the photo is the blond Ashkenazi girl, sitting between two dark girls, probably of Yemenite origins. The fact that she is the only one who is actually drinking suggests that the picture was taken with her as the focus. One can also ask, have the other children drunk already? Or perhaps they have not yet received their milk and will only do so after the photograph is taken. The fact that they all sit distant from the cup, and with the napkin and cup on their table, might suggest that for the sake

Figure 1.7 Milk Delivery to the Transitional Camps (*Ma'abarot*) in the early 1950s (Tnuva Archive).

Figure 1.8 Milk Delivery in the 1950s and 1960s (Tnuva Archive).

of the picture, the girl in the center is the staged model of the spectacle of drinking. The medicalization of the milk, along with the impression of sterilization, adds to the ritualistic aspect of drinking milk in school as a highly valuable commodity in the "pedagogical" consumption of the national good, in the sense that the consumption of national goods, in this case milk, marks the consumer as belonging to the national good (Figures 1.7 and 1.8).

Throughout its history, Tnuva has been closely tied to the Israeli state, and in many respects, the story of Tnuva was made to be the story of Zionism. The company's public relations brochure links the history of the company to that of the nation-state. Their website, for example, includes the story of how in 1948, David Ben Gurion, Israel's first prime minister, called for Tnuva to deliver milk in secret convoys to Jerusalem, which was under siege.[38] An agri-business with cosmic designs, Tnuva can also be understood as an institution promoting a native

Figure 1.9 Moshe Dayan, Minister of Agriculture, Drinks milk, 1963.

"lactic eugenics".[39] Children were administered milk as if it were a potent "cultural tonic" that would build strong, native bodies. Note in
this connection that children of the Sabra elite are called *yaldei tnuva*
("cream of the crop"). Appropriated as the national beverage, milk has
been transformed from a children's drink into an "energy drink" or even
"super food" for adults (Figure 1.9), even as drinking it turns adults
back into children, into native Sabra, and into symbolic orphans whose
biological mothers are replaced by the motherland. Consider Meir Wieseltier's lines in his poem, "Snippet of Pedagogic Poem": "I was not
born in Nahalal, I did not suckle at the breast of Tnuva".[40] Wieseltier,
who was born in Moscow, is mocking the mythologized native culture
and the inflated image associated with Nahalal, the socialist hometown
of Zionist leaders of the Second and Third Aliyah. Moshe Dayan, who
was appointed to a number of prominent roles within the Israeli military
and government, including the Ministry of Agriculture, epitomizes this
native model of Israeli virility at its most nationalistic.
   Similarly, Tnuva has usurped the process of lactation as a mother-child
centered activity, developing it as a male-centered industry with a global
consumership. With over 1,000 dairy products—in as many colors, fla-
vors, and percentages of fat—lining the shelves of Israeli supermarkets, it is
easy to forget that milk is a substance that comes (once came) from nature.
The more milk is invested with technological expertise, the more its aura
or auratic value rises in the libidinal economy of consumptive pleasure.[41]
For Israelis, drinking milk is an opportunity both to identify with the early
pioneers and their new relationship to the land, and to meld fantasy with
utility. It is a seemingly banal act filled with "ideological evidence" that

Figure 1.10 Tnuva, Tel Aviv.

effectively "whitewashes" the other aspect of the story of Israel as a "land that devours its inhabitants" (Wright and Wright 1999) (Figure 1.10).

The ideological dimensions of milk were made powerfully evident in the 1970s with the rise of the Israeli Black Panthers, who deployed it as a symbol of ethnic, class, and racial differences. According to the Panthers, delivered milk was redolent of Ashkenazi, European culture, and of an affluent, middle-class lifestyle. They staged Operation Milk in Jerusalem on March 14, 1972, redelivering bottles of milk from apartment buildings in Rehavia to the "asbestos neighborhood" within Kiriat Yovel consisting of low-income tract housing. On flyers attached to the bottles, the Panthers wrote:

> Operation Milk is for the children of the poor neighborhoods. These children do not find every morning behind the door the milk they need. In contrast, there are cats and dogs in wealthy neighborhoods that are provided with plenty of milk.

The operation was especially effective given that it took place in the 1970s, a period when political activists were prohibited by the police from staging large-scale demonstrations. Operation Milk generated a great deal of publicity and sympathy for the Israeli Panthers (Figure 1.11).

Tnuva's prominence in the Israeli economy cannot be overstated. Cottage cheese has, in recent years, become a staple of Israeli food for those of every socioeconomic status, surpassing even bread in its ubiquity. Tnuva controls roughly 70% of the Israeli dairy market, enough for the Israeli Antitrust Authority to consider it a monopoly. Nevertheless, in 2008, the Authority announced it would no longer regulate cottage cheese in the interest of generating market competition. Shockingly

Figure 1.11 Cow dolls on display in the Jerusalem Day Parade, 1998.

enough, this led to Tnuva raising their cottage cheese prices by around 40% over the next three years, resulting in a class-action lawsuit. In fact, the massive protests in Tel Aviv in the summer of 2011, which protested the increasingly high cost of living in Israel and came to encompass such issues as untenable housing rates, were catalyzed by Tnuva's price hikes for their cottage cheese, the baseline of a modern Israeli lifestyle (Figure 1.12).

In 2015, after extensive negotiations, Tnuva sold a major share to Chinese food conglomerate Bright Foods. Nevertheless, Tnuva CEO Arik Schor maintains that Tnuva will always remain fundamentally Israeli while they develop an international market for Tnuva products. Taken in the context of Tnuva's saturation of brand identity with Zionist rhetoric and biography, it becomes apparent that Tnuva has appointed itself the corporate emissary for the global consumption of Zionism.[43]

Milk is a symbol of inclusion of the native-made Israeli Sabra and his high seat of masculinity. Feeling strong and big, the Hebrew reader is contentedly tied to the milk and the breast in a metonymic relationship, whether it is the breast of God, the breast of the land, its mountains, as Shlonsky asserts, or the mother's breast. Indeed, it was impossible to foresee that part of the genius of the milk is its ability to drown its drinkers, in the same way that the cruel sweetness of the sticky honey was beyond the sight of the Hebrew reader. Within the over-consumptive ideological climate of Zionist Israel, these two substances will turn their consumers into oblivious slaves of symbols, addicted to historical depth and its magical possibilities. The fantastic promise of milk and honey will continuously make us believe in the language of Tnuva, that

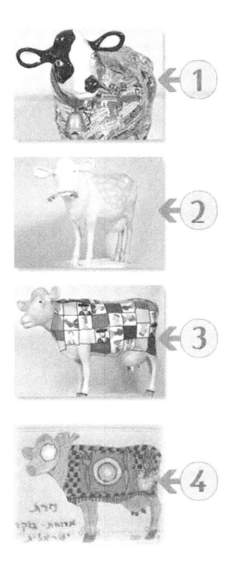

Figure 1.12 The four winning designs in the Miss Tnuva art competition, as part of the inauguration of "Tnuva House" in 2004.[42]

it is a way "to grow up in an Israeli home!" Healthy and strong, they will raise us, bring us home, and sweeten our wars, a native food for the normalization of life.

More than that, milk whitens all colors, especially red, that of blood. In Chapter 2, the poet Shelly Elkayam tells us how the smell of the covenant masks the stink/stench of dead carcasses, Abraham's slaughtered pieces of the Brit, in Genesis 16. Within the big melting pot that is Israeli culture, milk helps also to bleach ethnic colors and whiten its differences. The sweetness in the mouth, similarly, anesthetizes the senses.

The opening scene of Dror Shaul's award-winning autobiographical film, *Adama Meshuga'at* (Sweet Mud) 2006, sets the tone to the whole predicament of the private life in the kibbutz. In the light of dawn, the camera introduces Avraham, the respectful Kibbutz secretary, masturbating to/on one of the cows. Avraham is the epitome of both the victim of Zionist rhetoric and the product thereof. Said rhetoric perverts the understanding of consumption, national duty, consumptive reciprocity, and pleasure (among other things) by subsuming within the ideology of milk such diverse and scarcely compatible notions as sexuality, agriculture, theology, animal husbandry, nationalism, and moralism. Avraham is masturbating to all of these things. (He knows not which, nor how to parse them out.) It is all the more poignant given that Dvir, the 13-year-old protagonist, shares with us this early morning voyeuristic scene, while crushing a big lollipop in his mouth.

Losing One's Way: On the Road to National Belonging

The *'ayin* and the *chet* is a source of living waters for an accent.
Tikva Levi, "Poor Bertolt Brecht," Keys To the Garden[44]

On the Way to Ein Harod

On the way to Ein Harod
I lost my trilled *resh*.

Afterwards I didn't feel
The loss of my guttural *'ayin*
And the breathy *chet*
I inherited from my father who himself picked it up
On his way to the Land.

On the way to Ein Harod
I lost my *'ayin*
I didn't really lose it -
Guess I just swalled it.[45]

That ethnic identity can be exposed by one consonant is an important fact in Chetrit's intra-ethnic exchange among Israelis. Speech, accent, diction, and pronunciation among Hebrew speakers reverberate against a "cultural ear", comprising, not the visual gaze but its aural counterpart. They are all contested markers of identity in a country of immigrants, identifying the speaker's place of origin, class, education, religion, or nationality. In the theater of representation, accent becomes a site of interpretation, an encoding and decoding of cultural boundaries that seeks almost instantaneously to mark and appraise the cultural location of the speaker. Whereas accent, in general, articulates a distinguished mode of pronunciation, the specific pronunciations of the glottal sounds, *"resh"*, *"'ayin"*, and *"chet"* denote a part of Sephardic Hebrew that served as the basis for the creation of the Standard Hebrew Language.[46] Nonetheless, in the hierarchy of accents and pronunciation, where the heterogenic dictions of the melting pot that is Israel, the Arabic or Mizrahi accent, more than the Sephardic, is a marker of inferiority.

Chetrit's poem's "On the way to Ein Harod" addresses the subject of devouring through the vanishing of the Moroccan ethnolect of Hebrew pronunciation. The glottal sounds are at the heart of phonetic difference and identity difference accent, indeed, present in Mizrahi and Sephardic diasporas, it has increasingly disappeared from Sabra speech. His choice of Kibbutz is cunning; "Ein Harod" should contain the three distinct Hebrew consonants of accent differentiation: the glottal *Resh*, *Chet*, and *'Ayin*. Thus, once, for example, the sound of the *'Ayin*, is assimilated into the *'Alef*—it becomes indistinguishable from the *'Alef*, as it losses its glottal depth. The same for the *chet* and the *chaf*.

Chetrit locates the drama of the accent "on the roads" to Israel (his father) and on the road to Kibbutz Ein Harod (the son, the poetic "I"). The kibbutz, in general, has embodied the Ashkenazi establishment of the Zionist project from its early pioneering days, dating back to the beginning of the twentieth century, to the socialist labor party, accentuating the agricultural collective and the platform of social and economic equality. Ein Harod is a highly symbolic site in the Israeli project of Sabrahood/'Ivrut that ironically exposes the absurdity of Jewish displacement in geographies of homeland and homecoming. Kibbutz Ein Harod is located in the Jezrael Valley, near Harod Spring, in the lands of what used to be the Palestinian village Eyn Jalud. Its invocation accentuates the layers of Arab difference implicated in both language and history; differences in accent, name, and place. Ein Harod is one of the first Kibbutzim in the discursive practice of the Yishuv (pre-statehood Zionist Palestine); its lands were bought from Palestinian farmers by Yehoshua Hankin, one of the key "redeemers of land" of the Second Aliyah in 1921. Historically, Kibbutz Ein Harod could also be perceived as the founding platform of Zionist ideology; many famous ideologues were among its members, such as Yitzhak Tabenkin or Haim Shtruman. But not only does its establishment re- flect the ethos of the Kibbutz in the broader discourse, but in 1953, Ein Harod was also at the center of fierce, scandalous disagreements that led to a split among its members and created two Kibbutzim, repre- senting distinct movements and political parties: the labor, mainstream MAPAI (*me'uchad*), and the more socialist, leftist group, MAPAM (*'ichud*).[47] Amos Kenan famously used Ein Harod as the last holdout of humanity against the apocalyptic ruins of Israel in his novel *The Road to Ein Harod* (Kenan 1984).

Chetrit speaks to the loss of one's accent as the loss of one's self, which is also the condition for inclusion. If these three consonants embody the physical performance of Sephardic authenticity (I am using the term Sephardic in agreement with the traditional division between Ashkenazi and Sephardic pronunciation of the Hebrew language), it tells us about the desire to belong through accent. For Rogoff, the project of Zionism has thematized nativity around the axis of belonging as a model of "a diasporic homecoming of the imagination" (Rogoff 2000). At its center is the "production of belonging", an intensified socio-cultural mechanism of national discourse "which mobilizes the desire to belong through a new definition, an outsider's definition of what and how it means to belong" (Ibid. 149). "On the way to Ein Harod" presupposes such a struggle to male or female Sabrahood (Levi 1996a, 1996b; Dahan-Kalev 2001; Weiss 2004; Chetrit 2010)

We see the devastating effects of this whitewashing even in the structure of the poem: *bala'ati* (swallowed) becomes *balati* (swalled). Already the *'ayin* has been assimilated into the *'alef*, but even that disappears without a trace. In other words, the suppression of the *'ayin* is so profound that even the *'alef*, the site of its appropriation, is devoured. *'Ayin*, the name of the letter, literally means "an eye" and "a spring", but in its new Sabra pronunciation it becomes similar to *'ayin*, "negation, nothing, and naught". Chetrit's Ein Harod, accordingly, has been reduced to its homophone Ein Harod, the non-existence of Harod, ironically emphasizing that rather than coming to Israel to "build and be built", as the mythological ethos reverberated, the consummate site of adjustment and belonging translates into a location of anxiety (*harod*, literally loss and defeat). The *'ayin* is phonetically, literally, and metaphorically swallowed and assimilated. The result testifies not only to the loss of the Mizrahi accent—a bridge that connects the body and its production—but also to the slow process of diminishing the Mizrahi subject into (*'ayin*), nothingness. Along with the gradual loss of the glottal sounds, the speaker realizes that he lost his agency, in the same way that he realizes that Ein Harod, the place, does not really exist: always on the way, never really arriving, strongly suggesting that the Kibbutz never fulfilled its dream of becoming or of "bearing".

Accents juxtaposes a long history of engagement with Jewish texts; Judeo-Arabic is an important aspect of North-African and Middle Eastern history that preserved Jewish tradition of prayer recitation, and the general intimate Jewish life as in Arabic culture. But rather than just merely a change of acclimation, accent, for Chetrit, is more than a physical loss, a mental injury that forces him to silence the inheritance of the past, its melodies, and to flatten the depth of its reverberation. In many ways, Sami Chetrit has become this ideal reader and Hebrew reader, now, articulated through his speech. In the poem, he mourns his glottal *'ayin* and *chet* which he lost with the acquisition of his Sabra accent as he realizes the irreparable cost of this achievement.

Notes

1 *Eretz zavat chalav udvash*: Although considered a folk song, the popular tune was composed in 1952 by Eliyahu Gamliel (1926–2013) who also choreographed the accompanying dance. A second, less popular melody was composed by Emanuel Amiran (Fotcguv) (1909–1993) in the late fifties. (www.zemereshet.co.il/song.asp?id=541&artist=109)
  Gamliel's song was performed by many singers and musical groups, among them Nina Simone.
2 The *hora* arrived in Israel with the Eastern European immigrants, likely introduced by Baruch Agadati from Serbia. Though it originates in the Balkans, it is by now primarily associated with Zionist and Israeli culture.
3 Putting biblical verses to music was not so uncommon, even for the secular Israeli Sabras. In that era, these songs had a predominantly secular valence, much like songs such as "Kumbaya". This is in marked distinction to the *piyyut*, a hymnal genre of music comprised of biblical and religious themes, and currently highly popular.
4 Ariana Melamed takes a harsh stance against the reception of the song as an "absolutely natural… a historical documentation" (2008), and not as wish fulfillment in the face of an uncertain outcome. Fifty-two years after the event, she reconsiders the meaning of the lyrics and the blindness in which it was sung. (www.ynet.co.il/articles/0,7340,L-3512614,00.html)
5 http://web.nli.org.il/sites/NLI/Hebrew/music/wilensky/selected_songs/Pages/mol_har_sinai.aspx
6 Ilana Pardes ties the whole Exodus narrative to a biography of the nation, highlighting the role of the Bible as a narrative base on the formation of Modern nations. Approaching the narrative moment of birth, she psychologically alludes to the stages of one's life as well as the project of nation-building. Accordingly, Pardes is right in emphasizing the act of resistance of the spies as a crisis within the context of nation formation and imagined community.
7 A land flowing with milk and honey appears 16 times in the Bible, in Exodus 3: 8, 17, 13: 5; Leviticus 20: 24–26, 22: 4; Numbers 13: 27, 14: 8; Deuteronomy 6: 3, 11: 8–12, 26: 8–9, 27: 2–3, 31: 20; Joshua 5: 6; Jeremiah 11: 5, 32: 22; Ezekiel 20: 5–6, 15.
8 The masculine *zav* is differentiated from the *zavat* of *'eretz*, the feminine land.
9 Another fragment of the story appears in Numbers 32.
10 Also in English, "spies" from the French, "*pieds*", foot.
11 Legs are important in the mobility of the Bible; the ultimate act of hospitality, the washing of the feet of the guests, can be understood as an expression of reception within this language of feet, like a hand shake. But a whole tradition of *le-ragel*, has been developed, including pilgrimage, hikes, touring and spying.
12 https://gideonofrat.wordpress.com/2014/06/13/המרגלים-שחזרו-מן-החום/
13 I am indebted to Zali Gurevitch's inspiring work in the essay, "The Double Site of Israel", for the conceptual framework of dialectics of home and return at the intersection of place and speech.
14 Milk is a historically prominent local trope in the culture of Jewish communities, especially in Eastern Europe in the shtetls, as illustrated by Sholem Aleichem's series of short stories and later memoir *Tevye the Dairyman* (1894), about a pious Jewish milkman, which was later adapted in 1939 as the Yiddish play *Tevye der Milchiger* (Tevye the Milkman). It was subsequently adapted as a stage and film musical, "Fiddler on Roof".
15 The literary expression of the idea of insatiable and unquenchable thirst in Hebrew culture appears consistently in poetry, literature, and films. See, for

example, the very recent "Hunger Project" inaugurated in 2001 under the auspices of the Israeli New Foundation for Cinema and T.V. What follows is the general description of the project from the foundation's website translated from Hebrew).

16 Etymologically Shaddai could be derived from the root, *shdd* (almighty) or from the Ugaritic religion as one of the Canaanite Gods. The possibility that it is connected to the breast relies on the attributes of God as the feeder and provider.

17 Avraham Shlonsky (Trans. by T. Carmi) "Toil".

18 "*Ha-machsan shel Godeon Ofrat*," posted December 23, 2010, http://gideonofrat.wordpress.com/2010/12/23/ברכת-האדמה-וקללתה/

19 Published by Beit Hatfutsot and 'Am Oved to accompany the show that ran from November 1996 to November 1997 in the Beit Hatfutsot Museum. Rachel Arbel curated the show.

20 "Architects—Visual Images of Zionism," last modified November 14, 2008, http://ilschool.org/WebPages/fdaf95fd-527c-4bb3-9812-ee246e98786d.79929100-2aa3-43b1-b9f2-32e592d60a15.aspx

21 The New Year ritual highlights sweetness with a blessing of apple dipped in honey, and the holiday of *Shavu'ot*, the Feast of Pentecost and the celebration of Receiving the Torah, highlights that the Torah itself has been likened to milk and honey, referring to the verse, "Like honey and milk [the Torah] lies under your tongue" (Song of Songs 4: 11). In *gematria*, the numerical value of the Hebrew word for milk, *chalav*, is 40, the number of days that Moses spent on Mount Sinai receiving instruction in the entire Torah.

22 Appeared in *Commentary* 1966. www.commentarymagazine.com/article/three-stories-fable-of-the-goat/

23 Charka, "Agnon crosses the Lines," Haaretz, 25.01.2013. www.haaretz.co.il/1.1911582

24 www.youtube.com/watch?v=xvkTPDiE8_4

25 See for example, "*Ma'asiyot U-ma'asim—Hatsagah 'al pi Shai Agnon*," You Tube video, 42.53, posted by "Pausa Theater," October 18, 2013, www.youtube.com/watch?v=yRlPX5Us20g

26 "*Ma'aseh Ha-'ez*," You Tube video, 1:25, posted by "Yonatan Zehavi," January 4, 2005, www.youtube.com/watch?v=H2tUQhFGtU4.

27 Like Natan Yonatan, Pagis also draws the connection between the expression "A land that devours its people" and the accusation of inheriting/occupying the land.

28 http://shironet.mako.co.il/artist?type=lyrics&lang=1&prfid=745&wrkid=2956

29 The melody for the poem, which was composed by Sasha Argov, one of Israel's most eminent composers (1914–1995), was produced by numerous musicians, and has since become a popular song, often sung in collective gathering and national ceremonies. Most singers of the Yom Kippur generation are familiar with the circumstances of its writing.

30 "A land that devours her inhabitants", and "Her lovers devour her lovers", exhausts any distinction between subject and object, their numbers and genders. If not for the Hebrew article *'et* that marks the direct object, the sentence would appear symmetrical.

31 Arnold Band chose to translate the poems as "Exercises in Daily Hebrew", highlighting the specific register of the language. Band pointed out that the poem is a "sardonic critique of the debasement of the Hebrew language" (512), and that Pagis's irony and parody establish the violent nexus between language acquisition and culture; the neutral statements in minimalist poetics "explode with meaning". Band concludes, "Clearly the problem of

synonyms, and more broadly of semantics, is a *central obsession* of Pagis in this period, and for that matter throughout his career" (514). Band universalizes Pagis's position as a problem that is shared by "all languages, politics and politicians".

32 The poem is extremely popular among teachers of Hebrew poetry. A gripping recording that is based on the poem was produced by Eitan Stienberg and Etty Ben-Zaken, *Voice Drawings* (2013). Etty Ben-Zaken's vocal work includes the "Dan Pagis Project," with two musical compositions to "Exercises in Practical Hebrew", in Hebrew and Arabic. It seeks to produce its meaning through voice.

33 Christi Merrill, conversation, October 2010.

34 Halevi (1996), 167.

35 In Even-Shoshan's Hebrew-Hebrew dictionary, "honeymoon of bees" is an entry attributed to Shababo with a reference to this essay.

36 Of course, there are many other dairy and food processing/distributing companies in Israel, although Tnuva arguably is the biggest and most renowned, and most closely tied to the history—the story—of Israel.

37 In 1996, the company opened a "milk hot line" to reassure anxious consumers about the safety of their products. This came in the wake of a scandal involving the company's use of silicon as a preservative to extend their milk's shelf life.

38 "Tnuva," last accessed June 16, 2015, www.tnuva.co.il/site/EN/ homepage.asp

39 Thanks to Jennifer Robertson for coining this term (personal communication).

40 Cited in Laor (1995, 147).

41 Milk in capitalist production becomes a virtual image that can be positioned according to the Lacanian distinction between reality and the real. (Reality being the social conditions of people and the processes of production. The real is the abstract logic that determines, explains, and interprets this reality.)

42 Campaign Miss Tnuva was a competition to design "the most Israeli cow". It included 30 full-size models of cows, using Israeli motives such as Falafel Cow or Hamsa Cow (an amulet against the evil eye). The first prize was given to "The Cow of Stickers" by Hila Nachmani, the second to a "Cow with an Olive Tree", the third prize to "The Ingathering of all Jews", and the fourth prize to the "Cow of Israeli Breakfast". When the chocolate company Strauss-Elite, the leading Israeli sweets brand, argued that the cow belonged to them, the notorious red cow icon on its Israeli chocolate bar, they argued: "So far, Tnuva never took care of the cow. On the one hand it milks it, on the other it slaughters it. The elite, on the other hand, worked hard to turn the cow in to a non-cow"! www.ynet.co.il/articles/0,7340,L-2957089,00.html

43 "*Man"kal Shtraus: Mekhirat Tnuvah le-Chavrah Zara—Iyum 'Estrategi*," ([President & CEO of Strauss]: Selling Tnuva to a foreign company is a strategic threat," *YNET Economy*, June 15, 2015, www.ynet.co.il/articles/ 0,7340,L-4668794,00.html

44 In Alcalay, *Keys to the Garden*, 1996, 374.

45 In Sami Chetrit, *Shirim Be-Ashdodit*, 2003, 30. Translated into English by Ammiel Alkalay, *Keys to the Garden*, 1996, 358.

46 Accent is a system of pronunciation that refers to specific phonetics and the production of sounds, 'alef, 'ayin, chet and resh is an emphasis or stress on the given syllables of a word, for example the one distinguishing Yiddish and Sephardic intonation, e.g., sh'abbat or shab'bat.

47 Today both kibbutzim belong to the same kibbutz movement, the *Takam* (*Ha-tnu'a Ha-Kibbutzit Ha-me'uchedet*, or the United Kibbutz Movement).

2 Gifts of Wounds
Isaac, Ishmael, and the Legacies of Abuse

The Mizrahi Altar and Its Interrogating Mouth

Many Mizrahi, Arab Jewish writers, have responded to the paradigmatic forces of the *'Akedah* and the sacrifice by addressing issues of violence, sexuality, desire, and body image. In many ways, the idea of internal exile, or exile within the homeland has been grounded within formative biblical narratives. The notion of intrinsic belonging highlights the estrangement and alienation of writers of Middle Eastern and North African origin. Second- and third-generation Israeli Sabras as well have depicted ethnic and social concerns through countless tactics, literary devices, and genres. Genesis already sets the tone for several hierarchies of inclusion and exclusion, stemming from blood lineages, national identity, and geographies.

As I noted earlier, Mizrahi writing helps us explore alternative textual strategies to circumvent the power of intertexts and their tenacious connection to Zionist ideology. The space that these intertexts prescribe is not just restrictive and silencing, it is also full of discriminatory assumptions. In fact, Mizrahim are ushered into this intertextual space only after they have proved that they are well versed in canonical culture; they need to show that they know how to engage within the tradition of citation. Many writers, such as Shimon Ballas, Sami Shalom Chetrit, Tikva Levi, Haviva Pedaya, and Shelly Elkayam, to name a few, have earned advanced academic degrees in disciplines such as literature, Jewish philosophy, political science, sociology, and Arabic. Many are deeply engaged in academic careers that help to legitimize their literary pursuits.[1] Another remarkable characteristic of these writers is their involvement in political activism and public discourse, including festivals, conferences, and publications. As this work shows, a long list of filmmakers, poets, bloggers, artists, and musicians of the second and third generation have emerged, placing the experience of their Arabic culture at the center of their work. This list extends from Sami Michael, Bracha Serri, and Ronit Matalon to Ktzia Alon, Almog Behar, and Mati Shemoelof. They invent new spaces for new lineages of authorship, experimenting with alternative genealogies of knowledge, and gradually are less reactive to the Ashkenazi paradigm.[2] But perhaps something of the awkward position of women writers in relation to the canon can be exemplified in Ella Bat-Tsion[3] (Gavriella Elisha)'s untitled poem: "We, a group of poets, speak to/converse with God with our face backwards" (1993, 7).[4] If for Bat-Tsion the paradigm of divinity is binding, the question stands: how does one assume a "backward position" of speaking and what kind of conversation can such a position engender? More precisely, how do less represented writers work around the allegorical space of the Binding, and how do they negotiate new possibilities for dialogue within Israeli culture?

Two poems by Dr. Shelly Elkayam directly address such questions through a poetic dispute over the cultural semantics of the root *'akhal* (to eat) and *ma'akhelet* with reference to the ethics of quantity and duration. Elkayam, born in 1955, is a poet, essayist, activist, and a scholar of Kabbalah and religion. She lives in Jerusalem and is deeply engaged in issues including peace, women's equality, and writers' social rights.[5] She has published two collections of poems, *Nitsat Ha-Limon* (Lemon Bud 1983) and *Shirat Ha-'Architekt* (Song of the Architect, 1987), along with several children's books. Her poetry expands the feminist dictionary of subjectivity by introducing a new textual vocabulary of multisensory experience.

Whereto Do You Love Me / Shelly Elkayam

Wherefrom do you love me so, and whereto
Whereto do you love me, and why
Why precisely me and how much
How many years can one for years so many years and more
    what have I done.[6]
Tell me, what have I done if I had done so I would know how
    to do such love

If you put me in your heart like a knife (*ma'akhelet*),
From within your heart I will ask you a knife (*ma'akhelet)*
    question
Why, of all pawned items did you choose a knife (*ma'akhelet*).
What inside you demands the binding of the knife (the
    ma'akhelet).

On its face it seems
Easy and simple
That your heart
Has become a burning bush
Which has not been
Scorched (*ukkal*).

Whereof do you love me so, and wherein
Wherein do you love me, and wherefrom
Wherefrom precisely me. And how many
How many long years can one so many years and more years
   and more how did I do it.
Tell me what have I done if I did so I would know how to do
   such love.[7]

In Elkayam's poem 'Whereto Do You Love Me' the presumed woman's voice probes her beloved about his love for her. If her questions to him imply that he has the answers, articulating them assumes an agency—one of solicitation—on her part. It would be possible to read the poem as a powerful protest against the shortcomings of heterosexual love if not for two words—*ma'akhelet* and *'ukkal*—that reveal the intertextual depth of the poem and the long-lasting reverberation of biblical narratives in Hebrew poetry. For speakers of Hebrew, the *ma'akhelet*, the slaughtering knife, and אוכל *'ukkal*, from the unconsumed (inedible) burning bush, allude strictly to their originary narratives (Genesis 22 and Exodus 3: 2, respectively), transporting the reader to their specific narratives and geographical sites (Kartun-Blum 1996).[8] It is the cultural tropes to which these narratives have given rise that are so fascinating; the genealogy that they have articulated historically, spanning their archaic and modern conceptions, is the very predicament Elkayam addresses thematically.

Elkayam invokes the boundlessness of time by using excessive question, specifically question words. In the first stanza, for example, the questioning subject augments an additional question in each line, preceded by the connective *vav* (and). The result is the doubling of the number of questions from five to ten: "Wherefrom do you love me so, and whereto/ Whereto do you love me, and why". The last question, *kamahin*, in Hebrew, is a brilliant construction; *kamah* is literally "how many" or "how much", but with the ending, which also rhymes with the previous lines, it becomes *Kamahin*, "truffles", the fungus that grows beneath the soil. With the meaning of longing that *kamah* conveys, it emphasizes the incredible duration of her question, the answers to which are, like truffles, buried in darkness.

Elkayam's questions are jammed together, referring repeatedly to open-ended adverbial expressions of time: "How many long years can one so many years and more years and more how did I do it". Such a breathless interrogation, with its repetitive structure, reads like an assault on the limits of knowledge. Do the questions inspire endless possibilities? An obvious answer? Or perhaps, more tragically, do they point to an innate inability to answer at all? Like a parable, Elkayam's questions become her answers.

Elkayam deploys the root verb *'akhal* (to eat), juxtaposing *ma'akhelet* (slaughtering knife) with the passive *'ukkal* (referring to the forever

burning, and therefore un-fully-burnable bush), exposing their signifying role in Israeli consciousness and their violent agency in directing cultural trajectories. With these allusions, Elkayam enters into an ultimate
patriarchal space. She thrusts the two objects into the heart of the male,
and into that of the poem, in the process of activating the two mythical
master-narratives: the Binding and God's appearance to Moses in the
burning bush. The female's rhetorical quest for knowledge becomes her
subversive position from which she rethinks the meanings of these narratives and reads them as a woman, a Mizrahi, and a philosopher. Ironically, her marginal position within an objectifying narrative enables
her to appropriate the immense space of patriarchal knowledge that her
insistent questions have penetrated. In their excessiveness, they make
apparent that the woman in the poem repudiates them, rethinking their
value and significance, and even suggest that the narrator attempts to
chart the limits of love precisely because they have already been reached.

The *Ma'akhelet* and the *sneh* (see Chapter 1) have molded the Hebrew
imaginary around the root *'akhl* as a space of materiality and potentiality. The two sites unfold the grand narratives about the genesis of
individuals and people, as God enunciates a promise—one people, one
nation, one land—constituting the paradigm of Jewish historiography,
underscoring the revelation of ontologized identity and divinity. Language again plays a major role in denoting the holiest of holies: Mount
Moriah, on which both the first and second Temples were built.[9] Similarly, the site of the burning bush is *Har Ha-Elohim*, God's mountain
in the Sinai Desert. It is later referred to as Mount Sinai, on which God
gave the Torah to Moses. From within the burning bush God reveals
himself "historically", saying, "*I am* the God of thy father, the God of
Abraham, the God of Isaac, and the God of Jacob" (Yerushalmi 1989,
6), thereby already inscribing the opening lines of the meta-historical
narrative of Judaism and the patriarchal genealogy of the new nation.
The idea of the chosen people, with its emphasis on the mythologized
origin of the relationship of Israel with God, is a crucial aspect of the
biblical narrative and the historical consciousness it engenders, which
compensates for the relatively recent, non-mythical origin of the people
of Israel (Funkenstein 1993, 31–34).

Both objects, the knife and the burning bush, inseparable from the narratives, are therefore contingent upon them. Their discursive signification
cannot be overstated, as it is through these objects that the divine has
touched humans, transforming them forever. In these two sites, God's
presence is approximated, made discernible through voice, objects, and
visual appearance. The totality of these events communicates also the primordial love in the historical covenant that the relationship between God
and Israel would gain. But they are of course loaded with ideological debt.

Elkayam's intertextuality makes use of the fact that in Hebrew,
the knife, *ma'akhelet*, is grammatically female, and the bush *sneh* is

unambiguously grammatically male, alluding to the possibility of reading these objects as metonymic representations of male (which includes God) and female. Consequently, the masculine is inscribed with godly meaning, whereas the feminine is but a divine instrument. The first-person speaker in Hebrew, accordingly, can be understood as the collective female I, especially in regard to the question of being chosen:

> Why precisely me and how much
>   How many years can one for years so many years and more what have I made (Ibid.).

Elkayam highlights the assumption that there ought to be a connection between being "chosen" and being worthy of that status. The infinite dance of love between the masculine (like the burning bush, he appears inhuman, unconsumable, and un/consuming) and the feminine (like the knife, she is sharp, decisive, uncompromising, and threatening to incise) encodes the irreconcilability of sexuality as embedded in the dominant gender ideology in Israeli/Jewish culture. It engages the couple in an eternally disruptive entanglement between the consuming female and the inconsumable male. And, despite their linguistic proximity, the distance between the narrative of the *ma'akhelet* and the narrative of the *sneh* is tantamount to differences in the reading of the promise, the covenants, and the "chosenness". As they are configured in the poem, the narrative of the knife and that of the burning bush negotiate a new position; now the female approaches not only male culture but God himself with some long overdue questions.

> If you put me in your heart like a knife (*ma'akhelet*),
> From within your heart I will ask you a knife (*ma'akhelet*)
>   question
> Why, of all pawned items did you choose a knife (*ma'akhelet*)
> What inside you demands the binding of the knife
>   (*ma'akhelet*).

>   (Ibid.)

Elkayam's subversive reading of these intertexts redefines their connection in the contemporary Israeli context in which Israel, building on its traditional depiction, is imagined as a 'woman'. Elkayam asserts that resorting to love is but an illusory escape from the potent, potential violence inherent in both fire and knife. By positioning them in dialogue, she activates the broader semantic meaning of the root 'to eat' *'akhl*, animating its seductive capacity to conceal its devouring and violent nature. Both objects are arguably what literary theorists Shoshana Felman and Mieke Bal attribute to both the fire and the sword, namely, an "interesting challenge to truth" because they move between being a "thing" and being an "event". Like the fire and the sword-in-action—sacred and divine—the knife and the burning bush can become "the instrument of 'rupture,' the breaking off of relations, and of '*coupure*,' the cutting: penetrating and dividing" (Bal 1988b, 22). Elkayam's incisive monologue deconstructs erotic love by insistently posing unanswerable questions, slicing through violent patriarchal authority and warping linear time and semantics. But the *ma'akhelet* brings back a hovering threat of violence that redefines love along the lines of violence and abuse. Not only is *ma'akhelet* invested with domestic horror, but eating too has been strongly invested with sexuality and the language of love. This desire is evocative of the satisfying breast as a 'prototype of the expression of sexual satisfaction' (Freud 1958, 48 in Kilgour 1998, 245). Eating is tied to libidinal pleasure, survival, and desire for incorporation and fusion of boundaries. Food and hunger also threaten to transform the eater into the one who is eaten, as in the case of the narrator in Agnon's 'Pat Shlemah'.

Elkayam's *ma'akhelet* keeps the glimmering edge of its terror. For Elkayam's inquisitive female subject, the knife is her mouth, a mouth that cuts. Her discursive position becomes a violent act that insists upon knowing and therefore becomes an instrument of penetration and rupture. The poem's last stanza makes it clear that this relationship leads to oblivion. Especially for Israeli men who might still perceive Abraham as the ultimate unconditional host, Elkayam makes sure to speak to the arresting power of love and its potential to turn the loved into its victim. She tells us that love, especially from a woman's position, is severed by the knife and charred by the burning bush. Precisely because these all-consuming objects contain and thereby delimit the horizons of the new Israeli (Zionist) imagination, they have effectively constructed the dead zone of language.

The Smell of the Covenant

In many ways the poem "Whereto Do You Love Me" extends Elkayam's earlier poem-question, "How Many Years Can a Man", which opens her collection *The Poetry of the Architect* (1987).[10]

> How many years can a man (*Adam*) pace
> Among the Pieces of flesh[11] –
> The smell of the covenant
> Stronger for him than the smell of the carcass.

In "How Many Years Can a Man" Elkayam takes us back to the problematic, rarely visited site of "*Ha- Brit ben ha-Btarim*" (The Covenant of the Pieces/Flesh) in Genesis 15. Time, in this poem, stretches far beyond the path drawn by Hebrew poetry and the covenant. In Genesis, this covenant is the first dialogue between God and Avram (later Abraham).

Before this interaction, God speaks to Avram and the latter responds by acting in accordance with God's demands, going to the land of Canaan and building an altar to God.[12] This covenant is important because it constitutes Abraham's identity in relation to God through his newly invented nativeness. In this covenant, God maps out the borders of the Promised Land and lists the ten different native nations over which Israel will take control. Abraham is given both the land and the peoples of the land. God's first promise is "Fear not, Avram, I am a shield to you; your reward shall be very great" (Genesis 15: 1). In response, Abraham poses the question: 'O Lord God, what can You give me, seeing that I shall die childless' ... 'Know of a surety that thy seed shall be a stranger in a land that is not theirs' (Genesis 15: 2) and God asserts, "Look toward heaven and count the stars, if you are able to count them ... so shall be your offspring" (Genesis 15: 5). Further, God promises the land: "I am the Lord who brought you out from Ur of the Chaldeans to assign this land to you as a possession" (Genesis 15: 7). Abraham's second question is: "O Lord God, how shall I know that I am to possess it?" (Genesis 15: 8).[13]

Elkayam's corollary question in the poem, "How many years can a man ..." continues the spirit of inquiry in Abraham's questions. Not only is the poem explicitly framed by the impossible duration of time, pointing to the fact that it has been too long, time is also implicated by the strong smell of the terrifying vulture-attracting site of the covenant.

God tells Abraham to cut up into pieces (*batar*) and offer him five different animals. Abraham obeys, driving off scavenging birds, and after sunset, he is overcome by deep sleep and a deeper terror.[14] Regina Schwartz highlights that this "cutting covenant" is at the very heart of the violent discourse of biblical covenants, building as it does on the literal meaning of the verb *karat*, as in *karat brit* (Genesis 15: 18), originates from "to cut", both literally and in the sense of cutting a deal, i.e., establishing a covenant (1998, 21–25, 15–38). The cumulative effect of this performative spectacle is a horrific one. Elkayam's sensory allusion brings the reader into this divine abattoir.

The enactment of the covenant performs a body-act ritual that reinforces the promise of God's speech act. It is not difficult to understand Abraham's demand for a concrete sign as a kind of a failure of the imagination, to make the transition to seeing himself as a father of nations, especially now that God has introduced a cosmic metaphor of countless stars and grains of sand. After all, it is highly ironic for God to open a genealogical discourse of the nation with Abraham who is not yet even a father and is well beyond the age of conception. God's focus on the promise and infinite duration of that genealogy emphasizes the open-endedness of his speech act and its potential to become a cosmological myth. Having internalized God's prophecy of Jewish history through its lasting covenant, Abraham emerges from his deep sleep as the ultimate believer.

Although Elkayam's constructed site of the gendered covenant is increasingly informed by time, it is identified by its distinctive scent.[15] Here, the sacred space is transformed into a site of competing smells: that of the internalized covenant associated with the carcasses presented to God by Abraham. Her poem's discursive blend of truncated and contested history makes its meaning, not through textual signifiers, but rather through the evocation of selective cultural memory. The carcasses (*pgarim*) and their rotten smell are not and cannot be confined and restricted to the five animals that Abraham slaughters and dismembers. Figuratively speaking, decaying body parts remain strewn about the discursive space of Israeli and Jewish texts, even after all these centuries. Time, if frozen, is necessarily emptied of its historical value in grotesque ways. The smell of time, however, is progressive, evidenced both by the extreme, continuous obscenity of the carcasses and by the accumulated layers of historical *slaughtering*. The olfactory sensation of decay revives and binds the historical memory of corporeal experience. It draws attention to the fact that dead carcasses have paved the road of history and that their invasive smell asserts a testimony that we so assiduously try to ignore. Indeed, the poetic materiality of smells manifest in their molecular physicality; all smells are composed of particulate.

Elkayam is well aware of the power of this biblical narrative that has forcefully produced a precise geopolitical claim for Jewish land, tirelessly redrawing more than a map: indeed, the entire course of Jewish/Israeli national history. Elkayam's reeking site underscores the transactional aspect not only of chosenness, but faith itself, documenting an entire national narrative of death and dying. Intended to be read in conjunction with its biblical intertext, Elkayam's poem makes a strong claim about linguistic rupture and the value of affect that goes beyond language, forcing us to realize that we, disciplined readers, have long since joined Abraham in his pacing amidst the rotting pieces of the covenant. It is the very quality of the covenant, like milk and honey and other mythical symbolic cultural possessions, to forcefully eradicate any competing referents to their grandiosity. For truth-seeking poets like Elkayam, however, if the covenant is closely connected with blood and terror, then it should convey its meaning through the stench of its enactment and not through nostalgic and canonical textuality.[16] The grotesque paradox is that the cosmic force of God's promise lies precisely in its ability to make us forget what is deeply inherent in fulfilling it. The covenant, with all its horror, and in spite of the putrid carcasses, is out of joint with history and time.

Elkayam's metaphorization of smell is her attempt to mobilize a cultural critique that shifts from a prefigured, textualized "reading" to the performative aspect of texts (see also Clifford 1986, 11–13). Truly, olfactory knowledge introduces a less canonical dimension to the discourse around the covenant, and yet aims to capture the intimate threat of intertextual life, especially in its relation to the economy of bodies and time. For the question remains of how to account to the repulsive stench of death. Can it be accounted for through poetry, the foremost literature of the senses? For Elkayam, the poetics of smell—and poetry as smell—offer another testimony of history and its carnage, but, more importantly, of the way we are implicated as inheritors through a long intertextual performance of horrific binding that sets its divine gift along with an unpayable invoice.

Elkayam's radically reflective poems together help us answer the question of how eating that initially was intended to curb hunger turned into a monstrous act of devouring. Her poems are contesting the inescapability of such historical force. The *ma'akhelet*, the sacrificial knife that Abraham wielded in order to sacrifice his own kind, has become the signifier that feeds the collective consciousness of all their children. The overbearing presence of the *ma'akhelet* and the covenant in Israeli consciousness make clear the near-insurmountable challenge of envisioning an alternative covenant not conditioned by the knife.

For as much as ink inspires narrative, it is the cutting blade of the *ma'akhelet* that constitutes text and identity. Elkayam alerts us to the potency and potentiality of the *ma'akhelet* in modern Israeli culture and of its problematic eminence in Hebrew literature, especially with its connection to *'akhal* (to eat) and *'ukkal* (food). *Ma'akhelet*, the cannibal object, sabotages any narrative that is not already consumed by its own language. Can a self-aware *ma'akhelet* carve out new rituals to redirect these trajectories of life and death?

"That Idiot Yitzhak (End)"

The olfactory aspect of the *'akedah* figures prominently in the following poem by Yitzhak Laor, who moves restlessly from one version of the binding to another, the written and the ones to which he alludes. Yitzhak Laor is a leading intellectual who writes prose, poetry and literary reviews. Here, Laor imagined himself as Abraham's various descendants as part of a framework through which to ask or channel broader questions about Zionism, politics, and other global issues. His concern is the narrative that he will tell his son. He also focuses on the enduring effect of smell of the flesh as the main aspect of the sacrifice. In *"Ha-Metumtam Ha-zeh Yitzhak, (Sof)"* ("That Idiot Yitzchak (End)") (1999, 87), Laor reduces the binding of Yitzchak to the smell that the *ma'akhelet* (always in parentheses) has left on the hand as its enduring lethal essence. Laor's question is, therefore, not what kind of narrative such a smell can construe. After having written so many drafts (this is his last), the answer becomes obvious: there is no narrative except for the terrible realization that Isaac is an idiot and that the *ma'akhelet* continues to leave its indelible mark on the hand.

What would I have told my son about my father, about Abraham, about the smell of
His hand (the *ma'akhelet*)?[17]

This long linear genealogy through the smell of the hand that held the knife speaks to the banality of it all. Nonetheless, it is an augmented reality; proposing several (im)possible answers, Laor poses numerous questions looped in genealogies, narratives, and poetry, all combusting with a horrible smell that contradicts the possibility of constructing satisfactory answers.

Laor's poem is not just about citation or biblical referentiality, but also and specifically about the ways that intertextuality is reified and made into cultural capital. Meaning is produced and put into being around texts, and thus the shaping of intertexts, canons, and knowledge continues into modern culture in academic and other cultural productions. This, in turn, encodes a critique of the sacrificial dynamics at play in academic institutions, which "devour their people", preying upon the achievements and original thought of its ostensible beneficiaries while undercutting their ownership/accomplishment and burning them out predictably in arbitrary cycles. It comes down that, as the narratives evolve, we also become aware of the institutions that emerge from the discourse of smell.

Laor indeed has written several drafts of a story "against the fathers" but was stymied by the impossibility of a final version. For him, to tell the story of Abraham's covenant is to dwell on the pervasive smell and to bypass the immense historical force of the narrative. Laor's multiple poetic drafts are, in fact, the only narrative that can be generated, because the Hebrew poem is constituted by the same signifier: namely, the accumulated meaning of contextual history, materialized by the site of the sacrifice, always informed and situated by the presence (smell) of the *ma'akhelet*. As the ultimate intertext of every narrative, the indelible mark that the *ma'akhelet* has left on Abraham's hand follows from one generation to another as yet another dim silhouette of its lingering totality. Laor's critical question becomes a hypothetical narrative of the genealogy of the incurable smelly touch. The only realization it provokes is that of Yitzchak's idiocy. The fact that Laor's first name is also Yitzchak nominally ties the archetypical Yitzchak in Genesis to the present writer. In the poem, Laor's Yitzchak struggles to free himself of the cleaving effect of the *ma'akhelet*.

Castaways

Adi Nes (1966–) is a prominent Israeli artist known for his provocative, staged color photographs in series such as the *Soldiers* (1994–2000), *Boys* (2000), *Bible Stories* (2004–2007), and *Depositions* (2010). Nes, a second-generation Iranian, operates at the intersection of class,

Figure 2.1 Adi Nes, Abraham and Isaac (2004) *Biblical Stories* c-print © Adi
      Nes. Courtesy of the artist and Jack Shainman Gallery, New York.

ethnicity, and sexual difference and is committed to queering Israeli discourse around militarism, religion, and national identity (or the collapse
thereof). His work often casts dark-skinned male models, critiquing cultural politics of masculinity, male identity and (hetero)sexuality. In general, Nes is engaged in reworking the cultural dictionary of metaphors
and allegories, challenging conventions around founding narratives, and
re-contextualizing them in new hyper-realistic settings. *Tikkun* magazine called him, "the face of modern Israeli photography"[18] His work
features in leading museums around the world.

Nes's "Abraham and Isaac" (2004; Figure 2.1) is included in the
Biblical Stories and tells us what has remained of the covenant: Abraham
and Isaac, homeless vagabonds who wander with a shopping cart and
scarce belongings. The colorful image of early dawn or evening articulates with a unique light a sense of their loneliness and aimlessness. Unlike
Genesis' Abraham who knew where he was going, with a clear address
to Har Hamoriah, Nes's Abraham has no address and no direction. His
head is slanted down, while he is pushing the cart, and his eyes, rather
than looking forward, are cast down. Isaac on the cart is barefooted,
lying in a posture of full resignation and vulnerability. It is not clear if he
is asleep or awake, for his face is turned away from the camera.

George Steiner reconsiders the story of Abraham and the *topos* of monotheism in light of Hegelian thesis, emphasizing that Abraham left home and became "a wanderer on the earth, a passer-by severed from the familial, communal, and organic context of love and trust" (Steiner 1985, 6). In seeking a "singular, almost autistic, intimacy with God" (Ibid.), Abraham pays the tragic price of lost childhood and youth, but instead gains a home in abstraction, in word, and text (Ibid.). Whereas for Hegel and Steiner, Abraham's displacement is intrinsic to the dialectic of his choice, for Nes, it is a result of a linear, historical process of being close to the text of Abrahamic tradition as it is read in Hebrew-Israeli culture, a tradition that casts him (off) as threadbare and outmoded textual regurgitation. Indeed, in an interview for Haaretz, Nes expresses his intention to unlearn the national-religious construction of the narrative and to advance instead a universally *human* Abraham and Isaac (www.haaretz.co.il/1.1380911).

Nes's website places his piece in dialogue with Duane Hanson's sculpture *Supermarket Shopper* (1970). Hanson's piece is a grotesque culmination of the postwar capitalist impulses of an unhappy feminine consumer archetype. Hanson's cart is overflowing with processed food. Nes's cart is devoid of food, instead holding the refuse upon which Isaac reclines. Both Hanson's shopper and Abraham and Isaac are victims of overconsumption: the woman for buying into such convenient excess, and Abraham and Isaac not because of the story of the sacrifice, but rather because of the swelling and engorging history of narration that continues to impoverish them.

Reading as "Belonging"

On January 16, 1996, the late Israeli president Ezer Weizman addressed the Bundestag and Bundesrat of the Federal Republic of Germany in Hebrew. It was the first time that an Israeli politician had addressed the two German parliament houses since the unification. Weizman's speech managed to use the historical moment and put into a few lines the meta-narrative of Jewish existence, telling firsthand the story of the victim, *by* the victim, to his historical perpetrators, redefining at long last the encounter not only between the state of Israel and the German people, but between the arch-murderer and his perpetual prey. Turning it, therefore, into a pedagogical lesson of history is consistent with the way Israeli Zionist history has been written not, as Idith Zertal asserts, by the political leaders who literally "made history" by participating in its enterprise (Zertal 1996, 15), but by those who perform it.

Using the dramatized collective "*'ani*" ("I") Weizman swept through 4,000 years of Jewish history, skipping from one map of Jewish Diaspora to another, from one trauma to another redemption:[19]

> I was a slave in Egypt. I received the Torah at Mount Sinai. Together with Joshua and Elijah, I crossed the Jordan River. I entered

Jerusalem with David, was exiled from it with Zedekiah, and did not forget it by the rivers of Babylon. When the Lord returned the captives of Zion, I dreamed among the builders of its ramparts. I fought the Romans and was banished from Spain. I was bound to the stake in Mainz. I studied Torah in Yemen and lost my family in Kishinev. I was incinerated in Treblinka, rebelled in Warsaw, and emigrated to the Land of Israel, from whence I had been exiled and where I had been born, from which I come and to which I return.

(Weizman 1996)

He told the Germans frankly that "I do not forgive and I do not forget" and urged them to remember and be vigilant against the emerging racism and neo-Nazism. The speech was received with applause and praise.

In the dialectic intricacies linking memory, history, narratives, and reading, the transitions between singularity and plurality are fluid. But when it comes to reading and ideology, my question is, as *whom* do we read? Do we read as one individual or as the collective that defines us? To what extent do we bring with us the collective, or collectives, if we can choose? To what extent are we allowed not to bring them to our reading?

I am using Weizman's speech as a gesture that best exemplifies the notion of the Israeli "parody of aesthetics" not only in the artistic sense but in the wider cultural and historical sense. Evidently, the event is an exceptional historical moment with an opportunity for a performance of lasting effect, but alas, it is nonetheless consistent with the way Israeli ideology reproduces its narrative through identification and attachment. In the realm of art, literature, and media, a "parody of aesthetics" is what Adorno distinguished as art kitsch, "a typical imitative gesture that is produced by the "cultural industry" (Adorno 2005). In a capitalist society, art is subjective, coherent, and aims to destabilize the power system, (Adorno Ibid.). It can be argued that kitsch history is rather objective, always building on and further stabilizing the existing power system. It follows that kitsch history is no longer history but appears superficially as history and has the effect of history. Not only does it lead to the inability to distinguish between history and ideology, but it also tends to define ideology as history. What is true about art in the context of capitalism has even more immediate potency for history in the context of nationalism. It closely corresponds with the elaborated mechanism of identification that transforms history and story into myth and totalizing ideology, as Phillipe Lacoue-Labarthe and Jean-Luc Nancy argue. Myth, accordingly is "a fiction in the strong active sense of 'fashioning,' that proposes, and imposes models or types for identification. A creation of the collective myth, like any other work of art, is an instrument of identification ... the mimetic instrument par excellence" (Lacoue-Labarthe and Nancy 1990, 297–298).

As such, mythification is a threat to culture, in so far as it becomes the substance of false consciousness. Placed at the intersection of both the capitalistic cultural industry of Jewish history, with its emphasis on anti-Semitism and the Holocaust, and the national identification and narrated genealogy, the consumption of this identity displays its exaggerated sentimentality. It is seductive, captivating, and totalizing; kitsch refers to both aesthetics and morals, or to the ideological mode of production of old narratives and presupposed notions of identity, victimhood, and oppression. Weizman's immersion within Jewish history, therefore, depicts what has become the Israeli ethical reading of history with the appropriate degree of attachment.

Being the president of Israel—whose official role is entirely representative—might explain Weizman's choice to address his audience with a personalized Jewish history. But even beyond his role as president, for many Israelis "Ezer" represents one of a short list of men (along with Yitchak Rabin and Arik Sharon) whose biography embodies what in public discourse is called "the spirit of the Israeli nation" (*ruach ha-'umah*), and their biographies, although different, are told as the story of Israel. A nephew of Chaim Weizman (1874–1952), a key player in initiating and obtaining the Balfour Declaration in 1917, the president of the World Zionist Organization, and later the first president of Israel, Ezer Weizman was the first Israeli-born (*Sabra*) president (1924–2005). A native of Tel Aviv, he returned to politics after a legendary military career as an Air Force commander and as a Chief of the General Staff. Prior to his presidency, Weizman held several posts in the Likkud government. Placed at the crux of Zionist history, Weizman's national charisma, his militarism, and his genealogy, at the frontier of Israeli emerging nobility, arguably played a central role in modeling native culture, along with his Israeli accent, chutzpah, and confidence, and his provocative and charming approach with the media and the public. For many Israelis, he came to represent the ultimate archetype of Israeli manhood. After his death in April 2005, he was lauded as "the man of the people".[20]

Within contemporary Israeli discourse, therefore, the "I" of Weizman defines itself against a very specific "not-I", a marked imagined "you" that inescapably returns to a paradigmatic projection of the Others. This entity is not different from the historical enemy, who now moves from the third person "they" to the second person, "you". Such an "I" repeats a dialogic paradigm that predictably continues to reproduce the suffering Jew within a reductive Zionist meta-narrative. Rather than using the opportunity to deliver a liberating speech that would disengage the locked positions of the victimized, suffering Jew and the anti-Semite oppressive Other, Weizman is over-engaged in the continuous process of remembering-as-an-Israeli (and a Jew) in the way prescribed by Zionist ideology. The grand narrative that he tells, therefore, is more than a confession (as Moshe Zuckermann suggests) or an abridged version of Jewish testimony (to follow Shoshana Felman's concept) that turns the speaker into an eternal survivor on the witness stand of the stage of the world. "I was a slave in Egypt. I received the Torah at Mount Sinai. Together with Joshua and Elijah, I crossed the Jordan River...". Weizman's testimony reads as an absolute truth of the Jewish people—he turns this narrative into a legal document, a *speech act* that legitimizes his position today as a speaker in the name of all Israeli Jews, in the name of all Jews, in the name of the living and the name of the dead, present, past, and future (Felman 1992, 52; Zuckermann 2001, 131, see also 115–137). Such a testimony makes clear that Israel is a teleological outcome of Jewish history, as it helps to restate Israel's legitimacy since the establishment of Israel, and, tied to it, the continued occupation of Palestine since 1967. This point is especially evident in the following usage of Weizman's speech in websites and the Israeli classroom. We return to the school, then, for another history lesson.

Since Weizman's speech in 1996, parts of it have been incorporated as an introduction to "Chapter 67" of the website "The Miracle of Jewish History: A Crash Course in History",[21] highlighting, not the unprecedented moment of the encounter between two historical antagonists, but the survival of Israel and the Jewish people as a miracle. On another website, a teacher in a religious high school in Raanana (an affluent middle-class town, north of Tel Aviv), suggests: "I usually cut the paragraphs into strips. The pupils "arrange them in chronological order ... We begin reading... going around the room". Needless to say, these narrative strips are word-for-word citations of the speech, whereby the "I" student cites the "I" of Weizman, and the collective "I/we" of Jewish history in an acute operation that interpolates individuals into history. Here are a few examples of the strips that the students read:

a   Together with the warriors of my tribe, the Tribe of Ephraim, we conquered the land from the Canaanites; there I planted my orchard of olive trees. The trees grew and bore fruit, and I prayed not only for rain but also for the fulfillment of my dream to press oil and light the Menorah in Beit Hamikdash (the Temple).

b   Together with millions of my brothers and sisters, I was cremated and turned into ashes in Treblinka. I rose to the sky in a pillar of fire and clouds....

c   I was reborn on an Aliya Bet boat. Under the cover of darkness, we stole into the Promised Land once again.

d   I am a true traveler, following the steps of my forefathers. And just as I escorted them, over there and in those days, they too join me and stand with me, here and now.[22]

In this effective experience, as she witnesses, "the emotions expressed in the voices of the actors are truly moving".[23] This reading spectacle builds on the paradigmatic locations of history on a Jewish timeline that has turned into the spinal cord of Zionist etiology. It is patriarchal and masculine, linear and reductive, and focuses on the main ideological apparatus of Israeli historiography. In short, scholars of Israeli culture have asserted the use and abuse of the Holocaust in Israeli culture and the way it has been incorporated into the Zionist narrative (Eyal Sivan 1991; 1999; Tom Segev 1991; Idith Zertal 1996; 2010; Adi Ophir 2000; Zuckermann 2001; Ilan Gur-Ze'ev 2004). Zuckermann specifically observes that Weizman's speech "reflects the dialectics of Zionist instrumentalization of the Holocaust and the difficulty of addressing the subject" (2001).

Gur-Ze'ev explains that "The instrumentalization of the memory of the Holocaust along specific ideological parameters was deployed as the ultimate objective for creating the image of the 'new Jew' as the Israeli collective, sustaining this image and bringing it to its proliferation". But the paradox of the postmodern, multicultural Israeli situation, according to Gur-Ze'ev, is that the more Zionism succeeded in terms of the proliferation of the State of Israel, making space for an individualistic, anti-collectivist and anti-idealist spirit—melting down the constituting myths of Zionism—the more pronounced was the increase in the success of the mythification of the memory of the Holocaust, and its instrumentalization reached record high (Gur-Ze'ev 2004, 129).

In analyzing Weizman's text, we must ask what is the difference, if any, between the collective "I" that he uses and the "we" that is typical of the Statehood generation—a plurality that depicted the pioneers' feverish commitment to collectively build the country and to be built by it. The "we generation" (*"dor ha'anachnu"*) advocated plurality as a position that had dominated the discourses and practices of Hebrew speakers and had provided a symbolic model of nation-building strategies and ethics. All Israelis were inducted into the ideology of the cultural production of Israeliness. For all of us, the plural form of verbs, *especially* verbs, was imbued with a force of redemptive mobilization of both the cohesive past and, more importantly, the imagined future. In other words, we were all trained to read Jewish history both as Jews and as Israelis, in a collective voice, bringing the collective into the text and generating an emotional cathexis from sameness, plurality, and collectivity. Only *"anu"* or *"anachnu"* ("we") carried the promise of blending differences together; with its presumed inclusiveness that obscured the exaggerated postures of the Diaspora in the miraculous melting pot and the messianic ingathering of all Jews—all within the strict bounds of the Land of Israel.

Weizman builds on this plurality and also elaborates on the biblical imperative to remember, *zakhor*, which implicates all Jews within the historical experience (Yerushalmi 1989, 44–45). As the ultimate mode of Jewish historical consciousness, *zakhor* in Jewish culture is a religious commandment that also constitutes a secular symbolic space of memory and its future destiny (Gur-Ze'ev 2004, 127). Enacted through the Passover Seder ceremony and the reading of the Haggadah, the celebrated festival of *Pessah*, is the Passover of generations, is never distinguished from the historical event *in* Egypt, making Passover into the exemplary mythical event, the genesis of both the Jewish nation and its tradition of storytelling. With its secular Zionist layer it has redefined Jewish immigration to Palestine as the exodus and return to the homeland. It is the moment of the birth and rebirth of the reading Hebrew subject of history.

The biblical Passover event commences the discourse of national memory and memorization. But it is the Mishnah[24] that introduced the dictum that was later repeated in the Passover Haggadah, stating that "In every generation each individual is bound to regard himself *as if* he personally had come forth from Egypt" (Pesachim 10, 5). The grammatical style of the expression underlines the singularity of the subject, underscoring that such a process and processing of historical memory is an individualistic event, even and especially while becoming one part of a nation. The memory of the Exodus relies on the reenactment of this historical event and its accumulated transformation through the fusion of past and present. Its purpose is to elicit identification with what is perceived as history, so much so that one feels "as if" one came out of Egypt. In other words, in order to fully comprehend the idea of freedom, one has to identify in the totality of the experience of slavery. For the sake of cultural cohesiveness, the imperative is to identify with the experience of the slave, to transfer the story of the others into the experience of the self, to assimilate these others into the very internalized collective Jewish people as part of history and memory;[25] the Hebrew word "*chayav*", holds the full semantic space of the verb, meaning must, committed, obliged, and owed, to the point of being in debt; the adverb, *ke-'illu*, emphasizes the hypothetical analogy, "as if…".

Weizman himself reiterated this imperative but with a radical Israeli twist. He turns the individualistic process of memory into an utterly collective one. These are the opening lines of his speech:

> It was fate that delivered me and my contemporaries into this great era, when the Jews returned to and re-established their homeland. I am no longer a wandering Jew who migrates from country to country, from exile to exile. *But all Jews in every generation must regard themselves as if they had been there, in previous generations, places, and events.* Therefore, I am still a wandering Jew, but not along the far-flung paths of the world. Now I migrate through the expanses of time, from generation to generation, down the paths of memory.
>
> (My emphasis)

The imperative to identify turns into a site of multiple "previous generations, places, and events", similar in its infinitude to the open sided empty signifier, "there", which alludes to everywhere outside of Israel, framed by the "here" of Israel, and has accumulated the traumatic experience of Jewish exile (most often of eastern European, Ashkenazi Jews) especially of the Holocaust.[26] In fact, the master-narrative of Jewish oppression impacted the way other histories were told. See, for example, Israel's emphasis on the Farhud in Iraq as the primary mobilizer of mass immigration in the early fifties (Shohat 1988). The fluid transition between singular and plural reveals the crowded space of subjectivity as it has tightened around the sameness of the Jewish/ Israeli master experience and narratives.[27] This tight space gradually unfolds to tell us about the devouring potential of memories and myth. With its tendency to erase internal differences of gender and ethnicity, it keeps colonizing individuality from within, and especially that of its internal others.

If the Mishnah sought to preserve the immediate relationship between memory and the specific historical reference to slavery, Zionist discourse opened the formula to other mythological sites. In fact, with the multiple sites of memory that "as if" enabled, it has been appropriated to become one of the important models of national identification. In the national context, "as if…" articulates a thesis of identification that emphasizes both the totality and intensity of the process and its mechanism of projection. It might be possible to make a case for an intensified mythification of remembering in specific moments in Zionist culture, especially given the use and abuse of textuality in Israeli culture—itself a mythical construct—and the specific "history of their fictioning" within this ideology.

Rather than simply outlining special events within history, reading "as if…" provides the totally self-fulfilling (and willfully self-fulfilling) logic of an idea, "by which", as Hannah Arendt suggested in her definition of ideology of the subject, "the movement of history is explained as one consistent process….The movement of history and the logical process of this notion are supposed to correspond to each other, so that whatever happens, happens according to the logic of one 'idea'" (cited from Lacoue-Labarthe and Nancy 1990, 293 [Arendt (1951):1962, 469]). It provides a mechanism to reactivate old myths and invent a new "mythical consciousness" by mythic identification (Lacoue-Labarthe and Nancy 2004, 11). As a method of reading and memorization, "as if" has become the element that makes narrative, memory, and fiction into lived reality. Rather than "reading as if…" we must talk about "living as if…" where text, language, and actions meet. Strategies of reading and remembering, then, are more forcefully transmitted as strategies of living and political action. With its emphasis on subjectivity, "as if" promises the desire for ideological conformity to Jewish history.

Modern spoken Hebrew provides us with a fascinating development that appears to build on the textual idea of "as if" (*"ke-'illu"*), and continue the process (that we found in Weizman's speech) of realizing the ingrained connection between "as if" and Egypt, with augmented multiple sites of identification. In spoken Hebrew, *ke-'illu* became the trendiest and most used word, so much so that it was crowned as the queen of spoken Hebrew, and *ka-zeh*, such as, like, is the Princess. Since the early eighties, spreading from the postmodern Tel Aviv Sheinkin Street, *ke-'illu* threatened to turn Israelis into the *ke-'illu* generation, what a journalist referred to as "Isra-bluff", highlighting the hypothetical aspect of its meaning, as if—but not really, like, pseudo, a pretense. For example, "excuse me, *ke-'illu*, what time is it, *ke-'illu*?" or, "I went to see her, *ke-'illu*, and asked her *ke-'illu* what *ke-'illu* she will wear to the party. (In English, "I, like, love you".) Whereas a linguist like Maya Fructman argues that *ke-'illu* is a pause or filler word, a common device in colloquial languages, ("like" in English and "genre" in French), Yael Maschler found in her close analysis of talk-in-interaction that *ke-'illu* is a discourse marker preceding self-rephrasal. Rather than reflecting a "thin Hebrew", the elimination of vocabulary and expressions among young speakers or being an indication of cultural shallowness, the proliferation of *ke-'illu* over the past decade, she argues, indicates the transition from the *dugri* speech (directness, "straight talk") which stood for a self-confident, undoubting voice, to a voice that simultaneously recognizes and attempts to overcome the limits of one's language (2001, 295–326).[28]

Is it possible, I ask, that *ke-'illu*, "as-if" in spoken Hebrew, is an extension of the reading *ke-'illu*, as-if, that continuously committed to turn any trivial utterance into an internal web of identifications, to the point of eliminating its references and appearing non-referential? Rather than simply reacting against the overload of meaning in everyday life, as Ariel Hirschfeld suggests, I suggest that the *ke-'illu* has consumed its speaker who is now locked within citation, only now the citation that seems to disappear is overwhelmingly hovering in every aspect of life within infinite unspoken ellipses. They ironically speak for uselessness of repetitive, exhausting, and closed multireferential language. It reminds us of Pagis's concern with chains of synonyms.

"Life 'in the myth'"—within the highly dense Jewish tradition of textuality, within its organic and symbolic unity—has turned into "life 'in quotation'".[29] Always referential and allegorized within provided systems of meaning and interpretation, it is therefore more easily approved and legitimized. Within such an intense process of ideological mythification, the Hebrew language plays a radical role.

The subject of identification was extensively explored in psychology. In her early psychoanalysis of emotional disturbance, Helene Deutsch identified a disorder to which she refers as the "as if". Different from the philosophy of "as if" of Hans Vaihinger,[30] Deutsch's notion of the "as if", is a model of excessive identification and mimicry that is manifested in "pseudo affectivity" (Deutsch 1965, 273). The "as if" personality, she argues, gives the "inescapable impression that the individual's whole relationship to life has something about it which is lacking in genuineness and yet outwardly runs along "as if" it were complete" (Ibid. 263). The individual is able to perform normal emotional life because he is technically trained to impersonate normality. Identification, therefore, can significantly submerge the individual to the point of losing their judgment. It is this loss of judgment that is relevant to collective identification in the case of Israel; it will mean adapting fully to the national master-narrative and its symbolic and performative aspects. It takes us back to the notion of national kitsch ideology that I discussed earlier. The highly plastic quality of the "as if" mechanism, which relies on both its deep sense of emptiness and on its "readiness to pick up signals from the outer world and to mold oneself and one's behavior accordingly", enables the adaptability of the individual to changes in the environment, "capable of the greatest fidelity and the basest perfidy" (Deutsch 1965, 265). Identification and mimicry help to give content to emotional and moral emptiness and are the only way through which such an individual can participate in real experience.

Weizman has internalized the story; he is the Sabra par excellence. To be an Israeli Hebrew meant, and to a large extent still is, to learn to carry from a young age the burden of signification inscribed in every code and sign in the Hebrew discourse. It is a process that represents itself through a unity: crowded and intense, colorful and dynamic. It is this internalized excess that created a totality of inescapable meaning, haunting with its depth and infinite referentiality every aspect of being and every potential spark of becoming.

And Still, the Knife

> [P]erhaps it isn't love when I say you are what I love the most - you are the knife I turn inside myself, this is love. This, my dear, is love.
> Franz Kafka, "Letters to Milena"

David Grossman, the celebrated Israeli novelist, continues to grapple with the knife and the question of its measure. I will use the reading of two of his books to draw the extent and density of the trauma of reading as it is enacted in Israeli culture, both on a textual level and on a lived, concrete level. In his novel *Sh-etihyi Li ha-Sakkin* (1998), translated to English as *Be My Knife* (Vered Almog and Maya Gurantz 2001),

Grossman attempts a major gendered shift in asking the female to be his knife. The second person of the imperative "be my knife", *tihyi*, demonstrates Grossman's desire to fight the fixation of the knife with masculinity and to instead transfer the agency of the object from male to female.[31] This time it is not the biblical *ma'akhelet* that he is requesting, but rather the Modern Hebrew kitchen knife, *sakkin*, also grammatically feminine. With the allusion to Kafka providing the titular knife, it could help him dig into himself and express his love, one would think.

The novel starts: "You don't know me. When I write to you I don't know myself very well, either. I tried not to write, I did, I've tried for two days, but now I've broken down" (Ibid. 3). Yair, the protagonist, is a thirty-three year-old married man and father to Ido, who is five and a half. He lives in Jerusalem, selling old and rare books to collectors. His life is overwhelmed by the presence of books. Miriam is a woman of forty whom he observed at his high school reunion. Knowing that he found in her his ideal, indispensable reader, he starts to write her letters ("I want to give you things I can't give to anybody else" [Ibid. 3]). Miriam, the "chosen", responds fully and wholeheartedly to his letters. He gets hers "in one day" (4). Through most of the novel, Yair implicates her responses in his letters. In the third part, when he stops writing, she copies his letters in to a notebook and adds her unsent diary entries to him, still in the second person. She is the author. The reader is always aware of several levels of textual production, implicated and deduced in the readerly process.

Nevertheless, to be his ideal reader, as he joyfully tells her, is to be able to read him "exactly as I am writing to you" (Ibid. 6). In the cultural dynamics of the Israeli male gaze—its content of gender, love, and body—he assigns to Miriam an unprecedented role: to be his knife. At this acute moment, Yair is desperate to put order into a cultural, gendered dictionary of reality, whereby Miriam will provide an accurate scale to measure his truth. The critical question is - will she have the space to hold his story? Will she be able to enter his textual contract? In other words, will she use her sharp edge to carve the truth out of the overwhelming excess that increasingly threatens to drown him? (Ibid. 14)

> I wish that two total strangers could overcome strangeness itself, the mighty, ingrained principle of foreignness, the whole overstuffed Politburo sitting so deep in our soul. We could be like two people who inject themselves with truth serum and at long last have to tell it, the truth. I want to be able to say to myself, "I bled truth (*zavti 'emet*) with her," yes, that's what I want. Be my knife for me, and I, I swear, will be a knife for you; sharp knife, but compassionate, your word, not mine.
>
> (Ibid. 8)

The root *zav*, as I discussed in Chapter 1, is typically restricted to the biblical expression "*Eretz zavat khalav udvash*", a land flowing with milk and honey. In high Modern Hebrew, it refers mostly to bleeding, or literally, flowing blood. It is hardly used in colloquial language. Here, it signifies Yair's desire to replace milk and honey, the direct biblical allusion, but also blood, its modern reality, with truth (see Chapter 1). For that, he will need the disciplining knife, using it against both flooding mythologies of satiation as well as hunger-laden, starving ideologies.

But it is much more; Yair's desire is to unload his male genetic code out of his body and consciousness and onto Miriam's through his "gifts", his letters, which are at times like diary entries, marked not only by days but by hours. The epistolary genre serves Yair well; it provides him an ample space to expand his internally gazing superego, which acts as an unstoppable mouth that hungers to combat the emptiness inside while it fills pages with his compulsive and neurotic self. Through his letters, he performs what he calls a "verbal striptease" (Ibid. 79). A deep, sublime, at times pornographic act of exposure, as he calls it, a "masturbation with words", that allows Miriam to enter not only his psyche but also "his most wounded place" (Ibid. Eng. 197).

> I want to wake up to life, to give you all my genetic material, for better and for worse, with my words. The microscopic double helix of my DNA spiraling through every sentence of mine to you…help me, don't give up on me, now, now, be my knife…help me, save me from myself. I can't do it alone.
>
> (192–193)

And yet, playing with knives is never safe. Yair soon interpolates within a deep obsession to write himself against the knife and its crowded site of meaning. The question is will he be able to suspend the force of the *ma'akhelet* and its devouring economy and stay with the more neutral, loving knife, *sakkin*, of Kafka, as he initially intended?

I should note here that in the Israeli climate, Grossman's novel has been received as a smoldering, sweeping love story. The opening words of the novel elicited such a romantic effect that it became a romantic script, subject to imitation. A young couple even chose them to decorate their wedding cake.[32] Grossman's position as the author of love is uncontestable among Israeli readers of the book. And yet, when I taught the novel in my Women's Studies seminar, at Michigan, some of the students identified Yair not as an awesome lover or a romantic model, but as a "creepy stalker" who manipulates Miriam into his own emotional trap. Indeed, the fact that it is so easy for Israeli readers to be oblivious to the creepy stalking aspect can be explained by the way Hebrew readers, much like Miriam, are coming to the literature without guards, charmed by words of love and chosenness.

In Jorge Luis Borges's short story *Funes the Memorious*, the eponymous character gains his compulsive memory after he falls from a horse, injuring his head. His crisis is one of measure; he has to live literally, "exactly" in the scale of reality without abstraction, metaphor, generalization, or conflation, the antithesis to "as if". He embodies the one who is condemned to remember, as he attests "I have more memories in myself alone than all men have had since the world was a world... my memory, sir, is like a garbage disposal" (Borges 1962). Funes is the prototype for an ideology that does not privilege one viewpoint above the others, arranging them.

Yair's "injury" is his excessive giving of himself in writing. It is a highly generative process, a result of a historical process of transmission and accumulation in intertextuality. Unlike Funes, Grossman's is the subject of carefully selected metaphors and allegories, a reductive historical reading of texts and intertexts and their infinite citations in lived reality. It becomes obsessive—evident in the overdose of events and anecdotes in his letters.

"To be his knife" turns out to be an elaborate operation where Miriam is expected to see into Yair's soul and his empty halls and cracks, listen to his words, read and heal his wounds, and identify with him so fully that they can meet each other in the dark of darkness (Grossman 1998, 130). Yair insists that this meeting should take place not face-to-face but through writing and text. A few months after their correspondence, Miriam shockingly discovers that she is pregnant, and it becomes clear that even though she and Yair do not meet in the flesh, their words brought body to body (Ibid. 88), as she discovers, "our words mixed together" (Ibid. 306).

The turn of events in Grossman's novel occurs when Yair starts a war with his son, insisting on teaching him a lesson. The five-year-old drives his parents nuts. His father claims he is stubborn and slow, and disrespects him, so he will not let his son inside the home unless he receives an apology from him. The drama escalates as Yair is fully determined not to give in this time to his son's whims, described in compelling language of the mixture of woven narratives until Miriam comes with her last breath to rescue father and son from where they are lying flooded and waterlogged, almost unconscious in the cold, fierce rain.

What has started as a love letter, a *sakkin*, a knife, to turn inside and expose male interiority (a condition of love through her that enables Yair to dig inside himself—as Kafka puts it), turns the affairs of the Israeli *sakkin*, knife, into the dance of the *ma'akhelet*. He admits in retrospect, "[w]e are somehow too densely packed to push ourselves into a single word 'love'" (184). The ontologies of the knives brought Yair back to the story of Genesis where father and son are under the threat of sacrifice. Numerous allusions to the sacrifice are scattered in the last part of the novel. Miriam, the assigned, merciful messenger of hope, is now urgently summoned to the scene of the doomed male body. On this new altar, she will meet Yair and Ido for the first time. Life with the *ma'akhelet* has appropriated the posture of the Jewish Israeli man, survivor of the eternal covenant. For Grossman, the *ma'akhelet* destroys the Jewish Israeli man's agency, and so for Yair, the *sakkin* must be the object that can return it to him.

Ten years later, Grossman elevates the story to a new standard; in his other magnum opus, his novel *To the End of the Land* (2008), literally, "a woman escapes a bad message", he has given the mandate of the story to a female character, Orah, and like Yair in *Be My Knife*, her name derives from the same Hebrew root, meaning light. He will enlighten, his name a future imperfect promise of light-to-come, while hers is the feminized form of light. The book was highly lauded, so much so that Menachem Perry, the renowned Israeli critic, argued that it is the greatness of the book that escapes critique, *Bikoret Borachat mi-Sefer* ("A review escapes a book"). Thus, the title of his article, referring to the mediocre Hebrew literary critics.[33]

Orah is situated between two men; her husband, Ilan, and her first lover, Avram, as well as her two sons, Adam, with Ilan, and Ofer, with Avram. She escapes Jerusalem, her home, saying, "I simply escaped; Do you understand? I cannot sit and wait for them to come" (Grossman 2008, 153). When Avram, under the influence of propidium, a synthetic sleeping pill, asks her, "who is them?" she says "them… and gave him a deep look, and saw that he understood" (Ibid. 154). She "kidnaps" Avram, Ofer's biological father, who has never met his son, to join her on a long journey along the track from the northeast, the "end of the land", in Galilee, to Jerusalem - a trip she prepared to take with Ofer, before he was called to the army. The logical principle that guides Orah is a thesis that words defy death and so, as long as she tells the story, as long as she engages with the detailed memories of her son Ofer, if she talks and writes obsessively, she will be able to suspend his death.

The Hebrew title, which as I mentioned literally means "a woman escapes a message", is a quote of Orah's words closely tied to her position of resisting calamity. She refers to herself as "a *refusnik* of bad news", in the climate of wars, violent attacks, and death. The bad news is news about her soldier son in the war. Nonetheless, with the discursive reformulation from the familiar "to the end of the world" to "the end of the land" the English title reconstructs the limits of Israeli experience as one that is essentially confined within the boundaries of statehood. What's more, the conflation of time and place (the Hebrew "*'ad*" means both "to" and "until") further tightens the life-and-death urgency of Orah's deferral.

Is it possible that Yair's symbolic mouth—that which begs for a knife—now dwells in Orah? Motivated by a deep, blind intuition, Orah provides a robust, mad dance of storytelling, an Israeli version of Scheherazade telling against death, which of course lurks in the cracks of the story, trying to break through. It comes as the imagined nightmare of every Israeli parent, through the army messengers who arrive at the doorbell to inform parents about the death of their son: "them". And thus, *as long as* she tells the story no bad news can intrude.

As long as is a discursive element familiar to us from the Israeli national anthem, *Hatikvah*, and Naphtali Herz Imber's lyrics. It syntactically frames the condition of hope.[34] Five of its eight lines are one long sentence of "As long as" that opens a speech act of infinite temporality, conditioned by the yearning Jewish spirit, and as such, it continues to condition a performative promise/prayer to the land of Israel even in Israel, from within Israel.[35] Emerging out from its long diasporic longing, "as long as" is a saturated syntax and semantics laid out in exceedingly conditional terms of temporality. Orah's story is saturated with a different economy. For her, "as long as" is hard work, tightening around her vocal cords, deeply engaged in telling Avram her story, their story, the story of Ofer, or any story. And being a concerned mother, she is an excellent storyteller, taking us inside the intricacies of relationships, love, family, nature... in a sacred deliverance, where the adverb, "as long as" measures a critical race against body and language. It is as critical that Avram is a captivated listener. He is Avram, the wounded intertext of Abraham in Genesis; throughout her story he is slowly healing from the Yom Kippur war injury and trauma. Once clean of drugs, he is wise, compassionate, and attentive; he asks engaging questions and mobilizes her tale, but most of all, he is able to sense, with his precise, devouring senses, the invisible contract they keep with death, continue the hike, continue to tell the story, do not go home. They cannot stop. They are not allowed to stop. And so, storytelling on the long hiking trail of the land of Israel organically ties itself to legs and body, intimately diverging to endless paths of tales and anecdotes of people on the road, fragments of memory, becoming a transcended, stretched trajectory of life and textuality that keeps running against fate, as reflected in Grossman's voluminous 630 page book.

Tragically, while still writing his book, David Grossman lost his youngest son Uri, on August 12, 2006, during the last hours of the fighting in Lebanon. Grossman writes in the epilogue,

> I started to write the book in May 2003. I had a feeling, or better, a wish, that the book I am writing will protect him... After the end of the *Shiva'h*, (the seven days of mourning), I returned to the book. Most of it was written. What has changed was the sound box of the reality in which the last version was written.
>
> (Grossman 2011, 653)

From now on, *To the End of the Land* and the life of the author are inexplicably tied together. The storyteller is not only the author of the fictional Yair or Orah; but also the defeated, bereaved father whose son was sacrificed. The book's conclusion violently moves out of the story and to the bigger story, drenched in the politics of war, the story that is no longer able to distinguish between the metaphoric knife and the concreteness of war, and failed to measure its metonymic proximity to the male body.

Writing and reading the story as suspension from reality provides the much-needed illusion of postponing or even superseding death's arrival. Grossman's book presupposes that in attending to the story, to the very act of telling it, to oneself and to others, it will not only tell a compelling story but also generate a testimony of life, a practice already common in the attempt to generate an archive of memory of the fallen young men and women. It transforms writing into another front, a war zone, in a language that has to be more than language, a compassionate and coextensive shield, accessible and yet deceivingly unattainable, it is a language that has to fulfill the promise beyond the fated, fatal deliverance.

Kafka's loving knife, the *sakkin* with which Grossman was hoping to trim, carve, and correct his overbearing story, insists on becoming the *ma'akhelet*. It has crumbled his protective shield of words and has brought the monstrous angel of death with a terminal hunger; the narrative, now, has devoured the storyteller, for it is time to feed the hungry story. The metaphoric world of Grossman becomes (a) reality. Not only is the story unable to suspend death; *more so*, it is starving to be fed, a historical phantom with no limits that itself survives on the totality of provision under the cover of love, promise, chosenness, and the covenant. But more alarmingly, the distance between metaphors and reality is itself a fiction. The attempt to live outside the story has failed. The political is fed by the metaphoric in a devouring system whereby even the language is deployed to camouflage dead bodies while the knives and swords draw the contours of luring violence.

The Open Desert of Torture: Hagar and Ishmael

Menashe Sefer Nehushtan's striking watercolor *Hagar and Ishmael* (2004, 50 cm × 35 cm) depicts distancing as a mode of mobility, an ontological step forward into the unknown (Figure 2.2): the desert. In keeping with the new paradigmatic shift from inside out, from the interiority of the household of Avram and Sarai, to the open space of possibilities, Nehushtan's painting captures well the physicality of this departure, a movement *from*, rather than *towards*, and whether Hagar and Ishmael are looking down or forward, he makes clear that they are walking away. This turn is further emphasized by the fact that the boundaries between them are less clearly demarcated than those between them and the desert. The extent of their exile is visualized; it leaves us with the impression of the grave loneliness of the two bodies, with their backs turned to the viewer as they gaze into the vast desert

Figure 2.2 Sefer Nehushtan, "Hagar and Ishmael", 2004 (watercolors).

that surrounds them. In a conversation, the artist asserts that Hagar and Ishmael's turned backs constitute a gesture of protest against the utter injustice of human experience. Along the same line, my analysis of Genesis 16 traces the violent rupture of Abraham's intimate circle and the tragic collapse of the integrity of body, narrative, and categories. It is at this moment when Otherness is being inscribed.

Nehushtan's aquarelle highlights the emergent organic quality of the relationship of the body with the desert. Hagar is a staging ground for previous escape, as a new body and the ultimate locale of expulsion and otherness. Otherness, now doomed to reconcile the anxiety of hollowness and the burden and the crowding of its reference, begins its account in Jewish and Hebrew tradition. Ishmael and his enigmatic hand and body emerge in my reading as a *kolbo* of alterity, a model of overwhelming saturation. I start with a close reading of Genesis 16, focusing on the conflict between Hagar and Sarai. I am interested in the ways in which the exchange of women, sons, insults, and torture has produced a system of gift exchange that continuously mobilizes hunger, violence, and otherness through the invading hand. Once I develop this originary exchange, its ideology, aesthetics, and economy of exchange, I examine its ramifications in the broader cultural phenomenon of sexual abuse of children in contemporary Israeli culture. I look at Ishmael's hand, following the way the body, like the narrative, loses its integrity and acquires a special desire to break its trajectory from the womb and Hagar's and Sarai's bodies to new social exchange, moving from the most intimate locations of culture to torture and crying, and open desert. Violence through the hand is then articulated in a unique genealogy of what I call, "the hand-me-down narrative", through stories of invading hands that keep legitimately destroying bodies and structures, continually expanding.

Indeed, one must read the story of Genesis 16 and the birth of Ishmael with heightened attention to voice(s), pain, and affect. Against the conventional reading of foundational texts, against the historical muting and muffling of cries and laughter, my feminist reading seeks to activate them in the narrative, to dynamize and dramatize them within a wider discussion of patriarchy, reproduction, and sexuality. Laughter and crying, *tshok* and *bekhi*, are responses that implicitly carry the semantic burden of culture. In Genesis 16, they are situated as a "language" of women, singular to each; Hagar cries and Sarai laughs. Women speak through their bodies, even and especially when they are censored by the demands of fertility and gender roles. Yet, insofar as *they* are significantly rewarded for their ability to give birth—not only to sons, but to the expressions of laughter and tears, Hagar and Sarah produce through tears and laughter the "irreducible effect of femininity" (Cixous 1976, 883). My argument follows the biblical narrative as it moves, following Elaine Scarry's line of inquiry, from seeing to hearing (Scarry 1985). Reading with an attentive ear to the echoes and reverberations of these sounds in the whole narrative advances a thesis about women's performance in critical cultural moments of scandal (i.e., torture, hunger, and invasion).

Most readers are familiar with the story of the birth of Ishmael. After ten years in Canaan, Sarai is fully aware of her infertile body, *"hineh na' 'atsarani God mi-ledet"*, "God has stopped me from giving birth", although *'atsarani* also could mean "arrested", which conveys more strongly Sarai's bodily condition. She resolves to act on it, and following a common practice in ancient Mesopotamian legal traditions, (Teubal 1984; Frymer-Kensky 2002, 227), she proposes to Avram that he approach Hagar,[36] her Egyptian *amah-shifchah* (slave girl), so that she might bear him a child (Alter 2004, 78).[37] What is astounding in the story is the fact that Sarai, along with her soft imperative (*bo'-na*: please come) to Avram to go to Hagar, also says, *"'ulai 'ibaneh mi-menah"*, "perhaps I will be built through her". The verb *'ibaneh*, to be built, could also mean I will be "sonned" through her, if the noun that it contains, *ben*, son, were a verbal root. And therefore means, "perhaps I will be sonned (or mothered) through her" (Genesis 16: 2).[38] The desire "to be built" has been further mobilized and fully appropriated in the Zionist project. In Israel, like in Zion, the renewal of Jewish life has been imagined through the trope of building: the line of the most famous pioneers' song, *"anu banu artzah livnot u-lehibanot bah"* (We came to the land to build and be built in it), is the slogan of patriotic pioneering of the Land with its renewal ethos (Zakim 2006).

The text moves fast; Sarai tells Avram what to do, but he does not simply obey her. The next verse explicitly states that Sarai actively takes Hagar and gives her to Avram "as a wife". In other words, she is pro-active, going beyond the mere giving of instructions. Avram "comes" to Hagar, and she becomes pregnant. Once Hagar realizes she is pregnant, the whole scheme falls apart. The conflict takes place within the arena of eyes and gazes. Hagar looks on Sarai in such a way that Sarai feels belittled. Furious, and without confronting Hagar, she goes to Avram. Hagar is not her partner in this exchange. Sarai acknowledges her role in giving Hagar to Avram, and bemoaning its outcome, she exclaims: "*Chomsi aleikha*", "My wrong be upon you! I put my slave girl in your arms (bosom), and now that she sees she is pregnant, she belittles me". This dispute, she declares, is between her and Avram, with God as their judge. Tenderly, Avram reminds Sarai that "here" (*hineh*), Hagar is "in her hands", under her authority, and gives Sarai permission to do anything she likes, "*'asi lah ha-tov be-'enayikh*" ("do to her anything that seems right to you"). Sarai tortures her. The text is quite economic, shifting from Sarai as the first subject, to the implied "she", Hagar, the second subject, using the pronoun without referring to Hagar by name (literally, "and Sarai tortured her, and she escaped"). Does the text imply that Hagar is becoming a subject? We do not know what "to torture", means here, or how exactly Sarai tortures her, questions with which commentators, scholars, and recent feminists have grappled. Surely, whatever Sarai did, it was enough to send Hagar fleeing to the desert.

The desert extends the narrative beyond its core territory of the plot and the angel of God follows her there and later "[finds] her" (verse 7). When he finds out that she is running away from her mistress, Sarai, the angel, concerned with her well-being, tells her surprisingly to return to her mistress and "suffer abuse/be tortured at her hands" (verse 9). He tells her that because God has *heard* her torture/suffering, she will be highly rewarded—her seed will be fruitful and multiply, and she will give birth to a son, Ishmael. Hagar will become a foremother of her own people. She also names her son, Ishmael. Her otherness will be rewarded.[39]

The Son: An Acoustic Gift

Sarai's offering Hagar to Avram is the first step toward the conception of Ishmael. In this act, the text casts its characters by their cultural roles; it asserts twice that Sarai is Avram's *'ishah*, wife/woman, he is her husband, and Hagar is the Egyptian and slave girl. In terms of Sarai's dative position, when it specifies that she gives Hagar to Avram, it makes explicit three times that Sarai gives Hagar to Avram, using the preposition, *lo*, (*le* + third person pronoun) to him, "she gives her to Avram, her husband, to him, as a wife" (Genesis 16: 3), "as a wife" is a critical speech act that confirms her status.[40] Sarai's initiative to inaugurate the "be fruitful and multiply" of the covenant is an act of issuing a gift, obviously given her inability to bear Avram children. Sarai's idea to give her slave girl to Avram and to transform her into a reproducing-wife is an example of Marcel Mauss's "total prestation" (1967, 8–12), in which what is given is "part of one's nature and substance" and what is received is "part of someone's spiritual essence" (10). Mauss asserts that a system of exchange is not physical or mechanical; rather it is moral, spiritual, and even magical. A woman or child is part of a long list of things that can be given as gifts (Mauss 1967, 12), although "It is in the interest of patriarchal ideology not only that women bear children but also that they desire to do so" (Exum 1993, 121). In that sense, Sarai is perfectly in line with her role.

Unlike Derrida's notion of "unconditional hospitality", though, Mauss's "prestation" is entirely conditional. Three obligations mobilize the prestative exchange: the obligation to give gifts, the obligation to receive them, and the "*absolute obligation*" to repay the gifts (Ibid. 10). These three obligations carry immense value. In giving a gift, a person gives a part of the self away (Ibid. 11), and "to refuse to give and reciprocate, or to fail to invite, is—like refusing to accept—the equivalent of a declaration of war, it is a refusal of friendship and intercourse" (Mauss 1967, 10–11). Mauss's language of responsibility, bound by the principle of exchange, elucidates the overall meaning of the biblical narrative.

It is thus clear that there is a lot at stake in the gift Sarai is issuing, as well as in what she potentially stands to lose and/or gain. In Mauss's terms, by offering Hagar to Avram, Sarai sacrifices part of herself, in a speech act, a gesture of creation entirely her own, opening anew the possibilities of genealogy. And yet, as Gayle Rubin suggests, the exchange of women is predicated on the very notion that kinship is "explicitly conceived as an imposition of a cultural organization upon the facts of biological procreation" (1997, 35). Pregnancy is a site of immense promise for change, a change that is otherwise impossible. Will Sarai be able to produce this radical change, transforming Hagar's otherness—her class, body, nation, and ethnicity—into kinship, and the perceptions thereof glimpsed in Genesis, without changing the core of its meaning?

Sarai's words "*'ulai 'ibaneh mi-menah*", "perhaps I will be built through her", and "perhaps I will be sonned (mothered) through her" (Genesis 16: 2) provide a fascinating access to her subjectivity. It is here that we become aware as readers of the depth of her internalization of the patriarchal libidinal economy of womanhood; her agency is bound up in her ability and inability to give Avram a son. The subjunctive verb *'ibaneh* in the first person, from the root *bni/bnh*[41] and its double reading underscores the profundity of her overwhelming, aching desire to undergo an internal *process of becoming* through Hagar's conception of a son. "To be built" also works against the very possibility of being destroyed by and through barrenness, a tragedy that can ruin a woman as much as her marriage and tribal ties. Indeed, even according to commentators like Midrash Rabba (17: 2), Sarai is lucky to even be able to still be contemplating birth after ten years of unfruitful marriage. Sarai's fantasy asks a question about the possibility of change, a request to be transformed and profit through Hagar's motherhood. Accordingly, Sarai's fantasy, as a political and ideological category, already reveals both the scandal of patriarchy and that of her personal trauma. *'Ibaneh* is her idea of excessive, double "ideological profit", holding potential gains for both her and Avram. Fantasy here, as Zizek suggests, is a political category that constitutes desire, and it plays a role in maintaining both the consistency of subjects and the solidarity of groups (Zizek 1999, 87).[42]

'Ibaneh is a striking *inclusion* of Sarai's fantasy exactly at the moment in which her body is under assault by patriarchal ideology. Her words cunningly indicate that, much as Sarai hopes to be built through Hagar's child, she also desires to be "sonned", to become a mother through Hagar. Pregnancy here is imbued with the unlimited power of structuring social possibilities. Women's production of self, family, kinship, and gender are all presupposed by the reproduction of sons, and thus this short line transforms not only Avram's genealogy but also Sarai's into an author of her own history. Inserting herself in this neologism, in the passive, imperfect mode, Sarai opens the semantic and "arrested" boundaries of the imagined narrative of birthing to its new fantastic limits. Inasmuch as she is open to possibilities, she is anticipating rebuilding rather than collapse. Instead of concluding that she is bitter, resentful (Alter 2004, 77#2), and desperate (Radak, Kimhi 1842, 53), Sarai can be read as seeking new, hopeful heterogeneity, opening her world to this new potentiality.

In the exchange of women, Avram successfully "receives" Sarai's gift: he is able to conceive. However, as the language of the text suggests, Hagar's change of status from *'amah-shifchah*, slavegirl, to *'ishah*, a wife or co-wife implicates her in the exchange, and shifts the overall economy of power; the exchange remains between Avram and Sarai, and not between the two women. They are, nonetheless, all dependent on each other, and they are all fatefully invested in the act of conception. Hagar's son could be the reciprocated gift. For, at the center of these competing fantasies and investments, at the layered complexity intersecting patriarchal authority and women's agency, the son must be the perfect gift.

The Insulting Gaze of Hagar's Pregnancy

Contrary to Sarai's hope, not only does Hagar's pregnancy fail to "build" Sarai; it crushes her. A critical moment, it demands that we further explore her hurt. In the language of Genesis, this means to understand the language of eyes and gazes. It is not clear if Hagar's gaze at Sarai is a power-hungry one, but the Bible shows that it is problematically elevated by the internalized meaning of pregnancy and infiltrates Sarai as such. The expression "*va-'ekal be-'enehah*" ("I appeared (s)light in her eyes") literally speaks in terms of both weight and look, whereby ways of seeing and being seen perform a cultural insult that can lighten and diminish Sarai's status. The way Sarai articulates her position of being looked at by Hagar brings to mind Laura Mulvey's feminist concept of the "to-be-looked-at-ness"; the coded gaze of patriarchy fully internalized by the objectified woman (Mulvey 1999). Communicating from this bodily-situated position of being-looked-at, Hagar's gaze unequivocally asserts the message of heteronormative patriarchy internalized and carried over as an absolute ontological imperative.

The pregnant body constitutes its own gaze, which I refer to as the "pregnancy gaze", informed by the essentialized schema of patriarchal sexuality and the value attached to it. Pregnancy itself is an "impregnating/impregnated performance", never detached from the fact that the body is continually growing. An important aspect of this performativity in Hagar's gaze is the fact that it is manifested, in Sarai's words, in terms of weight; and Sarai consequently perceives this look as making her lighter. The pregnant female body is a fetishized stage that casts male's sexual power and, in Genesis, the power and intervention of God.

The pregnancy gaze can potentially be inflicted between two women, co-wives, sisters, sisters-in-law, in any polygamous household, from one pregnant women to any other woman, especially to the barren one.[43] It is a reversal of the more commonly believe in the evil eye, whereby the pregnant woman is vulnerable to strong feelings of jealousy and envy, attributing power from outside her body. They are two hidden discourses related at their core, forming the competing "eyes" that articulate without words, yet, with unambiguous meaning, confirming the female's ability and disability in terms of pregnancy. The pregnancy gaze, nonetheless, pays no mind to the infertile body. In patriarchal culture, it constitutes disability. More than that, it voids any unspoken contract of solidarity between women because it builds on the currency of pregnancy as a limited good, brutally barring the unpregnant woman from the core of social becoming.[44] Pregnancy and its saturated gaze turns an insulting eye on those women whose bodies are locked, arrested, or otherwise unable to partake in the cultural propagation of kinship. Hagar's gaze, accordingly, has managed to destroy that which it was supposed to build. While this destruction accentuates Sarai's difficulty in facing Hagar, her gaze, pregnancy, and its weight, it will become the precursor to Sarai's own pregnancy and to the miraculous significance attached to it.

If the pregnancy gaze is one of the most problematic acts, it will be through voice and sound that resolutions are managed. Hagar will cry in the desert of torture. And when Sarai learns of her pregnancy later, she laughs—and God hears her. For now, God's angel hears Hagar and Ishmael. In this way, voice and sound mediate the women's relationships with the divine. The narrative shifts from the overloaded arena of the gaze and eyes to that of hearing, in which the sound is sharp and clear. Hagar's cries and Sarai's laughter appear dichotomous in the extreme and they figure in the narrative as sharp and crystalized moments that catalyze action and resolution.

Nonetheless, Hagar's gaze effectively and radically shifts the relationship between the two women, for they enter into an intersubjective exchange of looks and power that works against the core of Sarai's investment in their exchange. Avram's permission for Sarai "to do anything" she wishes redirects the lines of exchange, as he gives or reciprocates authority back to Sarai, allowing her to reassert her power over Hagar. Avram does not actively say or do anything to Hagar, but he appears to side with Sarai. Rhetorically, he reconstitutes parental authority, putting it back in Sarai's hands, as if power is inherent to Sarai. Her name literally means to rule and to govern. Avram's permission provides Sarai ample latitude for action, and is thus consistent with the citational strategy of the narrative; it is open to the totality of possibilities. Later this permission is reiterated when Sarai requests that Avram expel Hagar and Ishmael, and God instructs Avram to do anything Sarai tells him to do (chapter 21, verse 12). It is a sweeping speech act that ends up broadening the scope of citationality.

Becoming pregnant implies that a woman becomes the mother of the covenant, and mother of the nation, developing into the *subject of her history*. The narrative thus advances Hagar's motherhood beyond her subordinate position to Sarai as obligatory in the process of building the institution of motherhood. Avram actively restores Sarai's power, responding to the way it has been diminished by Hagar, through her pregnancy. Hagar's intimacy with her conceiving body introduces her to a new discourse of power. If Hagar's change allows her to open her eyes and gain knowledge, it is through her new position of anticipating motherhood and through her relationship not to Sarai but to her own body.

Transitive Torture

Avram's answer to Sarai's complaint about Hagar is revealing, for he reminds her that "*Hineh, shifchateck be-yadekh*", "here, your slavegirl is in your hands", and thus provides her an explanation that functions as a permission, an alibi, to "do whatever you think right" (16: 6, Alter Ibid. 78), or more literally, "do to her what [seems] best in your eyes". Avram establishes the scope of Sarai's response to Hagar's gaze with a totality of open possibilities. Sarai's challenge lies in whether she will be able to contain and set limits in this moment when "everything", the everything that Avram has permitted, is hers. Sarai's desire for retaliation here stands to answer the degree of her insult by Hagar's gaze. Throughout the narrative, the centrality and repetitiveness of the idiomatic uses of eyes and hands flesh out the role of language in the narrative. The idiomatic expressions like "in your eyes" and "at your hands" articulate the space between the concrete, literal body and the abstract, idiomatic body, in such a way that substantiates the wider bio-political construct of domination. Abstractions of power are encoded and materialized in immediate, corporeal referents. The narrative focuses on female bodies; from Hagar's gaze and her eyes of s/lightening, it moves to Sarai's gaze, her eyes of measure (of what is best), while Sarai holds Hagar in her hands. The body and its parts serve to further situate and make visible different positions of power and control.

The scope of possibility stands in striking contrast to the brevity of the account of what Sarai does in return (one word in Hebrew): *va-te'aneha*, "she tortured her". The text is secretive, even censoring. It introduces in one word the whole event of torture, yet reveals nothing about the exact nature of it. And yet, there is an inherent measure of excess in the verb "to torture", regardless of whether the torture was physical or mental. As a transitive verb, *Le'anot*, to torture, is to inflict pain and suffering on the other—excessive and intentional—for the sake of teaching through pain and suffering an unambiguous lesson of power. "Teaching" here is tied to discipline and intimidation, for Hagar is meant to experience powerlessness that resets the hierarchy, aiming, as Foucault suggests, to renew the vigor of power (Foucault 1984, 199). Pain and the realization of pain are central to torture.[45] The verb *le'anot*, in *pi'el*, is semantically related to *la'anot*, in *pa'al*, which means to answer, respond, or react. This relationship brings to mind that torture is in itself a kind of figurative speech. It speaks through another language (pain) and delivers its message not through elaborated vocabulary but through its unlimited permission.

Excessive and intentional, torture invades, separates, excludes, breaks down, and breaks apart. In the context of modern history and moralistic, universal humanism, scholars like Talal Asad approach the pain of torture in terms of "scandal" that is driven by a force of retaliation (Asad 2003, 152, and 100–126). Such an act mobilizes momentous consequences that are critical in understanding torture today, but they also have relevance in reading Genesis 16 and the stories of Hagar and Ishmael. For, if torture manages to symbolically reset the superiority of Sarai over Hagar, it does so at the price of breaking down all potential structures and categories, including the one of gift exchange. Against the logic of calculated gift exchange, and within the patriarchal economy of female desire and fantasy, Sarai's torture means to highlight Hagar's (sub)alterity, bracketing her pregnancy within the kinship system of Avram.

But the physical scandal is manifested ontologically. Torture accordingly intends to strike a blow against the most intimate and sensitive texture of being, demolishing any protected interiority and engaging its object in interminable restlessness. On other occasions, torture appears in the Bible in contexts of sexual abuse and rape (II Samuel 13: 22). The emotional scar of the abuse will permanently undermine the integrity of the body and self, and manifests itself in Hagar's cry as her marker of difference. As the works on trauma by scholars such as Shoshana Felman and Dori Laub (1992), Cathy Caruth (1995), and Regina Schwartz (1998) suggest, torture becomes a long-lasting memory/injury as it settles in the body and spirit. Not only does torture violently dismantle the boundaries of Hagar's body, but it also goes beyond that to impact the disposition of Ishmael. And it is this torture that becomes his indelible wound with lasting effects. This is the act that "violents" the body, to invoke Mieke Bal's concept, in which "violence violents", and "violation is violent" (Bal 1988b).

In her book, *Trauma and Experience*, Cathy Caruth suggests a departure from "A notion of traumatic experience as a neurotic distortion" and a move towards a notion of torture as "a temporal delay that carries the individual beyond the shock of the first moment" (10). This, for Caruth, refutes the possibility that torture could be contained in any given time and place. Torture, performed to mark a person and body, is the ultimate traumatic event. Like trauma, it has repetitive after-shocks. Caruth elaborates:

> The trauma is a repeated suffering of the event, but it is also continual leaving of its site. The traumatic reexperiencing of the event thus *carries with it* what Dori Laub calls the "collapse of witnessing," the impossibility of knowing that first constituted it. And by carrying that impossibility of knowing out of the empirical event itself, trauma opens up and challenges us to a new kind of listening, the witnessing, precisely, of impossibility.
>
> (Caruth 1995, 10, emphasis in the original)

In order to understand the trauma of reading I utilize Effi Ziv's psychopolitical model of "insidious trauma" that seeks to develop a cultural theory that is grounded in collective and political systems of oppression such as sexism, racism, and homophobia. She critiques PTSD as it is practiced in the field of psychology, arguing that it tends to be linear, hierarchical, diagnostic, and often focuses on symptoms. Detached from the cultural political mechanism that has produced it, such approach ends up localized to one traumatic crisis of the past, depoliticizing and decontextualizing its unique emergence. "Insidious trauma" or "intractable trauma", according to Ziv, asserts that trauma is a continuous condition, a reality that is often camouflaged by the process through which it has become normative and natural. Such a condition manifests itself persistently not through a binary, chronological paradigm but through the rhizomatic model of less obvious traumatization in a wider socio-cultural context (Ziv 2012).

In Genesis, it is Hagar's trauma of torture that is repeated in Ishmael, thenceforward reverberating through the genealogies of Genesis. Torture, as a product of invasion and the absence of limits, is made possible by Avram's permission to Sarai to do anything she sees fit. This absence of limits is the crux of the narrative, for Sarai's act of torture leads to two additional moments in which boundaries and limits—bodily, psychological, narratological, and discursive—break down. The narrative consistently moves from Sarai and Avram's presumably firm unity, from the intimate female space of bonding, exchange, and hospitality, to departures, expulsions, and dispersions. As a liminal zone, the desert's limitlessness also opens up the challenges Caruth describes above. In its unending, wandering wilderness, the desert to which Hagar escapes is not only an overwhelming space of infinity that aims to devour her, reinforcing her inability to remain intact; the desert is itself a site of torture, as it is unable to provide her with any sustenance, compounding her crisis. Her exclusion will constitute her way of speaking enigmatically as a desperate cry from this place.

Hearing the Voice of Torture

Genesis introduces crying and laughter as two paradigmatic affects. To the extent that they are presented as binary oppositions, the text aims to differentiate the ontological condition of Hagar's crying from Sarai's laughter in their sons' prefigured narratives as inscribed in their names: Isaac, *Yitchak* (he will laugh), and Ishmael, *shama'* (God will hear), alluding to Hagar's crying voice.[46] Before giving birth to Ishmael, therefore, Hagar gives birth to crying, and yet, before giving birth to crying Hagar gives birth to the voice of pain, for the voice of pain, as Elaine Scarry tells us, transforms into crying. So although crying and laughing occur fully around the birth of Isaac, and the expulsion of Hagar and Ishmael in Chapter 21, Hagar's voice of torture begins to resonate strongly through the course of events in Chapter 16, within the context of exchange and its collapse.

Indeed, paying attention to voice and its volume has been clearly overlooked by scholars. If each act of crying and laughing is singular, untranslatable, and not readable (Derrida 1986), what can be said about the first act of crying and the way Genesis introduces it? The narrative follows Hagar's voice through the eyes (and ears) of the Angel. Pain, as Elaine Scarry theorizes, "that which cannot be denied and that which cannot be confirmed", is unshareable, for pain resists or even destroys language, "bringing about an immediate reversion to a state anterior to language, to the sounds and cries a human being makes before language is learned",[47] (Scarry 1985, 4–5). Nonetheless, when the first human in Genesis cries, God hears her.[48] He is her witness, hearing and implicitly siding with her unambiguously. The response to her voice of torture is the interference of the divine, miraculously signifying that if torture does not have an answer, at least it has an ear. This is important; it establishes God's ability to hear interior pain beyond language, place and time. So critical to Genesis, it introduces the genesis of crying with a compassionate and humanized ear.

And yet, even after hearing her, the Angel's response to her voice of torture is the most betraying, for, as we have seen, he sends her back to torture: "Return to your mistress and suffer abuse at her hand" (*hit'ani tachat yadah*) (Alter 2004, 79). The reward of her suffering is to be the one who gifts the son, and in the big picture, torture and suffering are reduced and minimized. The angel makes Hagar several promises; that she "will be fruitful and multiply" now uttered to a woman; she will have a son, Ishmael; he will be wild, his hand will be inside/against everyone, and everyone's hand will be inside/against him, and he will spread out all over the land. This moment has been understood as the genesis of a new lineage: the emergence of Islam's sacred history and ritual (Freyer Stowasser 1996, 44–45; Hassan 2006, 152–155). Hagar has been granted in this moment of epiphany the gift of motherhood as the ultimate matriarch of culture in the Islamic tradition. In Jewish-Israeli consciousness, however, Hagar's inclusion has been highly compromised; she will become the rejected genealogical branch—and the core of Judaism will continue from Sarai, the mother, to Rebecca, Leah, and Rachel.

A Manic Category: *Yado Ba-kol ve-Yad Kol Bo*

My analysis follows what I see as the heart of this narrative: the way violence is mobilized within an originary patriarchal system of exchange, and how such a system of gift exchange and "total prestation" has been corrupted. Unproductive transactions challenge this system and break down the boundaries of categories (kinship in particular), inventing new, disorderly possibilities. From the intended gift at his conception, Ishmael is exiled to otherness. I wish now to explore more fully how this otherness is articulated.

Ishmael is an ideological child. Even before his conception, he had been invested with a totality of competing expectations and obligations by Sarai, Avram, and Hagar. After his ten years of life in Canaan, the promised son will begin to unfold the much-anticipated lineage of the covenant. Sarai, the master planner of the idea, has not only been motivated by the desire to rescue Avram's lineage by providing him with a son; her emotional cathexis is in her son, to be a mother and "to be built" through and by another woman. For Hagar, a son would assert her power and transform her from a slave girl into a producing co-wife, bringing her socio-economic status closer to Sarai's.

Despite these human expectations, the Angel enunciates Ishmael differently. Wildness is a key aspect of his representation that sets him apart; it is saturated with discriminatory markers. He is "wild", "a wild ass", in the sense that the Hebrew adjective *pere' 'adam* distinguishes him from domesticated, obedient and controlled humans, and becomes singularly attributed to Ishmael as the signifier of his separation. But more than that, such "wildness" marks him as unnatural, inhuman, uncultured, and savage. Indeed, most biblical commentators have tied wildness to mobility and wandering, referring to the nomadic, tribal characteristics of Ishmael. Often, scholars conveniently read verse 12 of Genesis 16 reductively or even ignore the second part of the verse, the most puzzling attribute of Ishmael, "*yado ba-kol ve-yad kol bo*", his hand (is) in/against everyone and everyone's hand (is) in/against him. (Hebrew does not need the verb "to be" for it to be a full sentence.) This idiom is untranslatable, and even in Hebrew, it is hard to grasp its meaning, a fact that perhaps adds duplicity and obscurity to the signifiers of separation of Ishmael. What is the plurality of the "hand" that invades him? How singular is it? How invasive and violent? And finally, how relevant is it that he is wild? Ishmael's obscured representation within the system of exchange strongly suggests that who he is and what he is are less significant than the very fact that he is a passing commodity of exchange that continues to appear as if he is gifting everyone. In the unreadability of the phenomena, Ishmael tells us to consider his unique ability to interact as he becomes the exemplary token of exchange.

The figure of the hand—"the singular thing that belongs only to man" (Derrida 1987, 182)—is a premier organ of touch, a tool, and a sign. It has been for many philosophers "the exclusive attribute of 'man'", the "humanual" as Derrida calls it (Miller 2008, 147). Most fascinating and relevant to this chapter is the way its economy is tied to the gift, more specifically to exchange, and to the subject of violence. Briefly, Heidegger differentiates between the human and non-human hand. Hand is *thought*. But close to his idea of *being*, hand (and thought) are un-theoretical, or pre-theoretical presences that are related to the kind of knowledge of authentic craftsmen, farmers, art, and poetry. In his book, *Being and Time* he articulates being in the world as a "concern" (*Besorgen*), rather than observing it. Man is concerned and involved in the world by using his hand (Clark 2007, 241). And thus, "All the work of the hand is rooted in thinking. Therefore, thinking itself is man's simplest, and for that reason hardest, *hand-werk*, if it would be properly accomplished" (Heidegger 1968, 16–17) Derrida goes further, claiming that Western thought it organized around the hand and speech (Derrida 1987, 181). Moving away from Heidegger's logocentrism, Derrida critiques Heidegger's approach as purist, idealized, totalistic, and binaristic in its opposition of giving and taking.[49] Accordingly, Heidegger's idea that the hand only belongs to man excludes problematically the hand of the ape, a typically anthropocentric erasure.

What is important to Derrida is the connection of the hand to the reception, following the etymological connection between thinking and thanking. Giving and taking, accordingly, is a dialogue, a "transitive gift" (1987, 174–175). Giving and taking away are acts that take place in the same gesture. In fact, "Nothing is less assured than the distinction between giving and taking". But more importantly, it is critical to rethink the values of different oppositions such as "the gift that does good and the gift that does bad, of the present and of poison" (176). The binary that Derrida opposes works well in Genesis in the depiction of two different paradigms and models and builds meticulously on Mauss's system of exchange. For both Heidegger and Derrida, the hand is a strong marker of human (Heidegger) and sexual and ontological difference (Derrida 1987, 181). In Ishmael's description, Genesis uses the hand's maximum potentiality to become everything—receiving and giving, human and inhuman—at once. A signature, a password (Miller 2010),[50] the hand speaks directly to differentiate the singularity of Ishmael among the children of Genesis.

In this extreme articulation of Ishmael, an animated hand, *yad*, in singular, hovers between self and others, between one single hand and two and many hands. The literal and the figurative, the thematic and operative, are substantiated by the fact that this articulation is predicated not on a verb but on the preposition *b*, "in", "inside", "at", "within", "in the interior of", "contained by", or "against". This nominative grammatical construct not only escapes any reference of time, but it also opens the hand of Ishmael and everyone against each other's interiority, as a never-ending, intensified uninterrupted penetration of hands. The preposition *b* significantly keeps and updates the dynamic mobility of the hand, wild and reactive, as it defines all bodies as penetrable, activating a long list of implied verbs such as "exist", "is", "dwell", as "touch", "stroke", "enter", "breaking through", "invade", "attack", and "overrun". The totality of *kol*, "everything", "everyone", "all", "each", and "any" augments the total availability of Ishmael's body and hand, refuting any illusion of symmetry between Ishmael's hand and that of another, alluding instead to the chaotic, collective mishmash of hands, bodies, other body parts, and others' body parts, all present in one space, one invaded "body", as the text continues to call it. So the exchange is non-productive, because, unlike Serres's model of the "parasite", it has no direction, and acts only for the sake of the mobility of its own system (Serres 2007).[51] The irony, or rather tragedy, is that Ishmael has long disappeared and has never participated in any cultural exchange.

Within the domain of the female psyche that intends to challenge boundaries, status, and hierarchies, Genesis 16 introduces a new conception of male corporeality that moves horizontally and vertically, able to transform any encounter into an incurable invasion. The image of a hand that is "in all", *ba-kol*, in everyone and everything, is a compelling reference, yet it is also deceiving; it works as if it were an agent of exchange. Yet it is at once both totally empty and totally full, overfilled, a sum of its gradual accumulation, and together an uncompromising economic measure that both colonizes all and is colonized in every encounter. Such a hand moves across different discursive realms, through and between language, thoughts, materials, and actions. Paradoxically, Ishmael's hand is at the full service of the ultimate *gift*: "co-belonging". He and his hand are saturated with the intention of giving and taking to the point of enslavement to the tyranny of the system. In his urgency and anxiety to fulfill his role, his hand ends up losing all measures and transgresses all possible bodies and boundaries.

Even though it is Hagar who is tortured, Ishmael bears the hands of others within him. Insofar as Ishmael's conception was invested with too many conflicting obligations and transactions, it has proven to be incongruous. As he becomes so completely over-determined to satisfy that which he encounters, he becomes the token of exchange, an utter symbol of "unfreedom" (Adorno 2006), able to hold and contain nothing. "*Yado ba-kol*" and "*yad kol bo*" is a doomed forecast of his restlessness, a curse, which underscores the historical pathology of his mother's torture and her offspring's inability to escape its predisposition.[52] Ishmael emerges in this short description of dense, infinite, and manic hands as the figure of the occupying and the occupied human, constituting with his crowded body, a paradigm of otherness with a new economy. This over-dense and overcrowded corpus suggests that we read the idiom as a single word, "*yadobakolveyadkolbo*" with no spaces or breaks.

Kolbo: Between Emptiness and Oversaturation

The Hebrew linguistic articulation of the *kol bo*, "all, everything (is) in it", as an empty container works like the enigmatic vacuum that Genesis has left us, yet it is always within a system of commerce and exchange of an ideal commodity. As it continually remains empty, it tells us about its potential to constitute an alternative, much fuller body. That *Kol Bo* and *Yad Kol Bo* were the names of medieval Jewish legal books and commentaries tells us about the term's potential to become a purportedly comprehensive body of knowledge, built on the compendious meaning of *kol bo*. Two volumes of 1155 pages, *Kol Bo L'Yahrzeit*, comprise an encyclopedia by Rabbi Aaron Levine which includes "Everything you need to know to understand and properly observe the *yahrzeit*, anniversary of the death".[53]

The modern urban construction of the *kolbo* in Israeli culture brings a more sensational cultural body. Building on its highly self-referential elegant semantic and economic formulation—all, everything (is) in it—it has become a sign with a totality of provision that aspires to contain in it more than products, more than dreams, simply all that can be imagined. The name *Kolbo* has worked as a magical concept for small businesses and department stores. The first one in Tel Aviv, Kolbo Shalom, was Israel's first department store, built in 1965, and was until recently the most visible part of the central business district of the Tel

Aviv skyline and an important part of the Shalom (Meir) Tower. Kolbo Shalom mocked the city as it aspired to reach the height of capitalist fantasy by promoting itself as the tallest building in the Middle East, with an amusement park at the top of the building.[54] Kolbo Shalom, like the Tower of Babel, purported to represent a kind of synecdochic mandala that contains the totality of Israeli/Jewish aspirations. It also mocked all the other small humble kolbos, scattered throughout the state—*kolbo la-bayit* (kolbo to the house) or *kolbo la-yeled* (kolbo to the child, a children's store), small, local stores that named themselves a priori as providers of household goods for specific customers.

Kolbo is a convenient signifier. It is possible to read in it everything we desire without compromising its integrity for the simple reason that its manic signification is already in such constant flux, and therefore always static. In its socialist conception, for example, the Kolbo, now a little "kolboinik", has transformed into a native, intimate waste bowl, mandatory at the center of the dining table. Until the late seventies, this aluminum or steel bowl, turned at the end of the meal into an overstuffed and overflowing garbage pile, at the heart of the trashing practices of Kibbutz members. The concept of the *kolboinik* is still common in contemporary culture. In Yiddish and Hebrew, a *kolboinik* is a rascally know-it-all. A brief Google search reveals that *kolbo.com*, for example, is a website that sells "Fine Judaica, Books, Music and Ketubot (marriage contracts)". Other sites use the word *kolboinik* in advertising; it is a name of a handyman who can do all kind of jobs, a construction company, or a truck delivery service. Alternately, it is the title of an article about an international versatile designer. Lastly, *Kolbotek* is an established consumer affair and investigative reporting TV show on Israel's Channel 2.

Ishmael is the one who was born thin-skinned; as such he bears all of these meanings of the kolbo. God saves him, God blesses him, (his mother protects him) but his otherness has been marked, he and his mother are effectively excluded from the main body of Israel and its story and history. This exclusion and its concomitant openness defines him: he is an empty vessel for others, and the one restlessly involved in making others and the world his container, highlighting the transitions or transactions from outside and inside. Ishmael's status as the kolboinik, then, has far-reaching ramifications in our cultural imaginary.

The collapse of the boundaries of the body articulates an ideological crisis; the idiomatic hands that occupy Ishmael are forces of one's life and story that move against definitions, order, and law. Reduced and concealed through arbitrary, exaggerated positions of giving and taking, from in and out, the body becomes the zone of exhaustive violence and abuse. This violence is mobilized in a system that keeps producing otherness. In Jewish culture, Ishmael's difference has created a category of otherness. I am interested in the way the collapse of this category has become a permission to invade the body/corpus. It has been produced and reproduced throughout history in different locations to varying degrees, depending on the different politics of othering. I move now to contemporary literature in order to show how this direction of violence through the torturing, invading hand, continues to figure in Jewish-Israeli culture. First, I turn to the poet Yehuda Amichai to show how the idea of the *kolbo* and its implicit invocation of Ishmael operate through the motif of the megalomaniac hand that again tempers with the parameters of inclusion and exclusion.

The Autobus of History

> Then he stopped and turned around, and I saw him: the face of God was a hand.
>
> Héléne Cixous, Inside[55]

> Go, children I begot; get yourselves into the next century,
> When the cry and the laughter will continue, just as they were.
> I remember giving them a stern warning:
> "Never, never stick your hand out the window of a moving bus."
> Once we were on a bus and my little girl piped up, "Daddy,
>   that guy
> Stuck his hand into the outside!"
>
> That's the way to live: to stick your hand into the
>   infinite outside
>
> Of the world, turn the outside inside out,
> The world into a room and God into a little soul
> Inside the infinite body.
>
> Yehuda Amichai, "My Children Grew"[56]

Against the father's stern warning, "Never, never stick your hand out the window of the travelling bus", the daughter screams out loud, "Father, he entered his hand outside!" or more clearly in English, "Daddy, that guy stuck his hand into the outside" (Bloch and Kronfeld 1999, 58).[57] The oxymoronic construction, *"le-hakhnis hachutzah"* (to enter outside) is more unsettling in Hebrew than in its English translation. The verb to enter is never paired with going outside; rather, its complementary object is towards the inside and this difference is exactly what Amichai intends to convey. Unexpectedly, the validity of the poem's message is in the voice of the daughter as perhaps the only voice that can be truthful here to language and the boundaries that have been "violented" (Bal 1988a).

The opening line of the poem already invokes Genesis 16. Bloch and Kronfeld's English translation obscures the tight connection that the Hebrew establishes between *tse'etsa'im* (offspring or descendants) and the verb *tse'* ("come out", "go out", or "leave"). Amichai's imperative *ts'u*, in the plural, evokes the promises to Avram and Hagar to "be fertile and multiply", and whimsically multiplies as it builds on the semantic fecundity of the Hebrew language to bear its own offspring. *Ts'u* plus *ts'u* equals *tse'etsa'im*, exactly in the same way that the originary act of coming out of the womb and being born (*yatsa*) is etymologically tied to becoming an offspring, *tse'etsa*, and *tse'ets'im*, in the plural. One way to perhaps capture this proximity in English, albeit somewhat less precisely, is through the connection between "off" and "offspring", reading the line, "Off, off offspring (in plural) come into the next century..."[58] or, in Hebrew, "*ts'u ts'u tse'e'tsa'im la-me'ah ha-ba'ah*".

This tension in Amichai is all the more ironic, because he summons the children to come out to the next century where not only cries and laughter will remain fixed, but where, as he already knows, such categories as tears and laughter or inside and outside have been skewed. His traveling bus of history, a new traveling kolbo of human subjects, is, like Ishmael, utilizing a megalomaniacal hand that seeks to escape its crowdedness.[59]

Amichai's collection of poetry *Open Closed Open* (1998) pushes us to reexamine the question of measure of what should be open, what should be closed, and to what extent. The language here is in a dynamic process of signification, alluding to the fact that the cultural protocols that structure our perceptions have been violently distorted, warping the limits of body, self, history, and language. This distortion generates a long chain of predicaments, confronting us with powerful questions about how cognitive and semantic categories operate under such conditions. Obviously, the romantic bus that was "flowing in milk and honey" has been transformed into an intolerable, threatening space. With the collapse of boundaries, the synecdoche of Ishmael's hand becomes larger than simply a bus and body, larger than God and texts, a phantom that represents the condition of total restlessness in the face of complete confusion of inside and outside. To the extent that Amichai invokes Ishmael from the empty bus of history, he seeks desperately to engage in any exchange even if it ends up once again touching the abysses of its hollowness.

Orgy and the Making of the Other through the Assault on the Body

The textual abuse of Ishmael in the construction of otherness lays the blueprint for other(ing) cultural practices of violence. It goes back to the numerous patriarchal mandates—from God and Avram—to "do anything" to the body of the other. Sarai's desire provides a unique opportunity to investigate how "becoming" is an intrinsic construct not only to the construction of gender, but also that of nationhood

The homogenizing melting pot of Israeli nationality is a metaphoric space of becoming for both individuals and communities. Here, I transition from the discussion of Ishmael to a discussion of Zionism, focusing on children and young adults. I will tie Sarai's aspiration and investment in Hagar's child and the possibility of "being built" through another to the Zionist ethos of "being built" through the act of returning to Israel, and through subsequent participation in the project of nationhood. I stress the single verb "*ibaneh*" (I will be built) in Sarai's desire and its manifestation in the Zionist ethos, "*Anu banu artsah livnot ulehibanot bah*" ("we came to the land to build it and be built in and by it"). The fantasy of "becoming through" a process of being built, active and passive, is full of possibilities and inevitably holds within it a concomitant capacity for fulfillment and lack thereof, which the fantasy or promise often effectively effaces.

Moving from female desire to the collective, the national, imagined "we" nevertheless maintains a sexual desire manifested in the process of becoming. Although the project of Zionism has been articulated in myriad ways, for S. Yizhar, the moment of national birth was "an orgy, that which summoned all that is human in you" (Tkuma 1998). S. Yizhar—one of Israel's leading writers, teachers, politicians (a *Kneset* member), and public figures—thus ties the project of nation-building to the most libidinal ecstasy of collective sexuality. It was a total spectacle, impossible for one to resist, experienced from within and invoking the most altruistic tendencies in its participants.

The libidinal economy we saw in the story of Ishmael might suggest some similarities to the libidinal economy of national discourse. Indeed, that Zionism was not only a political and ideological project, but also a sexual one, is a thesis that was put forward by several scholars of Israeli culture. This process aspired to rescue the Jewish male body from its long years of diaspora and transform it into a heteronormative, hypermasculine native body (Biale 1992; Boyarin 1997; Gluzman 1997; Weiss 2002). For Raz Yosef, this dominant masculinity and sexuality is articulated through the exclusion of ethnic others (Yosef 2004). In general, the excessive ideological force deployed to create national and religious unity was crucial to the construction of Sabra identity. This ideology glorified the melting pot metaphor; it was immediate, cohesive, integral, and restorative, and provided a new genealogy that re-membered the "ruins and fragments" of the Jewish exilic past. The creation of the Israeli-born Sabra and the melting pot worked to erase gendered, ethnic, and sexual differences by rapidly assimilating them: the devouring mechanism at work.

Speaking of national emergence as an orgasmic sexual moment, as Yizhar does, underscores the linguistic predicament of appropriation and the more problematic distinctions between the literal and the figurative, pleasure and torture, and the violence inflicted on bodies and the violence of language and narratives. Since the 1980s, works explicitly confronting the experience and perpetration of sexual violence have been increasing in Israel and can be understood in part as representing a critique of utopian Zionism. The authors of some of these works also aim to rewrite a postcolonial critique of modernity. The body invaded and colonized by sexual predators directly contests the (masculinist) ethos of Sabra culture, which is still imagined as highly moral, nurturing, and protective of women and children. Throughout this chapter, my reading aims to pay attention to the physical body first before the metaphoric and allegorical. Acts of sexual violence are not easily verbalized or translatable into a shareable, communicative language.

I focus on three Hebrew narratives that articulate different degrees of invasion and sexual assault on the *yeled* (the child) of Sabra culture. "*Yeled*" designates a vulnerable space of youth into which adults can readily intrude. The signifier presupposes that children as a plurality are incapable of acting as subjects, and need to be initiated into the "knowledge" of culture via excessive feeding, a position that emphasizes the need for the patronizing adult.[60] Rescuing the other is an essential component of the discourse of modernity and colonialism. The positing of conditions or populations as inferior or necessitating rescue itself manufactures the conditions of subalternity it ostensibly aims to correct. The rush to civilize is both a symptom and agent of this phenomenon, which is also tied to the project of collective becoming; having built oneself up, the logical progression is to build up the other (Fanon 1967, 31–32).[61] The first story is therefore a rescue narrative, and its gift is sweet bread and jam. It contributes to the creation of the Israeli Sabra and brings him closer to the cultural resources (i.e., Hebrew literature and its author). The other three explicitly approach the subject of sexual violence towards young boys in the context of ethnic, gender, class, and age differences.

Victim of Rescue: David Shahar and "Midnight Story"

David Shahar (1929–1997), an award-winning writer, translator, editor and educator, is famous for his novels, especially the series of novels *Heichal Ha-Kelim Ha-Shvurim (1969–1994)* (The Palace of Shattered Vessels), his four short story collections, dating back to 1946, and a children's book.[62] His early stories are especially notable for the typical style of the Statehood Generation, which articulated the Zionist teleological narrative of return and redemption.[63]

Shahar's "*Sippur Chatsot*" ("Midnight Story") in his first book of short stories, *Concerning Dreams* (1955) is ostensibly an innocent story of hospitality—the tale of the narrator-author taking care of a young man, Danny. This is a typical narrative of belonging, consistent with the Israeli ethos of provision. Told as a memoir in the first person singular,

Shahar's author describes the midnight encounter between the author narrator and Danny, a nine-year-old boy running fearfully in the dark through the trash-strewn streets of Jerusalem. The story provides an excellent example of the typical Oedipal way in which Hebrew literature encounters its children and fulfills its role by providing a rescue narrative in a contextualized national framework of patronized and protected childhood. Shahar frames the encounter (my translation):

> The sound of barking dogs shattered the silence, and soon after, a dog appeared at the top of the small mound; he sniffed at broken dishes, nibbled on the trash, twirled his nose upward and sent a long howl to the stars. At once, a deep, fragmented choir of barking replied from all directions, startling the cowering silhouette of a person near the cedar tree. The person split away from the tree and hastily moved towards me. It was the figure of a child in a long, wide coat; the fringes of his pajamas encircled his skinny legs. I slowed down. The child stopped beside me, gasping and panting fearfully. Once the noise of barking calmed down, the child started walking more slowly, as if he were simply taking a walk. I turned to him, yelling out "Hey, *yeled*! Stop!" The child stood, looking at me. I approached and saw that his eyes were wide with fear, and his teeth chattered in a grimace. I put my hand on his shoulder, feeling his collarbone through the coat. *"What are you doing here so late?" I asked him. The child didn't answer. I repeated the question. He remained silent. I put my other hand on his shoulder, and shook him, repeating my question for the third time.* He continued to stare at me and finally said, "Nothing...just ... walking..." *A lump stuck in my throat. I swallowed my saliva, and felt an intense thirst.* "Listen, *yeled*," I told him, "Do you want to drink a hot cup of tea with lemon?" *The child came to life,* nodding his head in agreement and saying, "Yes, I do." I took him by the hand, rushing to my room, with his small hand in mine and a night wind blowing in our faces...At the entrance of the building the child turned to me and said: "There are so many stars in the sky. I never knew that there are so many stars in the sky. And that the sky is so large and wide. It's a little frightening ..." A bashful, hesitant smile formed on his face.
>
> (Shahar 1955. My emphasis)

In the grand narrative of rescue, in which the expansiveness of the sky and the darkness of the city take on a mythical dimension, the child is lost, amplifying the significance of the appearance of the author. Notice the implied sensuality of the description, for how are we to explain that the narrator must shake the child's shoulders after repeating his question three times? And why is it important that he, the narrator, feels a lump in his throat, that he is the one who is intensely thirsty? Obviously, the child is the one who "comes to life" once offered tea and lemon. And yet, the gesture of hospitality, offering him tea and lemon, bread with jam, and a sofa to sleep on (which the child refuses), brings him back to life. The double agency embedded in the author-narrator takes on a grandiose dimension. It is significant, too, that tea and lemon with bread and jam were the staple food of immigrants in the fifties, when scarcity of resources was part of the daily austerity.

Danny is running away from home because his parents often fight and quarrel violently, screaming and shouting rudely about the father's disloyalty to his wife. That night, the mother, who has had enough, finally sends her husband back to his mistress, saying, "Filthy pimp, take your hands off me and return to your whore!" (Ibid.). And yet, it is the child, Danny, who leaves the house, terrified, "running away from his bed" (Ibid.). Confronted with the betrayal, the violent, vulgar exchange of his dysfunctional parents, at this liminal hour, the child runs to the street as a more secure alternative. And here he stumbles upon our protagonist. More clearly, the temporary calm and relaxed hospitality that the narrator extends restore a sense of trust and friendship, which are so antithetical to the resounding shouts of betrayal from his parents' home. He obviously trusts him.

In Shahar's narrative, the pre-constructed ideological space of trust is meant to suspend any possible fear; it is structured on the principle of national security, national territory, as alternative space that pretends to ease the danger, and smooth the contradictions between Diasporic, ethnic, and even gendered culture and local, Sabra identity (see also Hever 211–232). The superlative of the metanarrative of Zionism is that Israel is a safe place for the Jews, and a critical aspect of this narrative is that the future generations of Sabra children are and will be unconditionally the safest. In this literary space, Hebrew and the position of the Israeli Hebrew writer are instrumental in transforming the stranger-narrator into a caring insider, and the street into the new safe and protective home of heteronormative Israeli childhood. Today, the general climate of fear has raised our anxieties and suspicions about any possible interaction of this kind. We hear the script of fearful parents advising their children to never have any contact with a stranger (especially male), let alone follow them to their house for tea and lemon, especially in the middle of the night. Strangely, it is the child's home that figures as a place of dramatic confrontation, miscommunication, and lack of trust. Thus someone, anyone—a stranger in the street, a writer—can kindly produce a counter place. Hegemonic and omnipotent, the stranger becomes worthy of trust, control, and confidence. Spontaneous, immediate, attractive, the street becomes a place of actions, constituting identity and unfolding new plots and narratives. The allegorical street opens the possibilities for a new kind of alliance. Not only does the plot unfold in the street; the street is also where a new consciousness evolves. Family is a site of (marital) violence, whereas society emerges as the protective neighborhood, the dialectical space between local and universal, confined and normative, epitomizing and modeling the cultural conscience of the time.[64] The narrator tells and owns the story, and therefore, he is able to host and feed the child. He takes him back to his home, which is unsurprisingly described as dirty, much as the parents are dysfunctional, and most probably ethnically marked. What is so outstanding in his invitation to a "hot cup of tea with lemon" when we read the story today? Within the context of child abuse and the increasing number of reported cases, Danny's willingness to follow the author seems almost inconceivable, suggesting an underpinning threat of sexual and other, looming violent acts. Rather, the outside invades, following the same trajectories of reading and identity formation, coming in from the street, the radio, the school or the media.

At best, leading the boy by the hand provides a sense of comfort and idealized friendship amidst his crisis, and yet with this extended hand, the author-narrator is not just leading the child to safety. His hand is the carrier of Hebrew culture, and through it, he transfers its implicit authority. Providing the tea and bread and jam (a local timely flavor of milk and honey) aims to work against the boy's parents' diasporic nature of family and morality. Hence, the sweetness of the author-narrator's gesture, indeed, camouflages the ideological climate in which the Hebrew author represented a new kinship, the safe zone of feeding and making-Hebrew (*'ivrut*) of the young reader. If we dwell with the incredible provision in this literature, we see the seductive force of even the sweetest and seemingly most benign narratives. These texts respond to a certain kind of starvation that itself makes the reader crave more sweetness, candy, etc. Reading the text through a contemporary lens of cultural relativism allows us to grasp the extent of that which is at stake in the encounter. There is always a cardinal perversion, lack or deviancy on the part of the parents that justifies the child's placement in ideological foster care. Hebrew literature played a central role in bringing the national outside space, the street, *shchunah* (the neighborhood, or block) into the home with its unique vernacular, layered with its rapidly developing subcultural inflections and its own intertextual codes of conduct, practices, and ceremonies. The cohesive unity was mobilized on the condition of inhabitation of the space and the total identification with its values. Along with the increased authority of the language, canonic Hebrew literature had conquered a central public space and appropriated it as the platform from which knowledge, logic, and standards of well-being are defined.

Shahar's story exemplifies not only the need for provision but how the ideological mechanism of Hebraization articulates the role of the author and of literature in the collective consciousness, a process that naturalizes the dependency on the system for a certain psychological Sabra's psyche and its inner logic: objective, sane, all-knowing. It is in this way that such a story and intervention create the condition of invasion, where one's body becomes the spectacle of the collective, when the hand of everyone is in or on this body. My reading here seeks to underscore the implicit violence in this invasiveness. In the name of modernity and progress, the savior narrative winds up robbing its subjects of any possible sense of agency. Small wonder, then, that the child is represented as unfamiliar with the outside space, bashfully saying, "I never knew that there are so many stars in the sky. And that the sky is so large and wide. It's a little frightening...".

Memory in the Second Person

> And I see the land unable to contain any longer all that we have
> buried in it, shaken and splitting open....
>
> > Katzir, "Schlaffstunde"[65]

From Jerusalem, we travel to Haifa, thirty-five years later, to Yehudit Katzir's native city and the locale for one of her most celebrated short stories, "Schlaffstunde" (1989).[66] The story reflects the ideological climate of moving from the national, "we" generation, to the personal, or individual wave, dominant with a more subjective voice of the hero and of gendered, women's writing in the contemporary era. German Jews, or *Yekes* as they were called, managed to create an autonomous space—"Little Berlin"—at the top of the Carmel Center in Haifa, a privileged area notorious for its Bauhaus architecture and German bakeries and cafes. The immigrants from Berlin insisted on speaking the German language and maintained their own community organizations within the Zionist urban context many years after their arrival to Israel. In recent years, several studies have elaborated on the long-standing discrimination against German Jews—stemming from their resistance to assimilation and unwillingness to abandon high German culture—within the ethnic politics of Israeli discourse (Segev 1991).[67]

Katzir's story illuminates the ideological shift from the hand of "friendship" to the more explicit molesting hand. From Shahar's totally protected public space at midnight, we move to the ostensibly sheltered geography of middle class German Jews, and to the grandparents' house in the Carmel Center, and from the humble bread and jam of Shahar we turn to the German Sachertorte, Schwartzwälder Kirschtorte, and Apfelstrudel (chocolate cake, Black Forest cakes, and apple strudel, respectively).[68] Shauli (or "Ulli", and also "Shulli", a nickname of "Sha'ul", "Saul" in English) will become the subject of sexual assault. Many insist on reading "Schlaffstunde" as a story of love, a tale of two cousins' "coming of age" in the summer between seventh and eighth grade while vacationing at their grandparents' house, in the Carmel Center of the 1970s. These scholars tend to miss the critical relevance of sexual harassment to eros, a direction I attempt to develop here.

"Schlaffstunde", the title of the story, refers to the mid-afternoon nap that many Eastern European Jews imported with them to Israel.[69] More than a siesta, Katzir's schlaffstunde frames actions and constitutes a specific mindset. Leaving for their bedrooms in the middle of the day, the tired adults free the stage for the children's subversive, secretive actions. It is during these hours that the cousins play, imagine, and discover their bodies. At 4:00, Uncle Alfred, the uninvited, detested guest, arrives at the ceremonial tea and finds the cousins in bed after their first sexual act. He consequently blackmails Shauli, in order to meet with him behind closed doors and to molest him. Alfred forbids the female narrator from entering so that he has total control over Shauli. Anxious and impatient, she eventually goes to the door, opens it slightly, and peers through at Shauli and Alfred. She recounts the story years later, on the occasion of their grandfather's burial, which, like the schlaffstunde— and similarly encompassing a broadly defined idea of "rest"—begins at 2:00 in the afternoon.

Katzir's short story strikes at a pivotal moment when the dead body is still present, while the earth is literally and figuratively open to snatch body, soul, story, and memory. The moment is revealing; after not seeing each other since the traumatic day, the two cousins meet at the funeral—he with his pregnant wife and she with her unfailing memory—and it becomes clear to the female narrator that she has to recover their story. In the invocation of the trauma, at the intersection of life and death, the sweetness and the utterly bitter, their story is like Katzir's version of Gustav Mahler's *"Das Lied von der Erde"* ("The Song of the Earth"), which Alfred sings in "Schlaffstunde". Mahler's symphony, which provides a recurring intertext for the story, draws on a Chinese drinking song to provide "a most intimate confession" and a "striving and sorrowful...heaven-stormer" (Hefling 2000, 79).[70] "Das Lied von der Erde" adds a sense of doom to the narrator's resolve to tell the story. The narrator aims to capture their first act of love, a moment that for many Israeli readers symbolizes the ultimate innocence of Israeli youth, so much so that the story has been received as a sweet (perhaps overly so), nostalgic love story depicting the best years in the history of its Sabra children (Shamir, 1990).

This attempt to reconstruct the trauma narrative from the very "collapse of its witnessing", as Dori Laub theorizes, works against any possibility of knowing what happened behind the closed doors, yet its impact is indisputable. The narrator aims not only to rescue stories and storytelling; she aims to lighten the load of the land, which is, as she writes "unable to contain any longer all that we have buried in it, shaken and splitting open" (Katzir 1990, 34, my translation). How much terror is generated in the open land and the exposed dead body waiting to be buried?

This terror—and the fear that the story will be buried as well—is a catalyst for the narration's unfolding. And death and burial thus also color other events in the story. There, at their grandfather's funeral and burial, alongside the graves of the grandmother and Uncle Alfred, the narrator recalls the children's attempts to poison Alfred in retribution. Death and the plotting of death unfold as leitmotifs and form the cousins' psychological landscape. This omnipresence of death invokes the subtext of the collective trauma of the Holocaust with its specific paraphernalia of mourning (Yahrzeit candles, the Diary of Anne Frank) and the full internalization of the "Germans" as the epitome of evil.

The open earth at the burial becomes the abyss of horror, invoked by the Israeli children in the dark, folkloric oath "I swear by God and in the black grave of Hitler" (Katzir 2006, 18). Katzir's choice to narrate the story to Shauli in the second person charges the text with an added urgency as she tells it to "you" as it happened, as it is remembered, as it can be told, a testimony and a proof, so that it would be remembered, and would be told, maybe even would awaken "you" from a long *schlaffstunde*. Conflating the burial of memory with the sleepiness of the *schlaffstunde* undermines the possibilities of narration. Obviously, the female narrator is the one who can speak Shauli's trauma, and in the politics of representing rape and sexual abuse, "Who is speaking may be *all* that matters", as Lynn Higgins and Brenda Silver assert. And yet, more problematic still is the unreadability of the invisible textual anxieties, contradictions, and censorships, begging us to be as attentive to the question "who does not speak and why?" This question is most relevant as she speaks for Shauli's injury and insult, forming a team against Alfred.

Standing at the edge of the open pit, against the threat of burying their story, their youthful past, and their love, Katzir is engaged in a dynamic and forceful act of storytelling. Shauli is still silent, in his psychopathological coma. Now is her moment to find a way to tell it and bring the psychic phantom of its secrecy out [in Abraham and Torok's term (Ibid. 1994, 171–186)]. As such, her story of love and death is also a song to the earth. And in this song of the earth *to* the earth, telling the story rather than burying it will ultimately rescue not only the story but the earth from splitting open. The question is, can she write *his* silence? How? I quote these paragraphs in full in order to capture how the narrator introduces her narrative of witnessing.

> Once, when summer vacation stretched over the whole summer and tasted of sand and smelled of grapes and a redhead sun daubed freckles on your face and, after Sukkot, the wind whistled into a gang of clouds and we galloped home through the ravine in a thunderstorm and the rain stabbed your tongue with mint and pine and the neighborhood dogs set up a racket, barking like

uncles coughing at intermission in a winter concert, and suddenly spring attacked with cats shrieking and the lemon trees blossoming and again came a *hamsin* and the air stood still in the bus but we got up only for Mrs. Bella Blum from the Post Office, a dangerous-child-snatcher who comes to us in bed at night with a wild gray hair of a dangerous-child-snatcher and narrow glasses on the tip of a sharp-as-a-red-pencil nose of a dangerous-child-snatcher and who smiles with a cunning flattery of a dangerous-child-snatcher and pokes dry-ice fingers into our faces, and only if we'd give her all the triangular stamps could we somehow be saved or if we prayed to God, who disguised himself as a clown in the Hungarian circus and rocked, balancing himself on the tightrope under the blue canvas of the tent, in high-heeled shoes and wide red-and-white checked pants and then disguised himself as an elephant, turned his wrinkled behind to us and went off to eat supper.

Once, when the world was all golden through the sparkling Carrera vase in the living room on the credenza, which maybe vanished with all the other furniture as soon as we left the room and we peeked through the keyhole to see if it was still there but maybe it saw us peeking and rushed back and a horrible gang of thieves was hiding out in the garage under the supermarket and only Emil and you could solve the mystery because obviously you were going to be an important detective they'd write books about and I'd be your assistant and we experimented with invisible ink made of onion skins and we heated the note in the candle so the writing would emerge and then we trained ourselves to swallow it so it wouldn't fall into enemy hands and we did other training exercises, in self-defense and in not-revealing-secrets even if they torture you and tie you to a bed and put burning matches under your toenails, and we mixed up poison from dirt and leaves and crushed shells and we kept it in yogurt jars and we drew a skull and crossbones on them and hid them with all our other treasures.

When the summer vacation stretched over the whole summer, and the world was all gold and everything was possible and everything was about to happen, and Uncle Alfred was still alive and came for afternoon tea and Grandfather and Grandmother went to rest between two and four and left us endless time, we snuck up the creaky wooden steps behind the house to our little room in the attic which was headquarters and we stood at the window where you could view the whole sea beyond the cemetery and you touched my face with your fingertips and said you loved me.

Now we're gathered here, like sad family members at a departure in an airport, around the departures-board at the entrance, where somebody's written in white chalk, two zero zero, Aaron Green, funeral....

(Katzir 1992, 1–3)[71]

In what appears as Katzir's stream of consciousness, the linearity of the text becomes a narratological device that permits different transitions from past to the present or from one individual to another, as if she moves between disparate memories in her story in the same way she skips from one grave to the next in the cemetery. "Once, when ...Once when... When... Now we have gathered here goes from ...". The repetitive, maximal usage of the conjugating *vav* ("and") in Hebrew not only contributes to the breathless narrative style of children, and to the descriptive temporal space of the story; it also blurs the distinction between a long list of relative clauses and their main sentence, creating an illusion of continuous linearity that serves the flow of the narrative. As a narrative strategy, it adds to the integrity of generative memory. It works against the erasure of memory in the here and now.

Telling in the second person is an important aspect of traumatic narratives, putting emphasis on pronouns that are strategically constructed around the interlocutor. From the description of the summer in "we", Katzir moves to the "you" and only then to the "I". The second person singular appears only in the second paragraph, leaving the opening—a long paragraph of almost one page—in the first person plural, in verbs and prepositions, to the narrator/readers "we". The use of the second person addressee draws the reader into her narrative's intimate tenor of conversation and into the female narrator's role as the vigilant witness who preserves biographies and histories, who contains the full memory of love from within the ruins of its trauma: remember? Once you could talk, you had a body, a mouth, she tells him, but this moment of coming of age was injured. Shauli's burning sexual assault has become a textual wound, an elliptic silence. Telling the story, therefore, is a woman's burden insofar as it aims, in the presence of death, to transcend reality and despair, and to reach her lover through the awakening of his deep pain. It also aims to erect a tombstone of love in the memory of love, at the intersection of the death of the spirit and sexual abuse, the death of innocence.

Sexual trauma is a scandal that shatters identity and every epistemological system; as I established in the model of Ishmael, it is a total event of an experience that undermines the integrity of the psyche because of the total loss of power that is caused by an invasion of the body. All defenses fail to provide any kind of protection, self-regulation, or mechanism of "sorting out". Because of its invasiveness, critical distinctions of 'inside and outside", "here and now", or "then and there" collapse and are forever impaired. At the heart of any trauma, there is an excess, which escapes any possible articulation in language or other symbolic systems in the face of an empty lacuna (Goldberg 2006, 14–23). Whereas the female narrator, like us readers, knows only a little about

what Alfred did to Shauli, the harassing impact of the event is nevertheless explicit and unmistakable. Katzir describes the partial witnessing in
these terms:

> You'd been up there for more than half an hour, closed in the
> room…. I couldn't control myself anymore. I went up very quietly,
> opened the door a little, and peered in. The two of you were sitting
> on the sofa. With big opera gestures Uncle Alfred was explaining
> something to you that I couldn't hear and from time to time he
> put his cotton hand on your leg. Then he wrapped his arm around
> your shoulders and put his face, which was always flushed, almost
> purple, close to your face which was ashen. Suddenly he looked up
> and saw me. A shadow passed over his eyes. I fled downstairs. I lay
> under the big pine tree, right over the oath we buried yesterday,
> and I looked at the green sparkling needles that stabbed the clouds
> which today were in the shape of a huge white hand. I waited.
> Time passed. More time, a lot of time passed, and you did not
> come down. … At last the door opened and Uncle Alfred came out
> breathing deeply as he went unsteadily down the steps. He but-
> toned his jacket and rang the front door bell. Grandmother opened
> the door, said, Hello Alfred, and he went into the house. Then you
> came running out, you lay down beside me, hid your head against
> my belly, and muffled your howls of anguish. Your whole body
> shook.
>
> (2006, 29–30)

Uncle Alfred is a caricature of the post-Holocaust German Jew, a symptomatic pervert, and a product of uber-European culture. His aspirations
were always directed towards the opera stages of Vienna and Paris. (He
brags that he has never missed an opera, always entering for free in the
second half.) In Israel, he remains the displaced Jew, Europe's orphan.
In that sense he symbolically stands for a certain Ashkenazi Jewish envy
of Europe; he is unproductive, sick, pompous, and foreign, with no wife
nor children, uncritically valorizing the products of a culture he has been
trained to view as superior. This attachment to the high culture of "civi-
lized" Europe camouflages a deep sense of starvation that no amount of
4:00 tea and Apfelstrudel will be able to recover. Katzir's description of
his hand is revealing. It is a "*tsemer-gefen*" hand (literally, a "cotton ball
hand"),[72] a soft hand of a spineless, impotent person. The cotton ball
hand highlights softness, but it has little to offer. It, too, is a misleading facade that hides the violence that hand will perpetrate. The hand
acts as a cipher for the toxicity inherent in the pursuit of "high culture"
and the fetishization of its purported superiority, eventually displaying
the full extent of the covert barbarism that results from the process of
"civilization".

By virtue of his ability to sing and consume high culture, Uncle Alfred gains access to the family, as he advocates his self-righteousness and goody-goody manners. And yet the narrator locates him squarely as the *galutí*, a diasporic "mama's boy of Europe" who is sleazy and unfit, an antithesis against which Zionism and the Sabra generation defined itself. His hand functions as a metonym and undeniably speaks for his sexuality; it is his im/potence that will make him violent. Tragically, Alfred is motivated to belong, or to leave his mark, as he has no children and his singing is, in fact, hopeless, and marked by his foreignness, he will leave this mark on the male Sabra body. The proximity between one sexual act of coming of age and the violating offense heightens the significance of the crushing violation that overwhelms and even stomps out the bliss of Shauli's sexual encounter with his cousin. The closed door and its acute silence is in stark contrast to their passionate freedom, which is manifested through their open communication: they even read each other's fingers drawing words of love on their backs with closed eyes.

Indeed, many Israeli readers see this violence as insignificant in the grand scheme of the story's romance. In this sense, the impact of "*Schlaffstunde*" extends beyond the text; the lethargy of the text and its characters infects the readers and renders them, like the unobservant grandparents, unable to critically and attentively read the situation. It is possible that nostalgia takes hold, overwhelming readers to the point that they become oblivious to the sexual assault. Even relatively astute scholars used words such as "sweet" to describe the historical period of the 1970s that forms the background for this story. But to insist on such sweetness of life is to gloss over not only the diabetic body of the grandmother—who ends up obsessively devouring the Schwartzwalder Kirschtorte, which ultimately kills her—but also the injured body of Shauli. The uncanny desire for German desserts traps the mind into a libidinal state of pleasure and desire. For readers and critics alike, the attachment to the love story, the sound of the singing of Mahler, the aroma of Haifa pine, and youth, numb one's alertness to violence. This numbness, I contend, is at the heart of "*Schlaffstunde*".

Israeli culture is, in "*Schlaffstunde*", enamored with the most beautiful love, even and especially when traumatized by the Holocaust. Ultimately, this love is insidiously corrupted by the sexual pathology of the older generation, especially that of Uncle Alfred. The story further seems to testify to the inability of the older generation to allow the young ones to thrive. Katzir's "*Schlaffstunde*" is thus a harsh critique of this fetishization of German "high" culture in all its sinister aspects. The story warns against the cultural mask that appears restorative but evasively distorts sexuality by "violenting" it. For it is not just Alfred who invades this idyllic Israeli trajectory, but a whole Germanophilic consciousness and worldview. This distortion is allowed because in spite of the Holocaust and in spite of the fact that "the Germans" in this narrative are explicit references to the most threatening imagined evil, in the Israeli imagination, German culture still holds immense potential for providing for Israeli culture.

Being both a literal site of death, and the container of human pain, wounds, and horror, the earth for Katzir is an ecologically overstuffed space that can swallow narratives, bodies, and histories. Man returns to the earth with his body, the Hebrew *'adam* from *'adamah*, man from earth, as articulated in Genesis 2: 19, constitutes the synecdochic connection of man, who turns into *'adamah* or *'afar* (usually translated as "clay", "dust", or "earth"). Katzir takes it one step further. Breathless, her narrator returns to the earth to regain their story and reaffirm her sexual body.

The relaxing schlaffstunde, the "perpetual peace", as Immanuel Kant famously called it, can perhaps reconcile the harsh reality of death and its totems in the story. And in so far as Katzier suggests a collective afternoon nap for all Israeli readers, can she promise that nothing terrible will happen behind closed doors, making sure that such a recess will not become a blinding curtain for acting out the dark libidinal desires and the secret crimes of society? Even still, my reading points to her story as a wake-up call to readers who have followed the alluring Germanophile softness, sweetness, and numbness—the sweet cake, and the schlaffstunde—which have rendered them unable to screen against the invasive hand.

The Reader of the Sacrifice: Albert Suisa's *Akud*

> Domination does not repress the desire for recognition; rather, it enlists and transforms it.
>
> Jessica Benjamin, *The Bonds of Love*[73]

The third text is Albert Suisa's first book *Akud* (Bound). It was published a few months after Katzir's *Closing the Sea* in 1991 and was awarded the prestigious Bernstein Prize. Born in Casablanca in 1959, Suisa immigrated to Jerusalem when he was four years old, to 'Ir Ganim ("the garden city"), "one of the many abysmal concrete enclaves hastily built during the 1960s" (Suisa 1992, 14).[74] "Akud" is also the first part of the book, entitled *Akud* (1990, 7–27) on which I first focus in my analysis.

Akud is divided into three sections that tell the coming-of-age narrative of three boys in the slums: Yochai, Beber, and Ayush. We are back in Jerusalem but in a working-class neighborhood of North African immigrants. The narrative provides non-linear, interconnected trajectories, all tied to the notion of binding and being bound, using the biblical root *'akad*, from Genesis 22. Suisa's work is an excellent example of the force of textuality in the consciousness of young adults. I argue that *Akud* is a story of a reader, of several readers, who wander their early adolescence through the alleyways of 'Ir-Ganim in the same way that they roam through pages of Hebrew script, fragmented verses and lines both real and imagined. Reading is a binding act. More than being physically bound to the altar, therefore, as the passive participle of *'akedah*, which conveys having the hands and legs tied together, Yochai, Beber and Ayush are forever bound in mind and spirit, trapped within their imagined bibles, together with their fathers, mothers, siblings, and friends. The biblical text foreshadows the story of the body. As the dwellers of Life in Citation, they are proficient Bible readers, they practice living within and between quotations, as if their life is a set of fragmented quotes that comprise their story.

As I probe in the introduction, there are many questions one can ask in terms of what the place of textuality can afford, how privileged it is, and what kind of potential for menace it holds. Yes, as much as each of Suisa's three protagonists is engaged in dialogic relationships with a whole culture of textuality, reconstructing and deconstructing a perspective about immediate life, Suisa makes it explicit that reality is nothing but "*Hayim ba-zevel*" (a garbage life). Reading informs every aspect of the three boys' lives in the neighborhood, serving as discursive "yeshiva" of knowledge acquired independently of formal institutions. And it is from this unsteady foundation that they launch their commentaries and interpretations.[75] In the tradition of Jewish commentary, Yochai, Beber, and Ayush each question, debate, and mock the meaning of their lives through the biblical text, and vice-versa, as if they are comparing the text to their own reality, a strategy that inhabits and informs their consciousness. Suisa shows the ways in which the Bible and Jewish texts undergo a process of "descending" from their sacred bookshelves to participate in life on the street, recontextualized by pornography, homelessness and sexual abuse.

In *Akud*, asking questions and attempting to answer them is critical to the formation of the subject position. One sees the full extent of this interpretive burden and its taxation on the subject in the case of Yochai. Yochai is haunted by the question "What did Isaac think on the morning of the *'akedah*?" (Suisa 1990, 19), and "What would the childhood stories of the sages be if they were to tell them?" (Ibid. 15)[76] Like Isaac, Suisa's protagonist follows his father. But because he is guided just as much by the narrative of Isaac as its absent voices, Yochai ends up running away from the itinerary his father charts for him, only to realize that the old story of the Fathers has already predetermined his movements; he is forever bound. "Akud" points to a permanent state, an adjective that ties Suisa to Isaac and to the tradition of Jewish narratives. Suisa's dilemma, therefore, is how to reconstruct a language for the historical silence not of the children of Genesis but of his own. What kind of narrative can be written from this tied, restless, poor, ethnic, and gendered position?

As I elaborate in Chapter 1, Mizrahi writing engaged in exploring alternative textual strategies to challenge the power of intertexts and their imposing force in contemporary consciousness. In no other Jewish-Israeli narrative is the position of the reader as a victim so clearly articulated as in the story of the Akedah. Can one escape this verdict? And for Suisa, in the poverty-laden neighborhood, can he construct an alternative home outside of the text? For Suisa, this search for home becomes a series of displacements. In Yochai's mind, the condition of unhomeliness—"a paradigmatic colonial and post-colonial condition" as defined by Homi Bhabha (1994, 9)—conjures up the homeless person, zeroing in on his space of neglect, decay, and ruination. Yochai's unhomeliness derives from his circumstances; he is running away from Bnei-brak, the boarding school and religious institution east of Tel Aviv that his father has sent him to. This flight culminates in his encounter with the old Polish man who approaches Yochai and lures him with sweets and soda into the dark seats of the cinema. He lures him by pretending to care for him, showing seemingly good-natured concern for his well-being. The description is defined by Suisa's limited ability to explicitly articulate the experience of abuse, leaving other external references such as the sweet licorice in Yochai's mouth and the violent images on the screen to speak instead.

The writing style stays true to the Polish immigrant's broken Hebrew, "'Ah, what cute boy!'" The man drew near, stroking his cheeks, 'Boy [yeled] (is) not from here, what they call boy?'" In his thick foreign accent, the man exoticizes and distances Yochai through the "not from here" so typical of monoethnic Ashkenazi binarism of belonging vs. non-belonging. Suisa ironically introduces the old man as an outsider to Israeli culture who claims his insider position by establishing Yochai as being from elsewhere. The question of origin is, indeed, critical within the paradox of displacement, which is soon translated into an asymmetrical hierarchy of power, defined by age, color, and accent, and plays a role in subjecting Yochai to the colonial, masculine gaze, saying, "Ah, what cute *yeled*, boy!... You still smooth boy, I like brown boys, in Poland there no brown boys" (Ibid. 26).

In the identity politics, names carry an ethnic marking that is reductive and often insulting. It is common, especially in the army. If the Polish man identifies the boy by his gaze, highlighting age and color, Suisa insists on identifying the Polish man by essentializing him further still. At first, he introduces him as "a slightly old man", later as "the man", then in the kiosk while Yochai is between his knees, he becomes "*hazaken*" (the old man). This vague reference of age with the definite article is slowly materialized on a larger national scale. *Yeled* and *hazaken* are both signifiers loaded with extended allegorical meaning:

"Yeled" reappears as a description and a term of address for young individuals. Shahar's narrator calls, "Hey, *yeled,* stop!" and Uncle Alfred repeatedly refers to the cousins as *yeladim* (children), asserting that they are too young for sexual acts. But as an address, "yeled" immediately marks the speaker's authority over the addressee. Suisa makes explicit that "yeled" is an empty category, appropriated to appear available and accessible to "adulthood". As such, "yeled" is an object of culture that can be instilled with whatever meaning is convenient. As in the case of women, and pets, "yeled" is accessible to the touch of others, and thus can be stroked and pinched. Within a degrading economy of twisted hunger, fantasy, and the value of the gift of sweet candies, the threat of the touch becomes even more immediate. Here is the entire description of the interaction between the two. Yochai has just escaped the school, wandering in the small town landscape (translated by Ramon Stern with a few modifications):

> From time to time, he (Yochai) would sit down at a bus stop to doze off, awaken after a bit and keep on walking, until he reached a small square with some falafel stands, cake and soda pop stands, and many taxis waiting there. He would have gone far away from there, would have kept going if he had not heard "Ah, what cute boy!" uttered in a melodious tone. Yochai stopped. A somewhat old man wearing a peak cap, with an extinguished cigarette between his lips, leaned against a wall plastered with old posters and smiled at him with a row of silver teeth. The man drew near, stroking his cheeks, "Boy (is) not from here, what they call boy?" Yochai wiped his nose on his sleeve, lowered his eyes to the sidewalk, and then stared all around. He had no strength left to run or keep roving the streets. Suddenly, without knowing why, he answered "Noah." "Noah, ha ha", the man chuckled, "Noah funny name boy. Come, I buy boy soda and cake." They entered some type of refreshment stand with mass-produced tables from the Jewish Agency and chairs like the stools at home, and the old man set him down between his knees, urging him to eat and drink, and amused himself with him as with a baby. He pinched his cheek once, and then touched him on the chin once, and said "You still smooth boy, I like brown boys, in Poland there no brown boys." Yochai felt a familiar bending in his stomach and a growing need to defecate. But his body had deceived him, and a brownish-pink jet suddenly burst out of his mouth and soiled the agency table.
>
> The man patted him on the back. "It nothing, it nothing" he said and asked for them to bring a glass of soda water, because soda water helps let out gas. Yochai drank and he no longer had gas, and his eyes gradually began to close as the man gently stroked his head. "I take boy to cinema", the man said, "and buy him lot of *bamba-lik*." He put the candy in Yochai's right hand and held onto his left, leading him down a dark theater hall. There were only a few people

in the theater, and there were no kids cracking sunflower seeds or whistling or slamming chairs. It was silent in the theater, and on the screen a man and woman were screaming out extremely loud, and the woman got very angry. But when the man started to hit her she did not put up any resistance, she even laughed and enjoyed it, and then he started pulling her hair and choking her –at that moment, Yochai did not take the *bambalik* out of his mouth, and in his left hand he felt a soft hairy and sticky substance, but he didn't bother to check what it was because his eyes drifted into a deep sleep, and he sensed himself in extended, infinite free-fall through a narrow opening, illuminated by a glistening light without source.

(Suisa 2012, trans. Stern)

Against the vagueness of the signifier "*yeled*", Suisa makes two other references that are relevant to our discussion. The tables in the kiosk help to complement the scene where Yochai is approached by *hazaken*. The tables of the *Sochnut*[77] are local, highly common, simple wood tables, but it is the chairs, the French-Moroccan *tabourets* chairs that are like the stools at home. (Again, the referential subtext reveals the narrator's emphatic position, describing the stools from Yochai's third-person limited perspective.) But sitting at the Jewish Agency table, the Polish old man, *hazaken*, slowly turns into a subversive allusion to David Ben-Gurion who was often referred to in and by the media as "Hazaken". Even though the reference hovers here between the most generic and the most specific, the juxtaposition of the Polish man's title and the chairs of the Sochnut leaves little doubt that Suisa is engaging an allegorical imagination of institutionalized Zionism. Ben-Gurion and the labor party gained enormous support from Middle Eastern immigrants in the early stages of Zionism. His policy, which advocated massive population growth and large families, was a radical catalyst during the Israeli baby boom of the fifties, especially among poor immigrant families who would get a special bonus after the birth of the third child. Many equated Ben-Gurion with his namesake, David (the King of Israel); naming male children after his first name was a common complementary practice, often resulting in the Prime Minister's presence at the *brit* (circumcision ceremony). Suisa here is aiming his sly critique at Zionism and its forefathers. From within this visual vocabulary and the intimately familiar frame of reference, Suisa highlights the dichotomized reality of Polish-imported Zionism versus the colonized Moroccan stool, allegorizing the identity of the sexual aggressor even before telling us the story. Indeed, Yochai, being sick and having lost control of his body, vomits on and literally "soils" the agency table. Nevertheless, inside the theater, with his mouth full of *bambalik* (licorice), he is exhausted and resigned. In a moment of numbness and sleepiness, while struggling to keep his eyes open that violence happens. It is in, by, from, and on the hand that the violence occurs, but what alarmingly becomes clearer throughout this narrative is the sedating effect of this violence to put its victim to sleep. But this sleepiness is different from the *schlaffstunde* in Katzir's story. Rather than offering a framework of the story, it continually affects the bound victim. With his mouth full of sweetness, the total colonization of Yochai's speech and body is complete.

In bearing witness to the ethnic subject's victimhood, Suisa leaves no doubt as to the ethnic difference that bind the *akud*. In his ontological condition of multiple exiles, Yochai runs directly into this pedophile Polish man. Located at the Israeli intersection of ethnicity, class, gender, and age difference, Yochai helps to problematize the allegorical space of intertextuality while exposing the limited possibilities for dialogue and continuity. "What the hell did the *tsadikim* do during their adolescence?" (Ibid. 15) is now a question asked from his own situated reality; will his innovative semantics and imagery enable Suisa to deconstruct the pathological and impaired language of these narrative? Can he dismantle their referential imposition?

Out on Suisa's Streets: Isaac and Ishmael

[a]nd Gersha says that still today they are sacrificing, but only in a different way....

Suisa (1991)

Suisa's second part tells the story of three protagonists that live in the neighborhood of Ir Ganim, in a housing project called Block 200, comprised of several crowded and run-down apartment buildings. David Ben Shushan is a macho bully and the leader of a gang of small boys who finds inspiration among the imagined captains, judges, and advisors of the Bible. When it happens that Muijo, the gang's errand boy, is absent from an emergency meeting, "a secret trial was declared, and they agreed not to ostracize Muijo, since there was no go-between better than him, but that he must be punished and sworn-in once more" (8). Ben Shushan gives the following speech:

Ya know, that when our ancestor Abraham swore in his slave Eliezer, ya know that he made him hold onto his dick when he swore?" Ben Shushan was greatly enthused, opening his eyes wide: "Hakham Jacob, my uncle, told me, well, he didn't say, but he pointed it out in Rashi's commentary and there it is written: "he held onto it." David raised his finger up to the heavens and paused for effect: "so shall Muijo be punished and he shall swear by my dick."

(Suisa 2012, 8, trans. Stern)

Ben Shushan's swearing ceremony grotesquely exaggerates the authority of its intertext. A speech act within another speech act, it ends up over-stating Abraham's measures of power with regards to sexuality, voice, and body; rather than the phallic touch, Muijo's act of "swearing by the dick" turns into the forced drinking of urine straight from Ben Shushan's member. In the symbolic historical transformation of male bodily fluids and texts, David Ben Shushan emerges as the modern Abraham.

The reading strategy of Ayush, Suisa's third and final protagonist, is different. In the following passage he effectively defines the necessity of his own silence. Ayush has identified with one of the Spies that were sent by Moses to scout the land of Canaan. Trembling with fear, he hypothet-ically makes his case about speaking or unspeaking one's truth. For "if milk and honey, very well, if dust and ash, off with his head". The stakes are high; the biblical reality dictates the limit of how far to go with his deep truth, how many challenging questions he can ask while hiding behind the sandbags of inquiry.

> Whenever he wanted to ask his father or teacher anything he felt in imminent danger. Somehow the question would always turn back to him: they would debate each other and bring it back to him instead of answering. But Ayush did not want to answer either, only to ask: he himself was an infinite reserve of things not yet said, seeds of memories yet to sprout, and beautiful body parts in his mind yet to be desired. But upon looking at his father deliberating over "yes" and "no," he thought that he, Ayush, was like one of the dreaming spies who came to survey the land and had already determined its virtue beforehand; if milk and honey, very well, if dust and ash, off with his head. *Surely his father, if he were there, would have taken the lead in stoning him. Thus Ayush held his tongue.* He would ask but not answer. He would only listen and question, for he felt that forty years wandering in the desert would not have forged and molded him into a rock. Rather, they would have made him soft and smooth like the belly of a Bedouin woman who, in spite of the many years she spends under the scathing desert heat, remains soft and milky white under her dress. Ayush felt that if he were there, he would surely have been one of those who went out every night to dig themselves a grave.
> (106–107)

What could be the dangerous answer to the question Ayush might have posed? What would the testimony be for which he would be stoned? Obviously, Ayush has reached a limit here; yet he is already at the edge of the earthly pit that threatens to devour him and his testimony along with the Israelite spies sent by Moses.

Yochai, David, and Ayush embody the restlessness of what I see as the *kolboinik* of contemporary textual Israeli culture. They will have to carry the burden of self-reflection and questioning with the distorted tools provided by their perverted realities and its Jewish textual tradition. They will continue to ask questions that will have to negotiate between their horrible experiences and the narratives that bind them. What kinds of life tactics do these narratives provide? And more specifically to the *akud*, to what extent can the victim liberate himself when his legs and hands are bound? Or still, double bound? *Akud* applies ample space for discussing these questions. Here is another example of textuality saturating space of questioning.

In the intimate moment of heightened self-reflection, mere days before his Bar Mitzvah and Yom Kippur, Ayush realizes that not only is he always predestined to err and sin, but he is also burdened by the sins which he inherited "even before his birth" (Suisa 1990, 13). His list runs through many of the narratives of Genesis, "the sin of Adam and Eve and the Serpent, the sin of the Tower of Babylon, the sin of selling Joseph, "for which we are all accountable..." (Ibid). Moreover, he is unwilling to confess to God some of his empathy for others whom the Bible condemns, as in:

> the cruelty of *Sara 'Imenu* against the poor, abandoned Ishmael, who wasn't the one to blame for her being barren and somehow wanting that her husband will have a son; and the shame of *Avraham Avinu*, who almost sacrificed a human being (and Gersha says that still today they are sacrificing, but only in a different way), and was cruel to Isaac, and Sarah, who herself was not the most righteous, and afterwards he is going to advocate for the righteous ones, *Tsdikim*, in Sodom.
>
> (Ibid. 113)

Note that Suisa's street, is another open space of the narrative, making it possible to relocate Ishmael and Isaac in the open landscape of the desert. The parallel is clear: what Abraham did to Isaac in the sacrifice, Sarai did to Ishmael. *Insofar as Ayush has become Isaac, he is carrying his brother Ishmael with him.* I have outlined how the narrative of Genesis 16 constructs the category of excluding the intimate son through the model of Ishmael's otherness. This model can help us understand *Akud*'s main thesis, holding a unique position of hovering between the tight, exclusive place of the covenant and the open, all-invasive body of Ishmael. An elevated position of sacrifice and exclusion, it tells us about contemporary violence, particularly the approach towards *Akud*'s ethnic, at-risk, homeless children and the meaning of the boundaries of their bodies. Suisa's street is different from Adi Nes's in his depiction of Abraham and Isaac with the shopping cart, as it complements the sacrifice not only with the verdict of total exclusion, but with the heavy burden of cited texts. Stern unpacks the aesthetic of ethnicity and the way it has normalized the pathologies and madness of everyday life. Measuring the impact of Suisa's work on ethnicity, he argues, "Ethnicity is a pollutant, a dangerous toxin that dirties both sacred language and the religious and nationalist awe surrounding the story of the binding of Isaac or *akedah*. The use of language, as much as the thematic vision of neighborhood and child psychology, throw Zionism and Judaism into disarray and transgresses both of their boundaries of purity" (Stern 2013, 357).

Indeed, *Akud*'s male characters resemble many aspects of the kolbo of Ishmael; hands here are occupying forces of one's life and narrative that move against definitions, order, and law:

> …until they reached the humble and remote outskirts of Ir Ganim Bet. That was when the father released his tough grip and stood introspective, panting. His limp hand lingered for a few moments on his son's shoulder in an uneasy, conciliatory show of embarrassment, as if to teach his son the subtle difference between father and enemy. Then both of them found time to wipe off their sweat and shake the dust and thorns off of their clothes. When in the presence of his father, Ayush always behaved like him. Each one put his hands behind his back, and headed home with his head looking down at the ground. *Yidek tayaklūk* –"your hands are eating you"—was an expression often used by Mr. Monsanegor, who believed that the dwelling place of most evils and passions was the hands. This was because hands are always liable to take hold of things that belong to others, to touch what is impure and forbidden, to pound and to smash, to defile and to touch improper areas of the body. Thus he taught his children to clasp their plotting hands behind their backs, not in their pockets. This was because behind-the-back is a place out in the open and since the body has nothing to do, the mind has the chance to think remorseful thoughts that are nice for a stroll.
>
> (Ibid. 94–95)

In the case of Ishmael, God saves him, God blesses him; his mother protected him. And in Suisa's case? His world—reductive and concealing through arbitrary, exaggerated positions—the body becomes the zone of exhaustive violence and abuse. "*Yidek tayaklūk*" –"your hands are eating you" is an attribution to the consuming hand, the one of self-devouring; its existential restlessness is acted out through greed, hunger, and sexual assaults. Yochai is sexually molested by the Polish old man, *hazaken*, initiated into the realm of abuse; Beber physically abuses Ayush several times. But with the collapse of body and category, even language joins to articulate the ideological crisis; *Akud* refers to a reader, subject to the lingering force of the text. Paradoxically, with all his attempts to be involved in reading, he is abjectly thrown up from it, unable to be included.

Twelve years after the publication of *Akud*, in a conference celebrating the book at the University of Michigan in Ann Arbor, organized by Ramon Stern, Suisa gave his keynote talk *"Bound together: My (Isaac's) Longing for Ishmael"*,[78] a brilliant and compelling analysis, in itself a literary event. Focusing on Isaac's *'akedah*, he advanced what he calls "the Ishmaelite option". Suisa distinguishes between several readings of the narratives in Islam and Judaism, religious and Zionist readings, and autobiography. According to Suisa, denied the right of the firstborn, Ishmael, rather than being bound, is *barred*. This exclusion explains that "the principle injustice was his rejection, on the basis of values, as undeserving of a place in the Abrahamic holy lineage. He, the first born, is deprived of the possibility that he might also be the designated holy sacrifice". This absence has constituted an internalized silence and yearning that informs the narrative and its discourse.

Suisa embodies the image of Ishmael, designating him, "a necessary component of the inner mold of the hegemonic narrative" in his attempt to radically critique and liberate Jewish Israeli consciousness. Emerging from his own passive and immobilizing silence, Isaac speaks now through the mouth of Ishmael, "his long lost brother". For, as he says, "Israeli literature was under the strict surveillance of an extremely silent and sullen Abraham and Sarah".

The "Ishmaelite Option", according to Suisa, offers a potential escape from the political binarist "ethnocentric genealogical circle" of the Others in Zionist discourse, Mizrahis included. Rather than simply engaging with the essentializing debate of victimhood or national Abrahamic inheritance, and going beyond foundational myths, reduced to, "the son of master and slave at one and the same time", Ishmael celebrates the desecration of his own seed and undermines both mother and father… this contempt is his defining characteristic. "His hand is against everyone, and everyone's hand is against him".

Anton Shammas also engages with the Ishmaelite option where Ishmael extends his hand to Isaac, as only these two brothers can "together confiscating his logos from [Abraham] and recreating it and re-shaping it in their own image" (Shammas 2012). Shammas' script is well aware of the grave ontological burden of the father and his narrative; the sons' desperate act is therefore to settle the historical account with this devouring alter by sacrificing the father instead.

The desire to maximize the agency of the participants is astounding: responding to a panel on Albert Suisa's book, *Akud*, Anton Shammas reintroduced the two *ne'arim*, young men that Abraham leaves at the foot of Mount Moriah, as a critical part of the trajectory of the narrative. Noteworthy is the desire amongst recent scholars, in general, to bring Ishmael into the narrative of the Akedah as a way of translating him into Isaac's bound position. This is a gesture of ironic inclusion and hospitality that seeks to negotiate with the constraints of the "bound" narrative in Genesis. Thus, for Shammas, the young men would have enough time to inform Ishmael of the intended plot so that he can appear as the angel and save Isaac, as he concludes, "Then, hand in hand, Isaac, and Ishmael, together for the first time, reverse the biblical narrative of Genesis 22, bind their father, and lay him on the altar, upon the wood" (Shammas, unpublished talk 2012).

Suisa's *Akud*, *Bound*, ties back into the Sacrifice, Isaac, and Ishmael more explicitly. It tells the coming-of-age narrative of the three boys in a working-class neighborhood of North African immigrants. The work is an excellent example of the force of textuality in the consciousness of young adults. They are not simply being bound by body, spirit, and mind; they are trapped within their imagined Bible and its grid of textuality. Reading here informs every aspect of the three boys' lives, serving as discursive street "yeshiva" of knowledge acquired independently of formal institutions. I read it as Suisa's harsh critique of textuality intersected with gender, class, and ethnicity, protagonists who have full agency as readers, but whose mindset overflows with a web of narratives: infinite allusions to texts, teaching, poverty, and daily experiences. His new epistemology of the street doesn't follow the logic of Zionism. Suisa's new, street-wise textuality responds to the collapse of the archive.

The 'Akedah inscribes the relationship of children and adults as unconditional acquiescence, prefigures utter obedience and rescripts the position of children responding to adults as if they were being issued the demands of the divine himself. But the kolbo warns us that Suisa's is but a second binding. He layers the discursive space of textuality, and with his critique proposes a way to decolonize this space and undo the narrative of the binding. His inclusionary novel accounts for Ishmael in the story of the binding; he identifies with Isaac and Ishmael who are both bound and invaded, eternally othered by the fathers. Again, children in Suisa's book are victims in different allegorical frameworks: biblical, national, sexual, and textual. Anton Shammas seizes on such a distinction to imagine a radical scenario in which Ishmael and Isaac turn the tables (altars?) on Abraham, undoing their bondage by sacrificing the father. For consistent with its devouring nature, the *ma'akhelet* does more than simply ask for blood. Looking at it from within the framework of reading and the root *'akhl*, I assert that the real victim in Genesis is neither Abraham, as Jewish tradition and philosophy have maintained, nor Isaac, as the young generation of post-Holocaust Hebrew writers have opined, nor Sarah, as recent feminists claim, nor even the ram, as the poet Yehuda Amichai suggests; but rather, the victim of the *ma'akhelet* is the Modern Hebrew reader, especially the Sabra native. Reading here is in the domain of debt economy, a demand of the text as it is circulated and imagined. It is an imperative to internalize and identify with its message of obedience, and read the text "as if" we are closely implicated weather as Abraham or his son. Reading from an ideologically saturated position implicates the reader of the story within the textual matrix and its genealogy as the eternally surviving offspring of Jewish culture.

Notes

1 In its extreme, this demand to be well versed in the canonic literature is apparent in the writing by Palestinian authors and the evaluation thereof; as evident in the reception of Anton Shammas's *Arabesques*, focusing on his virtuous multi-layered Hebrew (often acclaimed as being "more Jewish than that of a Jew") or in A.B. Yehoshua's 1977 *The Lover*, in which the young Palestinian Na'im memorizes Bialik's national poetry of longing for the Jewish homeland.

2 Consider, for example, the archival website "an invitation to Piyyut", one of Pedaya's projects, which is expanding and reaching beyond Mizrahi and Sephardic musical traditions as an all-inclusive enterprise.

3 Between 1984 and 2004, Ella Bat Zion, a poet, translator, and author, used the name, Gabriella Elisha. On her poetry, see Mendelson-Maoz (2006).

4 Bat Zion has dedicated the poem to Shelly Elkayam and Amira Hess. There is an active poetic dialogue between the Jerusalemite women poets who belong to the same generational group. They engage in subverting conventions about sexuality, love, religion, and ethnicity.

5 A founder of the movement East for Peace and a former delegate to international women's conferences in Nairobi and China, Elkayam is an outspoken public figure among intellectuals in Jerusalem.

6 In Hebrew, the verb *la'asot* means both "to do" and "to make". There is no functional distinction between the two. This extends to the construct of "making love". I have chosen to translate this verb as "do" throughout the poem.

7 The poem was published in Hebrew in *Hame'asef*, of the Hebrew Writers Society, the *Rosh Hashana* Special supplement, in 1993, in a concert with *Kol Yerushalayim*. Elkayam was the editor of that special literary supplement, following two years as literary editor of *Tarmil* 1990–1992. See *Hame'asef* (1993, 8). Translated from the Hebrew by Rachel Persico and Ruth Tsoffar.

8 The only other time that *ma'akhelet* is mentioned in the Bible is in the disturbing story of the concubine in Judges (19:29): "he took a knife (*ma'akhelet*) and laid hold on his concubine, and divided her, together with her bones, into twelve pieces, and sent her throughout all the territory of Israel". See Mieke Bal's illuminating discussion of this account in "The Rape of Narrative and the Narrative of Rape: Speech Acts and Body Language in Judges" (1988b).

9 Today, what is known as Temple Mount is at the heart of the Palestinian/Jewish dispute over Jerusalem.

10 "Shirah" in Hebrew means both "poetry" and "singing".

11 This refers to the *Brit ben ha-betarim*, the Covenant of the Pieces or Covenant of the Flesh as described in Genesis 15.

12 Genesis 17 builds on the covenant of the pieces to establish a second covenant around the sign of the *Brit Millah*, the circumcision of the male newborn. The two different versions of the covenant have caused scholars to attribute the first, in Genesis 15, to the "P" ("Priestly") writer of Genesis and the second to "J" (Yehwistic documents, referring to no later than about the eighth century BC).

13 In the covenant of the circumcision in Genesis 17 Abraham obeys God, and although he doubts to himself, laughing, he does not question God directly. The story of the binding of Isaac, which appears in Genesis 22: 1–18, develops further Abraham's persona as the ultimate obedient and amenable patriarch.

14 As described in Genesis, "vultures descended upon the carcasses, but Avram drove them back. Now, when the sun was setting, a deep slumber fell upon Avram, and there, fright and great darkness fell upon him!" (Genesis 15:11–12).

15 Hélène Cixous and Catherine Clément's discussion of the sense of smell as a disorder of women's hysteria becomes another gender marker, which discloses an attempt to anesthetize the body and pathologize femalehood (1986, 32–39).

16 The "intoxicating aroma" is also found in the *Misdrash* and *Aggadah*, particularly with regard to the Brit *Millah*, in which the rabbis wax romantic about the intoxicating odor of the mounds of foreskins.

17 The word *ma'akhelet* in its numerous parenthetical appearances is present in the original Hebrew.

18 Simona Kogan (2007). www.israel21c.org/photographer-adi-nes-connects-ancient-and-modern-israel/.

19 Gideon Hausner, the attorney general of the State of Israel, used a similar tone in his opening remarks at Eichmann's trial in April 1961. "With me at this moment stand six million prosecutors".

20 The Jerusalem Post, April 27, 2005, "Ezer Weizman lauded as man of peace and courage." www.highbeam.com/doc/1P1-108245583.html

21 www.aish.com/hisrael/history/Crash_Course_in_Jewish_History_-_Part_67_The_Miracle_of_Jewish_History.asp

22 The webpage concludes with a reference to Weizman's speech and is given within quotes, although there is no mention of the fact that the author added to her "free" translation of Weizman's speech considerably.

23 www.amit.org.il/learning/english/Holocaust/teacherssuggestions.htm

24 The Mishnah, meaning repetition, is a major source of rabbinic Judaism's religious texts. It is the first recording of the oral law of the Jewish people, as championed by the Pharisees, and is considered the first work of Rabbinic Judaism. The Mishnah was redacted around the year 200 CE by Yehudah Ha-Nasi. Rabbinic commentaries on the Mishnah over the next three centuries were recorded mostly in Aramaic and were redacted as the Gemara. The Mishnah and the Gemara together form the Talmud.

25 "In every generation (and generation) each individual is bound to regard himself as if he personally had come forth from Egypt" (Pesachim 10, 5). And it is said: *and thou shall declare unto thy son, on that day, saying, this is done because of that, which the Eternal did for me, when I came forth from Egypt* (Ex. 13: 8). It was not our ancestors only that the most Holy, blessed be He! redeemed from Egypt, but us also did He redeem with them; as is said: *and He brought us from thence, that He might bring us in, to give us the land which He swore unto our fathers* (Deut. 6:23) (Haggadah shell Pessah 1949, 44–45).

26 In his 1986 novel, *See Under Love*, also republished 2006 as *Momik*, David Grossman reduces the reference of Nazi Germany into *"eretz sham"*, the country over there, literally the land over there, whereby the nine-year-old protagonist, Momik, projects a whole scheme of imaginary Holocaust history. Grossman, therefore, generates a linguistic, literary, figurative, and philosophical construct of extreme otherness. The internalized paradigm of "here" and "there" is critical in constructing the child's consciousness of estrangement and alienation and horror (Grossman 1986).

27 This reductive dichotomy was also projected on the experience of Jewish communities under Islam as the only possible trajectory of Jewish life out of Israel.

28 In his popular song '"Avadim", Slaves, (1998) Berry Sakharof, "The Prince of Israeli Rock" (born in Izmir, Turkey) articulates the drama of living in the

false freedom of the addict, "everyone wants to be free, but free of what?" Amazingly, the song ties together the "such" and "as if", of the one addicted to/by the addiction of those who are in power, living with an open mouth between one dose and another.

> Because we are all slaves, even when we have
> "such' (ka-zeh) and "as if" (ke-illu).
> Opening a big mouth, waiting
> for the next pleasure
> We are all someone's addiction
> Who asks: "now feel."
> Opening a big mouth
> and waiting for the next dose.

29 Following Lacoue-Labarthe and Nancy (1990, 298).

30 Hans Vaihinger's thesis, *The Philosophy of 'As if': A System of the Theoretical, Practical and Religious Fictions of Mankind* (1968), was an influential study of human knowledge. Vaihinger argues that knowledge, including law and religious system, is functioning "as if" it was true, but it is fiction that has been constructed and gained validity through experience and pragmatic modeling.

31 See, for example, Gil Anidjar's critique in his article, "On the (Under)cutting edge: Does Jewish Memory Need Sharpening?" in Anidjar in *Jews and Other Differences* (1997) 360–396.

32 Yehuda Gizbar, for example, a blogger, wishes to meet his twin sister, a woman like Yair. https://gizbar.wordpress.com/tag/%D7%A9%D7%AA%D7%94%D7%99%D7%99-%D7%9C%D7%99-%D7%94%D7%A1%D7%9B%D7%99%D7%9F/

33 www.newlibrary.co.il/article?c0=14221

34 "As long as in the heart, within,/ A Jewish soul still yearns, /And onward, towards the ends of the east,/ An eye still gazes toward Zion; / Our hope is not yet lost: /The hope of two thousand years,/ To be a free nation in our land,/ The land of Zion and Jerusalem". I chose to use the popular translation as it appears in Wikipedia. https://en.wikipedia.org/wiki/Hatikvah

35 Five of its eight lines are one long sentence of "As long as"; the lyrics were adapted from the Austro-Hungarian Jewish poet, Naftali Herz Imber's poem which initially included nine stanzas and was written in 1877. It was spontaneously sung by Czech Jews at the Auschwitz-Birkenau gas chamber.

36 The verb *'atsar* can be also translated as "to stop" and to "arrest".

37 Other commentators define Hagar as a concubine. See also Robert Alter (2004, 78), and note #3.

38 Rachel, whose barrenness is accentuated both between Jacob's love and the constraints her father puts on Jacob to first marry her older sister Leah, gives her slave girl, Bilhah, to Jacob, using the same expression, "And I will also be built through her" (Gen. 30:3).

39 The chapter ends with a geographical account whereby Hagar names the place of her encounter with the divine, 'El Roi; a genealogical account which reports the birth of Ishmael, who will be named by his father, Avram; and a final demographic one which tells about Avram's age as he becomes a father: eighty-six.

40 Some feminist scholars suggest that Hagar obtains the status of a wife, similar to Jacob's wives (Schneider 2004).

41 If the verb *'ibaneh*, I will be built, is familiar to the native speaker of Hebrew, it is the plural form, *nibaneh*, we will be built, that is its most common

modern usage. Certainly, Hebrew itself "builds on" its root systems, conjugating in seven "buildings" (conjugations, *binyanim*), into which the verbal system is divided. But more than that, the whole Zionist project presupposes the individual collective enterprise of the pioneer song, "*'Anu banu 'artzah li-vnot ule-hibanot bah*", we have come to the land to build and be rebuilt by it. The root, *bnh/bni* is the way to participate in draining the swamps and making the desert bloom, as the desire to, as Eric Zakim argues in his book *To Build and Be Built: Landscape, Literature, and the Construction of Zionist Identity*, "transform both into something essentially Jewish increasingly came to mark a turn inward toward the reclamation of a Jewish subject tied to the very soil of Palestine" (Zakim 2006, Edna Politi's film, *Anu Banu: the Daughters of Utopia*, 1982). The whole Zionist enterprise can be reduced to this expression, being constructed and constituted here through the act of building, through the very full participation of working the land. The very essence of return and renewal, *Hibanut*, being built, is the process of transformation, conversion and becoming. Its meaning responds to *hurban*, annihilation and destruction of the Temple, Jerusalem, and other cities of Yehudah, as much as the whole crumbling Jewish life in Europe during the Holocaust. To build and be built, *Bnh/bni* is an important, verb for it carries a deeply sacred meaning and combines linguistic, material, and spiritual layers that are at the very heart of the call for return to Israel.

42 Zizek (1999, 87–101). Zizek's three key features regarding fantasy are: "(1) the tension in the notion of fantasy between its beatific and disturbing dimensions; (2) the fact that fantasy does not simply realize desire in a hallucinatory way, but rather constitutes our desire, provides its co-ordinates—i.e. literally 'teaches us how to desire'; (3) the fact that the desire staged in a fantasy is ultimately not the (fantasizing) subject's own desire but the desire of his/her Other; fantasy is an answer to the question, 'What am I for the Other? What does the Other want from me?'"(Zizek 1999, 100, note 1).

43 In the case of Rachel and her sister Lea, the Bible introduces both envy and jealousy: Rachel is envious of Lea's ability to bear children, and Lea is jealous of Jacob's love for Rachel. The envy has such an unbearable impact on Rachel that she cries to Jacob, saying, "Give me sons, or else, I will die" (Genesis 30: 1).

44 The miraculous manifestation of the pregnancy gaze is manifested when Mary visits between Elizabeth in Luke 1:36–56. Mary's greeting is utterly informed by her pregnancy, to the point that the baby in Elizabeth's stomach leaps upon hearing it.

45 As the English expression conveys, "to teach (you) a lesson". In colloquial Hebrew, in addition to the expression, "*'ani 'alamed 'otkha lekach*" the nastier one is, "*' ani' alamed 'otkha me-'eafo ha-dag mashtin*", I will teach you from where the fish pees, alluding to an obvious knowledge, and yet, highlighting the need for teaching.

46 Amichai's personification of the sacrificial ram as the third child of Avram and Sarah conspires to introduce *Yivkeh* (he will cry) filling the void of the name and the person who cries within the narrative, and from Amichai's perspective of reading it. See Amichai (1998, 119).

47 In contemporary Israeli ethnic politics, an increasingly popular strategy for Ashkenazis to devalue Mizrahi's claims of historical oppression is to state that the latter is *mitbachyanim* (whining or crying merely for the sake of receiving attention), in a form of gaslighting that is at the same time highly infantilizing.

48 It is important to differentiate between the verb *bacha* and *zahak*, in English both are often translated as "to cry", or "to cry out". Earlier, God reminds

Cain that Abel's blood had cried out unto him from the ground. The verb *za'ak*, lamented, implored, cried out—depicts the drama of Cain's murder and his denial of it. *Bacha*, as in the case of Hagar, means to cry (tears).

49 "Here, without analogy and without 'perhaps', Heidegger declares... thinking is a handwork" (Derrida 171).

50 Miller on Derrida's reading of Nancy (2008, 160).

51 For Michel Serres, the hand is "a naked faculty", or, as Cary Wolfe adds, "'an image of pure possibility', a readiness to take any shape" (Wolfe, introduction, 2007, xix). The hand is undifferentiated.

52 It will be instructive to move from the literal meaning of hand and body to the grammatical hand, the one that idiomatically figures in numerous prepositions and other idiomatic expressions such as *'al yad* ("near", or literally "on hand"), *'al yede*, ("by", literally "on the hands") *mi-yad* ("immediately", literally "from hand"), *kilachar ya*, ("incidentally", literally "as if after/following a hand") *be-yad* ("by", through, literally "in the hand"), and *miyade* ("from", literally "from the hands").

53 Pethahiah ben David of Lida, who in Frankfurt in 1727 issued his father's *Yad Kol Bo*. The book was confiscated but was restored with the approval of several professors and preachers.

54 More ironic, though, is the fact that the department store was built on the construction site of the destroyed Gimnasia Herzeliyah, the first Hebrew high school in Tel Aviv that was founded in 1903, and since then a legendary institution that stands for early Zionist Hebrew ethos and sublime culture. The education that Kolbo Shalom promoted was carried out via weekly celebrations of international cultures, such as the Romanian week, or Arab week, with food, merchandise and publicity attracting huge crowds.

55 Cixous (1986, 21).

56 My translation is loosely based on the translation by Bloch and Kronfeld. The original poem is included in his series, "My Son Was Drafted" in *Open, Close Open* (Hebrew 1998). The translation was published as an independent poem in the New Yorker (translated by Bloch and Kronfeld), (The New Yorker – 1999, Volume 75, Issues 28–34 – Page 58).

57 To enhance the clarity of the translation, Bloch and Kronfeld added to the impersonal subject, "he" and the more specific reference, "that guy". The original merely keeps the subject vague, "he" ("Daddy, that guy /Stuck his hand into the outside!") (Ibid.)

58 Amichai manages to add to this crowdedness and density of both the physical body and the grammatical body (in Hebrew the same word, *guf*), moving from the imperative plural form of the verb to the first person "I", to "their" third person "them", to her (my daughter) and ending with the enigmatic third person "he": "He stuck his hand into the inside". Unlike Bloch and Kronfeld, "Go, children, I begot: get yourselves into the next century" (Ibid).

59 In his series of poems, "Jerusalem, Jerusalem why Jerusalem" (2006), Amichai compares the city to the accelerated image of the spinning carousel, another time machine, where up and down, past and present, sacred and secular all blend together (Amichai 1998, 142–143).

60 Yael Darr, in her study of Pre-1948 Hebrew Children's Literature, notes that writers often addressed children as mature adults, demonstrating a tendency to "soldierize" young readers. This highlights the distinction between "young youth", who are not yet ready for army service, and "adult youth" in both the representation of heroism and the general experience of reading (Dar 2006, 157). *Yeled gadol* and *yaldah gdolah* ("big boy" and "big girl", respectively) are expressions of praise for Hebrew children.

61 In his study of how specific language and speech structures the psychopathological economic system of the white colonizer and the colonized person of
color, Frantz Fanon emphasizes the way the white man addresses the Afro-
American in syntax and vocabulary, talking pidgin "exactly like an adult
with a child and starts smirking, whispering, patronizing, cozening... a way
to 'fasten him to the effigy of him, to snare him, to imprison him, the eternal victim of an essence, of an appearance for which he is not responsible'"
(Ibid. 35).

62 Shahar was a fifth-generation Jerusalemite who served for many years as
chairman of the *Hebrew Writers' Association*. Later, in Paris, he was appointed the title of *Commandeur* by the Ordre des Arts et Lettres of the
French government. He died in Paris, where he spent the last years of his life.

63 On the movement of Shahar's work from the Hebrew margins to the literary
canon, see Shaked (1993).

64 Mr. Rogers the highly popular American television show host between 1968
and 2001, and a Presbyterian minister and educator, is a good example of
such a neighborhood hero in American popular culture. Rogers constructed
the nation as "neighborhood" with himself as the sympathetic, inviting host.
In 2002 he was awarded the Presidential Medal of Freedom.

65 Katzir (1990, 34). Katzir is a prolific writer of short stories and prose whose
work has been translated into numerous languages. Katzir also edits and
teaches writing at the Tel Aviv University.

66 "Schlaffstunde", was written in December 1989, and was first published in
the short story collection *Sogrim 'et ha-Yam* (Closing the Sea) (1990, 9–35).
The story was re-edited and republished in the *Haifa Stories* collection *Si-
purei Heifa* in 2005. It has been adapted into a play as well as a feature film,
Family Secrets (1998).

67 Most prominent among them is Tom Segev's book, *The Seventh Million*,
which was published in 1991 in Hebrew, and translated to English in 1993.

68 The story engaged so deeply with the details and texture of German Jews,
the Yeke culture, at the top of the Carmel, that it could be easily defined
as ethnic literature: competing in its themes and life style with the Sabra
culture, and aiming to document the last generations of its people. Nevertheless, German Jews were able to preserve their Germanic culture around
the neighborhood of Merkaz HaCarmel, the "Carmel Center", on the top of
the mountains in Haifa.

69 Scheduled between 2:00 and 4:00 in the afternoon, it has divided the day
into two parts, "before noon", and "afternoon"; shops, banks, post of-
fices, and other official businesses also followed this schedule, which was
especially comfortable in the summer season when napping hours were the
warmest time of the day.

70 Attributed to the pianist E. von Binzer, in Hefling (2000, 79).

71 English translation in *Closing the Sea*, translated by Barbara Harshav, New
York: Harcourt Brace Jovanovich Publisher, 1992, pp. 1–30.

72 *Tsemer-gefen* is a reference to cotton balls, which are a staple of Israeli households and used for nearly everything. The processed cotton fibers are used
for cleaning, medical purposes, insulation, etc. Metaphorically, the term
"tsemer-gefen" refers to over-protected, including protected children's—
softies and mama's boys.

73 Benjamin (1988, 219).

74 Suisa studied in the Hesder Yeshiva. For a few years he wrote for the Jerusalem weekly *Kol Ha'ir*, studying mime at the movement theater in Paris, and
now lives in Jerusalem.

75 My position is in stark opposition to the tendency to romanticize and po-
eticize Ir Ganim, as represented by critics such as Menachem Perri, *Akud*'s
publisher.

76 According to *Midrash Tanchuma*, Isaac was thirty-seven years old at the
time of the *'akedah* (*V'yera*).

77 *HaSochnut HaYehudit L'Eretz Yisra'el* (The Jewish Agency for Israel) is an
enormous, quintessentially Zionist enterprise. Established in 1929 and representing itself as a nonprofit, the Agency boasts of having "brought home"
more than three million Jews, founded more than 1,000 settlements, edu-
cated more than 300,000 children in the youth movement *Ali'yat Ha-No'ar*,
and established 1,500 educational and cultural institutions.

78 Albert Suisa (Unpublished lecture, March 28, 2012, University of Michigan,
Ann Arbor).

3 Ruth's Homecoming

Metabread, Transformation, and Offspring*

> And God said: My children are rebellious, annihilating them is impossible, returning them to Egypt is impossible, exchanging them with another nation I cannot do, so/but what shall I do to them, behold, I shall surely torture them, and purify them through a small starvation (*ra'avon*).[1] "And there was famine (*ra'av*) in the land."
>
> – Ruth Rabba, Introduction

Doing Textuality and the Performance of Reading

The chronology of violence that I am developing in this work and its demanding quality asks us to move to hunger and the request for food as a metathesis that will integrate the different ideas and will produce an analytical tool to study the subject. I set the Breadscape as the framework in which I explore these demands, the space of hunger including the substance of life, bread, but also, here, in this specific culture, the book, its language, and its location, the land. Citation emerges in this Breadscape as the practice that promises the vitality and sustainability of the grain, the seed, the word, but as a *tsatetet*, it has become a disease that embodies all the symptoms and the treatment in a way that we can never distinguish between them: the symptom became the treatment.

This chapter takes a novel position, situating *The Book of Ruth* as a continuation of the story of the conception of Moab in Genesis 19. Once read together, the crises around death and scarcity of food fully expose the insidiousness of Ruth and Naomi's trauma. It will require a major shift in consciousness in order to overcome it. My main question is how the Bible does it, what kind of change it introduces, and how the deep-seated trauma of generations—death, survival, and hunger—is resolved. In that sense the domestication of Ruth's otherness into Judea and Judaism, both literal and

* Shorter versions of this chapter appeared as, "The Trauma of Genealogy: Ruth and Lot's Daughters," published in *Women in Judaism: A Multidisciplinary Journal* 5, no. 1 (2007); and "The Trajectory of Hunger: Appropriation and Prophecy in the Book of Ruth," in *Sacred Tropes: Tanakh, New Testament, Qur'an as Literary Works*, edited by Roberta Sabbath. Brill 2009.

symbolic, is predicated not simply on her graceful desire to follow Naomi's God, people, and identity, but also on her ability to allow Boaz's bread to speak its perfection to her through its performance of measure: he gives her *pat shlemah, a* perfect, whole bread.

Genesis tells the story of the destruction of Sodom and Gomorrah, the emergence of Lot's family from the ruined city, and Moab's precarious historical conception. Ruth's primordial trauma, dating back to the trauma of her people, emerges out of this narrative. The accumulated grief in her own life —the sickness and death of her husband, his brother, and their father; the loss of her home; the loss of her sister-in-law Orpah; and the potential loss of Naomi, her mother-in-law— are, in the light of the trauma of the past, inescapable reenacted losses. I will demonstrate how from the brink of the abyss, she overcame these losses, and turned into the ultimate agent of transformation. The epigraph that opens this chapter presupposes that hunger (*ra'av*) even a little, petite hunger (*ra'avon*), is for the Rabbis a transformative event. As intended by God, purifying through hunger, especially in *The Book of Ruth*, is an act that, within the paradigm of sin and punishment, can change consciousness and bring one to repent.

Hunger, petite or big, is a constitutive condition, like narratives and language. And from its very first articulation, Hebrew language and the biblical story have been associated with flavor and palate. It is not only that abstractions are embodied through specific materiality, as Benjamin suggests (Benjamin 1996), but more ontologically, the story of Eve in Genesis provides us with the first libidinal lesson, and has taught us that "knowledge could begin with the mouth" and that "knowledge and taste go together" (Cixous 1991, 151). But unlike the primitive meal of the forbidden fruit, however, the milk and honey are the Abrahamic ambrosia through which God reveals himself as both feeder (land) and food, and hunger is the trope of reentry into the feeding paradigm, a movement we already encountered in Genesis in the narrative of Joseph. Rather than a meal that tests the limits of desire or provides via prohibition the libidinal education, as Helene Cixous puts it (Ibid.), milk and honey constitute an invitation to live with the land that will provide the sumptuous food. To the extent that the configuration of land, milk, and honey have become a different feeding code of cultural sustenance, hunger and its solution is the prism through which the Bible introduces Ruth back into her new agency of body and life, kinship and nation.

Ruth, a Native of Moab

The Book of Ruth tells the story of a stranger's journey from her birthplace—the state of Moab—to her new homeland in Bethlehem— literally, the house of bread. The story is thusly about Ruth's radical transformation from a stranger, a daughter of a nation that has been cursed by God for more than ten generations, into a native. It moves from the deadening intersection of hunger, malady, and death to that of satiation, birth, and communal jubilation. The narrative begins when Naomi, her husband, Elimelech, and their two sons—Machlon and Kilyon—decide to migrate from Bethlehem, in Judea, to Moab in search of food, a journey of around fifty miles to the northwest. Surprisingly, the text does not directly mention the food that they find in Moab, or even that they find food, just that they settle there.[2] After the death of the father, the sons marry the Moabite women, Ruth and Orpah. The two sons subsequently die, and upon hearing that there is no longer famine in Judea, Naomi, now a widow and childless, decides to return to Bethlehem after living in Moab for ten years. En route, Naomi allows her daughters-in-law to return to their father's households; they don't like the idea, but Orpah returns home. Ruth insists on accompanying Naomi, affirming that Naomi's people, God, and nation are from now on hers as well, and they continue together. Once in Bethlehem, the hungry Ruth gleans barley from the fields of Boaz, a member of the clan to which Elimelech, Naomi's deceased husband, belongs.[3] Boaz and Ruth meet, he bakes her bread, and she later approaches him sexually and they subsequently marry. Ruth becomes pregnant and gives birth to Obed, grandfather to King David. The book ends with the description of the women of Bethlehem praising the child as "the son of Naomi", claiming that Ruth is worth more than seven sons.

At the beginning of the story, Ruth is not simply a woman and a widow; she is a pariah. As a Moabite, she belongs to one of the most symbolically "polluted" of the biblical nations. She is constructed as a foreigner in *The Book of Ruth*, a status that puts her outside of the purview of the legal system, wherein she has no national or political rights (Kristeva 1991, 103). With the status of the outsider she is not obliged to obey the law and is free to leave and return to Moab. But she comes instead with Naomi to Bethlehem. In the Bible, Ruth is rewarded for her loyalty to Naomi; not only is she redeemed by Boaz, but she is also incorporated into Judean culture and ultimately becomes the ancestor of King David and of the future messiah. In this way, Ruth enters the *communitas* of the Hebrew people and, from her previously condemned cultural location, she is assimilated into the heart of the sacred canon.

I first trace here the narrative dynamics of *The Book of Ruth* and demonstrate how its complex and loaded theological, psychological, territorial, and genealogical content makes it an ideal text for the study of Israeli ideologies of hunger and satiation, or the Breadscape. I argue that *The Book of Ruth* delivers an important moral lesson about the rewards of inclusion and belonging, setting an important cultural model for the adoption and appropriation of narratives, their subject (Ruth and her offspring), and the literal and symbolic treatment of hunger and feeding. For Bible-reading Israelis—and as mentioned, all Israelis are Bible readers, whether religious or secular—the story of Ruth serves as an important prototypical model of '*Ivrut* (Hebraization) a building block in the construction of a collective national ethos and consciousness.

In stories of famine and hunger, when feeding finally occurs, the readers are also fed. Hunger and satiation are familiar sensations; readers identify with them, feeding and being fed (and fed upon) through the process of reading. Ideologically, such stories also serve as existential allegories or didactic models. My reading of hunger and satiation in *The Book of Ruth* exposes the ideological operation of gendered (or even sexualized) foreignness and its treatment within the culture of the Bible. I approach the story as a narrative of trauma and survival in their various symbolic and allegorical manifestations, and in the process I unfold an already unfolded script of prophecy that transforms the breadless into the satiated, the homeless into natives, and lonely, childless foreigners into cultural protagonists.

The literary value of *The Book of Ruth*, like that of the Bible, lies in *Ruth*'s potential to be adapted to contemporary realities while at the same time adhering to historical practices and their relevance (see Gurevitch 1997, 204).[4] The book reflects a historically sedimented understanding of history and culture through reading and re-reading. The dating of *Ruth* has been the subject of ongoing controversy, the gist of which is whether the book is pre- or post-exilic. For the sake of this work, I contend that *Ruth* (like *The Book of Job*) is a work of historicized fiction that was most likely written during the time of Ezra and Nehemiah (between 500 and 350 BCE) and set in the historical period of the Judges, some 250–450 years earlier.[5] Several compelling reasons have been advanced for a post-exilic dating of *Ruth*. These include the vocabulary and style of the narrative; the idyllic representation of the genealogy of David; and evidence of legal customs, such as the levirate marriage, the gleaning of the fields, and the redemption of the land.[6] Moreover, a post-exilic dating of the text supports the view that the original and explicit purpose of the book was to make a case against the ban on intermarriage imposed by Ezra and Nehemiah. As a pro-miscegenation response to specific socio-political realities, the book is a fascinating document that makes apparent the internal use of history and historical narrative for political and ideological purposes.

What mobilizes the plot and guides the depiction of the characters and the resolution of the story in *Ruth* is the insidious trauma of hunger that tells the story of Moab's origins. In the commentaries and scholarship on *Ruth*, this connection and the impact of Moab's emergence of the catastrophe have gone unacknowledged. With that in mind, the radical act of inclusion and incorporation that the book teaches us becomes a wide-scale testimony to survival against the existential threat of total annihilation. It shows that what makes *this* book radically different from other books is that it presents a narrative model in which hunger, at the

heightened intersection of its physical, sexual, metaphysical, and epistemological manifestations, brings a woman "home", turning the struggle
of her survival into her arrival-cum-inclusion. Ruth's arrival in Judea
builds on the connections with the patriarchs Abraham, Isaac, Jacob,
Lot, and Judah, and the matriarch Tamar. In the attempt to transform
the exiled foreigner into an indigenous local who will share the promise
of the covenant with God, the book engages several paradigms and symbolic systems, such as geography (territory), Jewish genealogy (kinship),
and naming (native language). They all play important roles within the
trope of return and arrival in the Zionist discourse.

In *The Book of Ruth*, the trauma of hunger animates two intersecting maps: a geographical map of Judea and Moab, and a genealogical
map of biblical figures and ancestors. The geographical map traces the
movement of Elimelech's family's journey to Moab, and then, ten years
later, back to Bethlehem. The book highlights their movement out of
Judea and across national and ethnic boundaries. Dynamic geography
and genealogy are thus intertwined, rendering the text dialogical while
historically situating the narrative. The genealogical map illustrates the
connections among the patriarchal lineages of the tribe of Yehudah, the
kinship of Elimelech, the people of Moab, and five generations later,
King David.[7] The genealogical ties provide a template that links past,
present, and future generations. Women are not excluded from these
lineages. In fact, one can count at least ten generations back from Ruth
to Lot, and from Boaz back to Yehuda, Tamar, and Peretz (in *Genesis*).
One can also count forwards to David, and even to Goliath in *The Book
of Kings*, who, according to the Rabbis, was the descendant of Orpah.[8]
The genealogical map is part of the larger project originating in *Genesis* of writing the *Sefer Toldot Ha-'Adam*, The Book of Man's History
(Genesis 5:1), namely the construction of the house of Israel.

Moving across geographical or familial boundaries is often an act of
choice that underscores one's freedom to invent new alternatives. However, movement impelled by hunger is dictated by urgency. Migration
for the sake of survival is motivated by the quest for food, land, or—as
in the case of Ruth—a husband. It often entails the crossing of borders,
an intensified confrontation with ambivalence, and the reconciliation of
identities. More significantly, hunger forces possible transgressions of
taboos such as forbidden foods and proscribed marriage partners and
kinship rules. As a symptom, hunger also marks the boundaries of the
body, disrupting categories of identity, knowledge and order. The question, then, is how does the trauma of hunger of Moab and Ruth become
satiated?

In her book, *The Curse of Cain*, Regina Schwartz approaches the subject of difference in biblical and sacred narratives by focusing on the
construction of the Other, arguing that "acts of identity formation are
themselves acts of violence" (Schwartz 1998, 5). Here violence involves

not only violent acts like war or rape but also the very conceptualization and articulation of the Other. Markers of difference are never symmetrical. Within the traditional Jewish mindset of "us" and "them", the Moab of ancient Judaism can hardly be understood as a tragedy of representation and violence. From its early conception, and throughout the Bible, the Moabites are positioned along with the Amalekites and Philistines as the ultimate absolute enemy. Located along the northeastern part of the Dead Sea, in what later became the Moabite Desert, Moab entered into the Israelites' discourse of hunger as they wandered through the desert. There, God imposed the Moabites' exclusionary status beyond ten generations because "they did not meet [the Israelites] with food and with water on the way, at [their] going-out from Egypt" (Deuteronomy 23: 4–7). This tense encounter around the absence of food and feeding positioned Moab as the absolute other in the collective memory of Israel. As such, the Moabite situation, to the extent that one even bothers to consider it, has become "natural" and its trauma invisible. *The Book of Ruth* struggles, among other things, with this invisibility and the undiminished potency of this memory, circumscribing Ruth within national boundaries while at the same time expanding the limits of tolerance around her otherness.

Moab, therefore, is at the most extreme end of the Israeli exclusionary system, and represents a "category of 'unbelonging'" (Rogoff 2000, 5). To the extent that Israeli culture has developed a discourse of belonging and a constitution based on shared terms of inclusion—whether institutional, disciplinary, national, regional, cultural, sexual or racial—it has also developed a discourse of *unbelonging*. No mere articulation of exclusion, this is a discourse involving an "active form of 'unbelonging' against which the anxiety-laden work of collectivities and mutualities and shared values and histories and rights" defines difference and other epistemological constructs (Rogoff 2000, 5).[9] Systems of meaning that are disrupted as difference and otherness manifest as new ontologies (Kristeva 1995, 119). Foreignness challenges tolerance and defines the parameters of inclusion and exclusion; it becomes the border of culture, its limits and its symptoms.

Hunger as a Cultural Limit

In the Bible, the rabbinical retelling begins: "Ten years of famine came to the world... and one was in the days when the Judges ruled..." during the time of Naomi and Elimelech (Bereshit Rabba 25:3, Ruth Rabba 1:4; also in Blumental 1947, 8). Hunger for food is always tied (by the rabbis) to hunger for the Torah. Rabbinic commentary explains that since the time reference, *va-yehi*, it came to pass, is mentioned twice, two kinds of hunger are at stake: "one hunger for bread and one hunger for the Torah" (Yalkut Shimoni Ruth 597, cf. Fogel et al. 1995, 3). A later Hasidic source deduces that hunger is also a spiritual phenomenon. "Famine struck the land" means that "the soul of Judaism hungers with pangs no less severe or lethal than those of an emaciated body" (*Ohr Yohel* in Zlotowitz 1994, xx). The Hebrew term *ra'av* means "famine", "scarcity", and "hunger", and it signals a condition that moves from land to mouth and from human to God. *Ra'av* ties together various institutions to various moral economies.[10] Material scarcity was perceived in moral terms. *Ra'av*, which is also associated with a place, believed to be ruled by the angel of death and its laws, further motivated Israelites continuously to move in search of food and refuge from evil.

Migration in this context is often associated with theological wrong-doing, whereas permanent dwelling is an indicator of a harmonious, balanced relationship with God. The term *ra'av* therefore raises questions about both its own metaphorical and historical status and the elaborate discursive mechanisms that deploy hunger in the internalized Jewish, and later, Israeli, imagination. More precisely, how are hunger and its multilayered meanings and immense magnitude represented? Can the description of the dry and barren land elicit the entirety of the symbolic threat to survival? Can the empty granary do that? What about the empty stomach or the mother's dry breast? Can hunger be quantified? If so, how? By the number of missing loaves of bread? By the rainless days? Or perhaps, one should go back to Pharaoh's dream of his seven "emaciated and lean-fleshed cows" or seven ears of wheat (*Genesis* 41: 2–8).

These questions are crucial in the attempt to explore the textual representation of hunger not only as an extreme event but also as an insidious trauma of persistent scarcity and the cognizance of its threat. As an extreme trauma, hunger is an all-consuming experience. It is an overwhelming crisis that tightens the connections of the human body to nature, the land to moral and ecological commitment, and local traditions to a wider geography. As mentioned in the previous chapter, the main aspect of Trauma Studies and PTSD that the model of Insidious Trauma allows us to critique is their reductive approach; the pathologization of psychological trauma as an individual condition is reductive and naturalizes a decontextualized evaluation of such trauma. But contextualizing hunger, or any type of trauma for that matter, has been on the mind of scholars and was considered crucial, in the words of Felman. It Laub in their work on Holocaust testimony, to "gain insight into the significance and impact of the context on the text" (Felman and Laub 1992, xv). The need to contextualize trauma in a wider cultural perspective cannot be emphasized enough for, as they explain, "the empirical context needs not just to be known, but to be read: to be read in conjunction with, and as part of, the reading of the text" (Felman and Laub 1992, xv). Their point is carried further by Cathy Caruth, in her work on trauma and memory; namely, that the "truth" of a traumatic event such as hunger forms the center of its pathology. In other words, at the core of this pathology is truth, as it was remembered and not as it was experienced. Caruth's emphasis here is on the persistent recurrence of traumatic memory in its literal manifestation (Caruth 1995, 4–5).

Redressing: Sodom, Moab, and Bethlehem

> Because from Moab we came, and to Moab we'll return, a hard soil of which we know nothing. Only foreigners can pay attention to that which takes place outside the walls, to build rooms, walls, and corners. Because only foreigners know that they themselves bring destruction upon themselves, and that Sodom is the synonym of foreignness, a fantasy of Lot's family like all other families. (73)
>
> Michal Ben Naftali, *Childhood, a Book*

I wish to situate Ruth's trauma of hunger within the historical Moabite framework and introduce *The Book of Ruth* from within the story of Lot in *Genesis*. Indeed, several scholars have alluded to the internal connection between the story of Lot and *The Book of Ruth*, focusing exclusively on the incestuous act of Lot and his two daughters (Frymer-Kensky 2002, 257–263). I suggest that the Genesis story should be read as a preface to Ruth, not simply because Ruth is a descendent of the incestuous and food-withholding Moabites—a fact that defines her otherness—but because it provides the etiological framework that informs her identity as a survivor of multiple cultural traumas; insofar as Ruth's life story threatens to continually reenact the traumatic collective memory of her ancestors, it strongly embodies her ancestors' collective memory. Unfolding between the city and a mountain cave, the story of Lot also helps us fathom the depth of the anxiety that motivates the story of Ruth, including the decision of Naomi and her family to relocate from one place to another.[11]

My reading of the stories of Ruth and Lot together is inspired by a shift in the ethnographic position of reading to what I have defined, in the context of reading cultures, as "ethno-reading" (Tsoffar 2006a). Ethno-reading is a methodology of reading that seeks to expand the contextual framework of representation to include the socio-political and the poetics of knowledge production about the other. It engages in providing new opportunities to increase discursive audibility and visibility that otherwise remain unavailable. Ethno-reading seeks to alert us to hidden violence that has been silenced. It aims to introduce new practices of reading the other, building on emerging practices in post-colonial anthropology that respond to the crisis of representation, and that remain attentive to issues of positionality. In the language of Trinh Minh-ha, for example, "speaking nearby", is an ethical perspective that replaces "speaking for" and "speaking instead"; it seeks to represent rather than objectify, obscure, and further otherize the subject (Chen, interview, 1992, 87). Ethno-reading, especially in narratives of crisis and trauma, may respond positively to Caruth's suggestion of a practice of listening and speaking from trauma, "not as a simple understanding of the pasts of others but rather, within the traumas of contemporary history, as our ability to listen through the departures we have all taken from ourselves" (Caruth 1995, 11). Within the Israeli politics of reading the Bible, ethno-reading means to step out of the canonical, Jewish, often ethnocentric reading, and rethink Ruth, in this specific case, from within her own intimate history of survival.

In the well-known story of Lot in Genesis 18–19, God has resolved to destroy Sodom and its sinful inhabitants and instructs Lot, Abraham's nephew who came with him from their native land Ur, to flee. Lot is singled out, emerging as the only possible survivor of the approaching catastrophe. As his name, from both *malat* (escape) and *lut* (cover, hidden) indicates, Lot is God's only concession to Abraham. Indirectly, the story of Lot addresses the subject of collective punishment by articulating the moral justification for God's vindictive decision. Genesis 18 introduces the grand-scale, all-encompassing plan of the destruction through Abraham's famous dispute with God, where he challenges the totalizing, uncompromising decree against all the peoples of Sodom and Gomorrah. If God is proving that, as part of the covenant, he does not "cover anything from Abraham" (Genesis 18: 17), then the divine's motives for moral punishment appear transparent, accessible and comprehensible to humans. In fact, as Martin Harries argues, "Abraham is the privileged spectator of the whole story of Lot", the one who is not destroyed by the sight of the catastrophe (Harries 2007, 1–3). Abraham's bargaining seeks to rescue the few innocents (*tsadikim*) who might be in the city, but also helps to process destruction. His dispute strengthens the ties between the narratives of Lot and Ruth, as it frames them within the unique cosmogony of sin and punishment, wherein hunger and famine, of any magnitude—as Ruth Rabba introduces in the epigraph to the chapter—figure. The critical question, however, is what of the traces of sinful Sodom will forever remain in Lot and his story of escape? How will these traces be carried over as the trauma of his history?

As Genesis tells us, processing the idea of the destruction, escaping the city and letting go of it are highly problematic for Lot. It reveals the fascinating way in which the narrative builds up his incompetency and eventually his becoming (an)Other. At first he hosts the angels in his house, and then he experiences the assault of the men of Sodom, and their being blinded around the door. Lot offers his daughters to the rowdy men pounding outside his door—"both old and young all the people from every quarter" (Genesis 19: 4)—in exchange for the male angels whom they were eager to sodomize. But, as Derrida reminds us, the scene of "sodomy and sexual difference", highlights that Lot himself is a foreigner (*ger*), who cautiously employs the law of hospitality, occasioning a tense negotiation based on a hierarchy of guests and hostages (Derrida 2000, 151–152).[12] By offering his two virgin daughters, in part to prevent the commission of homosexual acts, Lot sets into motion the process culminating in the total collapse not only of his parental role and agency, but of his chances to be less of a foreigner.[13] The response of Sodom's people to his offer would avenge "the foreigner" who "came to play the judge" (Genesis 19, 9). Admittedly, in order to agree with Derrida's regard for hospitality without overlooking the misogynist angst of offering the daughters, an act that has preoccupied feminist readers, we need to value the law of hospitality as an absolute, unconditional, cultural imperative. A law that b(l)inds! It is this heightened intersection of competing economies of sexual differences, female bodies, kinship, hospitality, and otherness that underscores Lot's failure to gauge violence and adversary.

Lot continues to struggle with having to let go and move forward during this life-threatening voyage.[14] First he lingers (*va-yitmahmehah*), so long so that the angels themselves not only urge him to leave, but "with God's compassion" take his hand, and the hands of his wife and daughters, and lead them out of the city. They again instruct Lot to go towards the mountains and not to turn back. Afraid that the journey will be too long, Lot requests to go to the nearby town of Zo'ar. Lot is melodramatically explicit, terrified and pleading for his life:

> No, pray, my Lord!
> Now pray, your servant has found favor in your eyes,
> you have shown great faithfulness in how you have dealt with
> me, keeping me alive—
> but I, am not able to escape to the hill-country,
> lest the wickedness cling to me, and I die!
> Now pray, that town is near enough to flee to, and it is so tiny;
> Pray let me escape there—is it not tiny?—and stay alive!
> (Genesis 19: 18–20)

Hesitation, paralysis, and the language of profound fear dominate the description of the journey. The family's narrow escape culminates in the transformation of Lot's wife into a pillar of salt. For the overwhelming drama of destruction and escape—enhanced by ear-shattering blasts and the smell of burning sulfur—is further amplified by the prohibition on looking back, not only at the city, but also at the wife and mother who is left behind. Throughout this highly anxious episode, the destructive God appears all fire and brimstone, overthrowing "those cities, and all the plain, and all the inhabitants of the cities, and that which grew upon the ground" (Genesis 19: 25). Once in Zo'ar, presuming that even its mountains are too dangerous, Lot finds refuge with his daughters in a cave.

The mountain cave (a symbolic womb), is a compromised setting for hope and terror, for it is isolated enough to create a claustrophobic feeling that death is closing in, exaggerating the already overwhelming response and sense of total *kilayon* (annihilation) (which comes to be the name of Naomi's son). In the cave, the daughters reveal their *poverty of thought*, an utter lack, since, as the older daughter suggests,

> Our father is old, and there is no man in the land to come in to us as befits the way of all the earth! Come, let us have our father drink wine and lie with him so that we may keep seed (*zera'*) alive by our father.
>
> (Genesis 19: 31–32)

With the disappearance of their mother from the genealogical record, and within the context of their "crisis consciousness", the daughters' economic imperative is to "preserve the seed (*zera'*)" of the father (Genesis 19: 33, 35), as their father becomes less and less a biological father and more a Father of humanity, the only living provider of *zera'* (seed, semen). But their distorted perception should not surprise us: their state of mind operates on the "enigmatic core" (Caruth 1995, 5) of their traumatic experience, which often creates a "crisis of truth" as a result of an inherent, inexplicable void of knowledge, the distortion of the event, and the collapse of understanding (Caruth 1995, 3–12). In fact, Laub's insistence that historical "truth value" of knowledge is not critical in testimony of trauma is relevant here as well, as it speaks for the depth of its affect (see Laub 1992, 59–63). The daughters serve as living testimony of the historical trauma of that sinful society and its aftermath. Anticipating total destruction, they must, as survivors, "document" with their bodies the absence of their mother and the erasure of their past. The Rabbis sympathetically decree that the daughters did not know that only Sodom was destroyed (Psikta Rabbati ['Ish Shalom] 42: 5, in Lubin 2003, 309).[15] Nonetheless, the text is less forgiving; although unconscious, and the Bible is careful to state twice that he "did not know", Lot is implicated in the incestuous acts of their impregnation.[16] Lot goes on to become another patriarchal figure in Genesis; his otherness nonetheless has been imprinted: unlike his "perfect" uncle, Abraham, he is positioned outside of the bounds of the covenant and becomes the father of Moab and Amon. Although they have managed to escape Sodom, the depth of the psychological impact of the trauma will persist. But if the Bible accentuates the narrative's terms of survival—blurring the distinction between the crisis and its resolution—it also helps to exonerate Lot's incestuous part in the act.[17]

Fertility and impregnation are the daughters' *tikkun olam* (repairing the world); they give birth, in their eyes, not only to the line of their father, not only to their nations, but to the entire human race. If their act stands in polar opposition to their mother, now a pillar of salt, it still highlights that all three women were highly impacted by the departure and their acts are all transformative. Lot's wife is at the very edge of the etiological narrative of Moab, as its subtext of their history: the Moabite matriarch and an eternal testimony of female nostalgic, compassionate, and libidinal ambivalence. For her daughters, she had become a mobilizing factor whose threatening image had to be reinterpreted through their shaken body and spirit.

Indeed, in Michal Ben-Naftali's *Childhood, a Book* (2006), the author aims to inhabit the psycho-cultural space of the biblical narrative as "the daughter of Lot's wife", a girl from Tel Aviv going back to Moab, deconstructing and constructing a voice, body, and presence, unprecedented in Hebrew or Israeli culture. Her feminist voice identifies with the daughter, speaking directly to the mother, as both a daughter and as the mother that she has become (a problematic position) as she affirms, "facing the mother, childhood is flickers of soaring up and crash-landing" (Ben-Naftali 2006, 21).

Ben-Naftali's search for a childhood that precedes the story of Lot is an attempt to dive beyond narratives, but being informed by them, she is aware of the epistemic lack and its impact on body, flesh and language. She builds on Lot's name as an ontology of that which will always remain hidden and beyond reach. Her dispute is therefore about living with in limits of consciousness, for which she brings Lot's wife home from years of desertion and abandonment. She tackles Motherhood, and her "gift of scarcity", that "face-hiding kindness", that has imparting the nothing she is lacking, against the deadening silence, the closed heart, the lack of language, and the confiscation of the body (Ibid. 2006, 9–10).

In her poem "I am the Daughter of Lot", Bracha Serri (1940–2013) inserts herself into the genealogy of the Other. Her "*Midrashir*", a midrashic poem, as Almog Behar calls it (2008)[18] is an audacious protest against ignorance around issues of gender, ethnicity, class, and political position. Her poetry directly engages stereotypes about Yemenite women, their class and ethnic exclusion, and their lack of formal education:

> I am the daughter of Lot
> you are all smitten with blindness
> and I have not known a man.
> You are men of Sodom.
> Smitten with blindness.
> (Serri 1990, translated by Yonina Borvik and Ammiel Alcalay,
> In Alcalay 1996, 290–291)

Moving between the sexual and non-sexual modes of "knowledge", she introduces a body that seeks to escape the collective, and at the same time, as she so fully identifies with Lot's silent daughter ("alone", in singular), she emerges as the one who knows:

> I am the daughter of Lot.
> I know the men of my city.
> Smitten with blindness
> and stupid.
> Bursting to break down the door.
> Striking the messengers
> instead of drawing conclusions
> to avoid disasters.

(Ibid. 291)

Against the backdrop of her other poems of the nomadic woman (Serri's third collection's title is *Seventy Wandering Poems* (1983), Lot's daughter emerges as a refugee from ignorance, and herself, against all odds, becomes an enlightened prophet.

Indeed, the story of Lot brackets patriarchy and emphasizes women's traumatic subjectivity. Hunger, per se, is not explicitly the central issue. Rather, it is a sense of total scarcity and the desire to constitute a promising *zera'*—a seed, sperm, or semen—and offspring that dominate the narrative. Felman and Laub have argued that the representation of trauma is problematic because it is unrepresentable (Ibid. 1992). To a large extent, in the Israeli-Jewish imagination, the trauma of Moab does not count. The story is never told from that perspective. And the layers of Moab's otherness help to further veil the trauma. Rather than being perceived as a symptom of pathology, a given crisis becomes the very essence of representation of the other. Such a fragment of crisis dramatizes and underscores their difference with a negative representation. It has reduced and essentialized Moab.

To a large extent, the story of Lot anticipates Ruth's inability to refuse the power of ideological determination and its totalizing authority; her story too is introduced within the uncompromising threat of complete annihilation. I wish to emphasize that what is shared between these two biblical narratives is not only the Moabite origin of the protagonists, or the sexual act of origins, as others have claimed, but more critically the underlying etiological pattern of identity formation based on otherness, catastrophe and its insidiousness. Moab emerges from within the total ruination of humankind, and ten generations later, now represented by Ruth, is still a nation (and land) utterly concerned with dire threats to life and reproduction.

Road Trip: A Process of Becoming

Canonical readings celebrate the fact that Ruth chooses well, that she sticks with Naomi; the extent of Ruth's traumatic hunger, and her experience of scarcity and anxiety have been overlooked. The scarcity of offspring not only frames the whole narrative, but it is also best manifested in the dialogue between Naomi, Ruth and Orpah, on the road to Bethlehem.

8 And Naomi said unto her two daughters-in-law: 'Go, *shovnah*, return each of you to her mother's house; God deal kindly with you, as ye have dealt with the dead, and with me.

9 God grant you that ye may find rest, each of you in the house of her husband.' Then she kissed them; and they lifted up their voice, and wept.

10 And they said unto her: 'Surely, we will return with you to your people.'

11 And Naomi said: 'Return, *shovnah*, my daughters; why will you go with me? *Are there yet any more sons in my womb, that they may be your husband?"*

12 Return, *Shovnah*, my daughters, go your way; for I am too old to have a husband. If I should say: I have hope, should I even have an husband to-night, and also bear sons;

13 would you wait for them until they were grown? Would you, then, refrain, from marrying? No, my daughters; it has been far more bitter for it for your sakes, for the hand of God has turned against me.'

14 And they lifted up their voice, and wept again; and Orpah kissed her mother-in-law; but Ruth clung (*davkah*) to her.

15 And she said: 'Behold, your sister-in-law is gone back to her people, and to her god; return after your sister-in-law.'

16 And Ruth said: 'Do not entreat me to leave you, and to return from following after you; for wherever you go, I will go; and wherever you lodge, I will lodge; your people shall be my people, and your God my God;

17 where you die, will I die, and there will I be buried; God will do so to me, and thus shall he add, for only death will tear us apart.'

18 And when she [Naomi] saw that she [Ruth] was absolutely determined to go with her, she stopped talking to her.

(Ruth 1: 8–18, my emphasis)

Naomi offers her permission to break the pact of kinship with her daughters-in-law and sends them to their homes and people with her gratitude and blessings. When they cry and ask to continue with her, she makes sure they understand that to come with her will be futile for, as she articulates unmistakably, "'Return (*shovnah*) my daughters; why will you go with me? *Are there yet any more sons in my womb, that they may be your husbands?*" (Ruth 1: 11). Naomi's speech is highly perplexing; she explicitly states that in returning to Bethlehem together, their shared genealogical destiny is sealed. She uses a wide rhetorical space to articulate her position, and provides three reasons for them to go back, answering her own question and refuting any possibility, any slim chance of giving birth to a child who would be a potential partner for conception. She starts with her age, for "I am too old to have a husband". But then she elaborates, "If I should say: I have hope, should I even have a husband to-night, and also bear sons; would you wait for them until they were grown? Would you, then, refrain from marrying?" the Hebrew feminine verbs, "*teshabernah*", and "*te'agenah*" (from *sh.b.r.*, to break, to wait, and refrain from marrying) dramatize the social condition of women who are in agony and abandoned, long awaiting their spouses (*Agunah* is the unfortunate Halachic status of a woman who was deserted by her spouse without divorce, unable to remarry).

A careful reading of Naomi's words reveals her unequivocal certainty that change—from hunger to satiation, from empty to full, from barren to fertile—is not only impossible but beyond imagination. Knowing the extent of her daughters-in-law's historical and genealogical trauma, she frames the chance to change in stark, realistic terms.[19] Naomi's soft, yet unsentimental tone responds to the core of her crisis, the death of her sons and her realization that it is impossible to find sexual male partners for the next generation. Trying to make sense of the situation, she tries to protect her daughters-in-law. Her words reveal the depth of her sorrow, saying, "No, my daughters; it has been far more bitter for it for your sakes, for the hand of God has turned against me" (Ruth 1: 13).[20] Here the trauma of Ruth is clearly accentuated through fertility, and the concern for offspring. Naomi unequivocally spells the utter improbability of providing any possible viable outlet to Ruth's and Orpa's desires for motherhood.[21] In the same way, Ruth's response to Naomi must be heard from within the particular context of her people's trauma and survival.

Orpah returns to Moab. Ruth insists on remaining with Naomi, and it is in this singular moment that Ruth resolutely (re)asserts her assimilatory belonging in a totality that crosses national, religious, and territorial boundaries:

> 16 And Ruth said: 'Do not entreat me to leave you, and to return from following after you; for wherever you go, I will go; and wherever you lodge, I will lodge; your people shall be my people, and your God my God;
> 17 where you die, will I die, and there will I be buried; God will do so to me, and thus shall he add, for only death will tear us apart.'
> (Ruth 1)

Ruth's invocation of God seals her speech act, transforming her words into a contract, an unbreakable vow of her identification with Naomi and of her new identity conceived within her commitment to change. In addition to being materialized words—shifting from verbal utterance to the substance of a contract and oath—Ruth's speech also demonstrates to the reader the depth of her desire, the powerful sound of words that cling as she, Ruth, clings to Naomi (*davkah bah*). Ilana Pardes's analysis draws on the meaning of *davak* and the semantics of love in Genesis 2: 24 and *Ruth*. "'To cling'" she concludes, "means to recapture a primal unity, to return to a time when man and woman were literally "one flesh" (Pardes 1992, 102). If trauma and its wound inhibit the possibility of change, impacting a paralysis, Ruth's speech puts forth an imagined script that moves from being to becoming. This subjective monologue of clinging, therefore, encodes a poetic text of becoming, a desire to be open to a new signifying process: as Butler elaborates, a desire that would further mobilize the discursive principle of "intervention and resignification" (Butler 1999, 43).

And yet, as a testimony to her history, her monologue must be heard with a sensitized acuity to a discourse that is unable to be represented, yet nevertheless is written (Caruth 1995, 3–12). Personal narratives, such as the following exchange between Naomi and Ruth, compel the reader to engage with and to participate in the unfolding events, and to consider the possibility that their words, perceived as a testimony, can facilitate an understanding of trauma, its effect and impact, and the human responses thereto. The profound and prophetic force of Ruth's words reverberate with the crisis of hunger and famine, the experience of death, the collapse of identity (both Moabite and Judean), and the total threat not only to history but to the future. Ruth is asking to recover everything that has been lost, a mother and a husband, offspring, food and bread, land and home, people and God, her name, and her story. Her speech act, a contract of identity, becomes her claim of inclusion, a virtual passport into the affective core of her healing at this intersection of emergence and change and within a culture from which she has been kept at bay. Stepping into a new trajectory, she will have to continuously prove that she is able to embrace it.

Boaz's Metabread as Historical Compensation

One of the lessons in *The Book of Ruth* is that the cursed nation of Moab cannot generate a solution for its hunger. In contrast, Boaz's bountiful fields in Bethlehem, once they recover from the ten-year famine, provide the epitomal measure of satiation. In Boaz's fields, Ruth is a hungry foreigner, still identified as "Ruth, the Moabite *na'ara* (young woman)" (Ruth 2: 5–6). The exchange between Boaz and Ruth is revealing: not only does he immediately assume the role of her protector, but he also blesses her in God's name, thereby confirming another level of her inclusion. This gesture of hospitality works on several levels, and is indeed bountiful. Note its semantic value:

> *Yeshalem Jehovah pa'alekh, u-tehi maskurtekh shlemah me'im Jehovah elohay Yisrael...*" "May the Lord reward your deeds. May you have a full recompense from the Lord, the God of Israel, under whose wing you have sought refuge.
>
> (Ruth 2: 12)

Having just acknowledged the immensity of Ruth's gesture ("all that you did for your mother-in-law after the death of your husband" [*Ruth* 2: 11]), Boaz uses three words in this blessing—*yeshalem*, *maskurtekh* and *shlemah*—each signifying a full reward, payment or compensation. The root *shalem* holds an unparalleled space in Hebrew, and signifies that which is perfect, complete, and whole; in its *pi'el* verbal form, it means to pay back, to compensate, and to reward. Other important nouns are derived from the adjective *shalem*, grounded in historic superlatives such as the name of King Solomon, *Shlomoh*; the name of the city Jerusalem, *Yerushalayim*; and the word for greeting and peace, *shalom*. In this short verse, not only does Boaz triply verbalize Ruth's worthiness for her reward, he thrice invokes the name of God. Unlike the failed economic exchange between Hagar and Sarai, Boaz is issuing a gigantic, unfathomable compensation to Ruth, and he summons God as the paymaster of this exchange.

The triplicate structure of his utterance is soon repeated in the configuration describing her way of consuming his gift: the grains he roasts for her. Boaz's reward to her is an act, which not only responds to her historical and traumatic hunger, but also marks a radical shift in the story of her emerging subjectivity. I will demonstrate how this shift is manifested linguistically. As she sits "beside the reapers", the book recounts:

> *va-tokhal, va-tisba' va-totar.*
> And she ate, and she had her fill, and she had leftovers.
>
> (Ruth 2: 14, translation is mine)

These three consecutive Hebrew verbs encrypt a whole narrative about the meal of the hungry woman, the end of her hunger, and her ability to leave surplus. It imparts a picture of great existential resolution. Symbolically, Ruth's new experience of satiation sets a limit on the all-consuming trauma of historical hunger. Recognizing the singularly potent economy of this passage, the Rabbis elaborated on the meaning of Boaz's gift of bread, referring to it as *lechem malkhut* (the bread of kingship, a royal bread), the emblem of the future Davidic kingdom. In another teleological commentary, these three consecutive verbs are deployed as grandiose models of and for Jewish history: a) *va-tokhal*, she ate the bread of the kingdom that would emerge from her in the days of David; b) *va-tisba'*, she had her fill in the days of Solomon; and c) *va-totar*, she had leftovers in the days of Hezekeyah (Rashi, in Shabbath 113; 2). Another commentary posits an even more monumental scale of Jewish time that occurs first in the days of this world, then in the days of the Messiah, and finally, in the days of the world to come (Ruth Rabba 2: 14).

However perceptive the Rabbis were in recognizing the critical significance of Ruth's satiation, they nevertheless overlooked its connection to her history of hunger, which I find crucial in understanding her shift in status and subjectivity, from breadless to well-fed, and from scavenger to an agent of feeding. According to the Midrash, "Boaz gave her just a "pinch of parched [roasted] grain between his two fingers", and Ruth's stomach was blessed, for she was satisfied by such a small morsel and even had some left over" (Zlotowitz 1994, 99). The Rabbis concluded that "it seems like there was a blessing in the intestines [gut] of that virtuous woman" (Ruth Rabba 2:14, also Fogel et al. 1995, 30). Her portrayal as a completely satisfied woman corresponds with another rabbinical interpretation of the name Ruth, as the "saturated" or "satiated one" (Berachot 7b; also Kristeva 1991, 71).

We can establish that within the project of hunger and feeding, these material verbs represent the psychological resolution not only of her trauma, but also of the insidious trauma of preceding generations: a critical moment where Boaz's gratefulness meets Ruth's and takes it a few steps further. Against a backdrop of the traumatic collapse of boundaries imposed by widowhood and famine, the narrative aims to restore *the* perfect moment: the totality encapsulated by *pat shlemah* and the triplicate repetition of her reward and subsequent satiation. It is precisely the overdetermined nature of her compensation that underscores the significance of the bread and extent of her symbolic hunger and desire for inclusion. Boaz's gift enables Ruth to return to her mother-in-law, not as the impoverished gleaner who shares her grains, but as a satiated provider of perfect bread. The verb, "eating her fill", *va-tisba'*, introduces the possibility of actually healing or closing the symbolic wound in Naomi's family, which in turn, allows for the opening of new discursive spaces in a new geography and genealogical trajectory.[22] This transition from closing to opening signifies the new modality of Ruth's identification with Boaz and Naomi. At the same time, the surplus or leftovers of her reward of grain become a gift that she takes to Naomi, thereby resolving allegorically, the harsh judgment inflicted upon Moab and introducing the possibility of inter-cultural hospitality.

Breadscape: *Rut*, 'Ivrut, *Hit'abrut*

Ruth's satiation is a compelling textual resolution to the trauma of hunger. The economical precision of eating one's fill, of having enough, acknowledges mind, body, and soul, making Boaz's bread into the ultimate signifier of nourishment. Here we encounter the second kind of *tikkun* (repair) through *lechem* (bread) and its eating. Boaz's bread is the metabread of culture; its role within the narrative symbolically addresses the deep abyss of mythological scarcity.

Here we can recall Sarai's desire to become a mother through Hagar in Genesis, and her words, "*'ulai 'ibaneh mi-menah*" ("perhaps I will be built through her"), or "perhaps I will be sonned (mothered) through her" (Genesis 16: 2). Whereas Hagar's gaze belittles her, sabotaging the possibility of being born through Sarai's hunger for a son, *The Book of Ruth* reintroduces this possibility, proving that such a construction of motherhood is possible, albeit with a twist. Truly, other women have used slave-girls to conceive, as in the case of Rivka and Bilhah in Genesis 30: 3, yet the quintessentially successful instance of such becoming is provided here, telling how Naomi, the mother-in-law (although not Boaz's mother), has "been built" and becomes a mother through Ruth, so much so that once the neighboring women acknowledge the grand redemptive act of Ruth's son, they end up even attributing the son to Naomi. "Naomi took the child, and held it to her bosom. She became its foster mother. And the women neighbors gave him a name, saying, "A son is born to Naomi!" They named him Obed (Ruth 4: 16–17). The same women who could not recognize Naomi after ten years in exile ("Is that Naomi?" [Ruth 1: 19]), are now not only naming her son; they re-inscribe Naomi as the matriarch of Judean-Moabite history, alluding to the possibility of the "shared" son—a perfect act of gift exchange—through which a son, a name, and a narrative are being restored. Ruth does that which Hagar is unable; she secures her fertility and her lineage and allows Naomi to be built through her, making this act emblematic within the narrative of her inclusion.

For women, the promise/possibility of undergoing change, of passing and transforming to 'Ivri (Hebrew) in the Abrahamic sense is not only through the act of moving and passing—*la'avor* (in the active verb)—from one place to another, but through *hit'abrut* ("conception", from the same root, in the reflexive). *Hit'abrut*, the Bible tells us, is the process through which a woman becomes 'Ivrit. Ruth's otherness helps to articulate more clearly this process of becoming. In other words, contemplating belonging from her excluded, hungry place makes us better understand how belonging has turned into a dynamic process of continual growth ("being built") and change. Women's becoming, against the odds of scarcity, hunger and death, promises the return to story and history in the full biblical sense.

My main question when moving from the biblical text to the modern Israeli "Ruth" concerns the depiction of the "Zionist bread", and its appropriation within the trauma of Jewish hunger and exile. It is possible that *tikkun* through *lechem* is what Agnon intended in his short story, "*Pat Shlemah*" (Whole, perfect bread"), a bread of the same wholesome quality as that of Boaz. Agnon's narrator desires, as he describes early on, "*ma'achal metukan*" (Agnon, 143), which is both a prepared dish, from *le-hatkin* (prepare, fix, install), and at the same time from *le-taken*, and *tikkun* (to repair, correct).[23] "*Pat Shlemah*", the intended meal, hovers between its minimalist bread, *pat* (a slice of bread), and a meal. Alas, the bread/meal for which the narrator awaits in his long, surreal night in the restaurant in Jerusalem, never arrives. He continues to wait and imagine it over the course of a long night, lonely, hungry, isolated from his family, and lost in his mind. Agnon's *Pat Shlemah* can perhaps explain the depth of meaning of the pre-Auschwitz Zionist desire for the metabread as both the emblematic condition of becoming in the context of conversion, and, for women, the juxtaposition of one that will further legitimize the discourse of maternity and the nationalization of motherhood within the new discourse (Berkovitch 1997; Kahn 2000; Rosenberg-Friedman 2008; Shiffman 2013).

'*Ivrut*, as mentioned in my introduction, is a gigantic enterprise of feeding that is anxiously obsessed with never leaving the reader hungry. Here '*Ivrut* is the mechanism of converting and transforming the newcomer Ruth in to her kin, and into the Jewish lineage. The Breadscape associated with her, Naomi, and Boaz is therefore full of potentialities for further appropriation, indeed it so readily responds to textual promises, the historical trauma of hunger, and the Zionist national ethos of plentitude. Contemporary Zionist reading has transformed the story of Ruth and her bread into the Zionist bread, building on it the metabread of Israeli modernity. At its core, '*ivrut*, as an ideological mechanism of appropriation, is presented as a national feeding process that deploys language, nation, territory, and citizenship. Ruth's satiation is an expression of the mythological value of the bread, once emerging from the land. '*Ivrut* is built on the premise that Israel is a Jewish state for Jews. The nationalization of *Ruth* has contributed to the construction of the Israeli family and its heteronormativity around female reproduction and its political demographic role in motherhood. Motherhood is a national concern, and women's citizenship is occasioned on playing an active role in resolving "the demographic threat" (Berkovitch 2001, 242–243). It is conditioned on her ability to participate in the discourse of motherhood as it is tied to being Jewish and to successfully contribute to Jewish cohesiveness while excluding other minorities from its core. She must both adopt and give birth to Judaism.

The Author's Feast: From Shai Agnon's "Pat Shlemah" to Appetizers

> One does not tell the story of the sacrifice in the usual way of storytelling.
> Baruch Kurzweil, "The Fire and the Wood"[24]

> The unarticulated became comparable.
> Theodor Adorno, *Critical Models*[25]

The Fire and the Wood, by Shmuel Yosef Agnon, the Nobel laureate writer (1887–1970), was the last work that was published during his lifetime (1998 [1962]). It is mostly a collection of Hasidic tales, as well as a semi-fictional account of Agnon's family history, and other more personal stories. The first half of these are stories he has transcribed that were told to him over the course of his life. Putting to text the oral tradition of his antecedents, Agnon commemorates the narratives as if to lay them to rest.

In the epilogue titled, "an Apology" Agnon confesses to the reader: "As a matter of fact, I hesitated at first to publish an unfinished book. It is as if I were to invite guests to a *se'udah* (banquet or feast) and then served nothing but appetizers" (Agnon 1998 [1962], 272). Certainly, Agnon developed a reputation for fastidiousness, often revising his texts such that several published versions were concurrently circulating, ("Agunot", "Forsaken Wives", for example, was published in four different versions), but his issuing of an apology is a significant gesture that merits close attention. Overall, in this volume, Agnon serves the reader 269 pages of stories, many of which deal, to varying degrees, with the *Akedah* (The Binding of Isaac).

Shortly thereafter, Baruch Kurzweil (1907–1972), a prominent literary critic, reinforces this conflation of food and text. Kurzweil adds, "after Auschwitz, it is impossible for the author to invite guests to a meal" (Kurzweil 1970, 322–323).[26] He reads from within the Agnonian oeuvre and from the deeply felt historical moment of "*The Modern Akedah*" (Ibid. 112). The total destruction of the Jews, he writes, a collapse of knowledge and consciousness, also "destroyed the foundation of the Agnonian epics" (313), eradicating the possibility of reading his (or any) text as a meta-historical or timeless synecdoche of human experience. Arguably the foremost epic, at the cathexis of Jewish life, is the story of The Binding of Isaac by Abraham in Genesis 22. Kurzweil's new observation is that one has to read otherwise. But what does it mean to read otherwise, especially with regards to the story of The Binding? And if we stay with food, what about the scarcity of nourishment?

The fact that Kurzweil cites Adorno's assertion from 1949 as an epigraph in the original German shows that for him, the parallels between the poem and meal are straightforward. He thus reframes Agnon's apology with Theodor Adorno's assertion that to write a poem after Auschwitz is "barbaric". Kurzweil's intervention is not to instruct the reader in how to read Adorno, but rather to reintroduce Agnon's flaw as "a pact of authenticity", bringing Adorno closer to the Hebrew subject and linking the story of The Binding with Auschwitz. For the Hebrew author, always a cook, the full meal as we understand it is no longer possible. Kurzweil's somber paradigm shift is therefore an ethical one, engaged with the provision and consumption of food and texts: their material economy and their immanent impoverishment.

Indeed, Kurzweil's position points to a radical moment in the development of literature through the trope of feeding. But even before Auschwitz we encounter attempts to articulate a totalizing thesis of food and its limits unique to the literature. Shmuel Moshe Melamed (1885–1938), an American socialist writer and philosopher, asserts, "Hebrew literature speaks in a language of hunger", (Melamed 1945, 562). Melamed engages in writing a linear history of Jewish/Hebrew hunger from the Bible to his present—the reality of Eastern-European Jewish life at the beginning of the twentieth century, "from Egypt to Kabziel, from *Genesis* to Masa Nemirov…" (Ibid). "The history of mankind begins with the verse, "By the sweat of thy brow shalt thou eat bread". This is his fate in life…The Rabbis viewed life through the prism of hunger". As a mode of storytelling, depicted by Hebrew texts, he highlights three moments: "Egypt" and the story of *Exodus*; "Kabziel" the fictive satirical shtetl of *kabzanim*, beggars, of Mendele Mocher Sforim; and "Masa Nemirov", the Ukranian town of Nemyriv, the site of a Cossack massacre of Jews in 1648, and the namesake of Hayim Nahman Bialik's renowned poem that responded to the 1903 Kishinev pogrom and was later renamed "*Be-ir Ha-haregah*", the City of Slaughter [1904].[27] Melamed's main concern with these allusions is to make cultural distinctions between the Jewish and Christian raison d'etre as he differentiates the Jewish passion of hunger from the Christian passion of love. He concludes that the ultimate "mother question" or "question of all questions" in Hebrew literature is "*What, then, do we eat?*"[28]—a biblical expression that conveys an immediate concern for the sustenance of food and feeding (*parnasah*). Melamed even goes so far as to unleash his passion in his argument:

… Hunger, hunger, hunger—that is the central motive. …Hunger gives birth to moral… The theme of hunger in the scriptures was used as the foundation for our literature, in every generation and especially during the diaspora. As long as we are a wandering people, going from one country to another, we will never stop singing the song of Kabziel and the shtetl of hunger…. Hebrew literature speaks in a language of hunger.

(Melamed 1945, 556–562)

Indeed, exile, displacement and homelessness have all articulated conditions of hunger in the Jewish Diaspora. The end of the First World War precipitated a massive wave of immigrants from Eastern Europe to the Americas, enticed by the prospect of financial growth and social security. In the East, by 1917, emergent Zionism and especially the Balfour Declaration mandated the establishment of a national home for the Jewish People in Palestine, foregrounding the conjoined experiences of migrancy and dispossession to Jewish literature of the time. Hebrew writers of the late enlightenment (the *Haskala*) and the beginning of the twentieth century conveyed this condition in terms of physical poverty, orphanhood, and widowhood. The "Song of Kabziel", alludes to the dire lamentations of a crumbling vernacular reality that sustains Jewish life. In fact, the emphasis on the creation of the "new Jew", constructed in opposition to the "old diaspora Jew", has been articulated as the native, socialist and secular Israeli protocol: speaking fluent native modern Hebrew and undergoing a physical process of healing and recuperation along Max Nordau's terms of muscular Judaism. A strong, healthy body was a critical condition to this transformative enterprise. It was predicated on ending the long history of hunger.

It is amidst this historical process of signification around (mal)nutrition that Yosef Haim Brenner's first short story "Pat Lechem" ("A Loaf of Bread", 1990), should be understood. Indeed, the story underscores this discursive predicament in literary terms. It tests the limits of poverty on a deteriorating scale that ends gravely. It tells us that Reb Hayim Podovalend's reality is of abject poverty, once a successful wine cellar employee, he has pawned all his belongings and now "all is enshrouded in hunger" (1990, 6). Brenner does not skirt around the details of hunger and despair, as Reb Haim is at the end of his rope. His wife is sick on her deathbed, his daughter is begging for a piece of bread, and the house is freezing in the dark of night and during a snowstorm. He goes out to the Jewish house of learning with the hope of pawning his prayer shawl and tefillin. Unable to control himself, and in a hazy state of mind, when he sees the half loaf of fresh bread on the window, he cannot help but steal it.

The utter shame, mortification, and distress that such a theft entails—and Brenner again is at his best in this description—undermine the very moral foundations of Jewish existence. Hunger, within Brenner's scant aesthetics, violently inflicts chaos on mind and body; in its extremity it leads to the collapse of all moral codes. Brenner's stolen loaf of bread, at the intersection of poverty, disease and anti-semitic pogroms, is the evidence for the hopeless deterioration of any Jewish consciousness; the bread falls on the wet, filthy mud, and with the night enveloped in death (*laila takhrichim*), "howling with unrestricted heartbreak", Reb Hayim begs "what is the limit of mercy?" The story ends with a gush of rain, and an outburst, as "they all cried ... a very big wail of despair" (Ibid. 10).

Historically, it is precisely this starving outcry of the diaspora to which the Zionist discourse responded. Insofar as the twentieth-century Israeli discourse of Hebrew modernity made Jewish textuality into an ever-dynamic and productive site of legitimacy, it has been articulated in terms of provision; the land is never separated from the Book and its language, Hebrew; nor, are the granaries fully distinct from the bookshelves on which the Book rests. Each occasion the existence of the other, affirming the rabbinic assertion that "without flour there is no Torah; and without Torah there is no flour" (Avot 3:21).[29] This provision is articulated as we see, not only symbolically, reaffirming the omnipresent animated entity of language in general, but also materially, engaging directly in the cognized, physical level of specific semantics that contains the cultural pantry of food, especially bread and its variants.

This understanding of hunger articulates a model in which we can draw connections from the bread of Brenner and the hunger of Kabziel, with the appetizers and impossible meal that Agnon describes. In doing so, it sets up an internal critique of Zionism, returning to biblical narratives, including the Binding, and reading them "otherwise", as Kurzweil suggests, while continuing to juxtapose food and reading and bread and narratives in contemporary culture. The concept of this immense discursive space is what I call the "Breadscape". The Israeli Breadscape is a unique, dynamic site of inquiry that draws on a synthesis of meaning that embodies texts as food, and that allegorizes the book (and God) within a secular framework of literary provision. Within mythologies of hunger and satiation, Breadscape conceptualizes their signification and their multiple constitutional manifestations through language, objects, symbols and images. Yet, these mythologies do not stop at the mouth; they open multiple sites of demanding cultural cavities, a broad spectrum of scarcities and desires for land and offspring, belonging and possession. The Israeli Breadscape, this work shows, is a multilayered site; both real and imagined, it covers a huge cultural space full of social, ecological, religious, and national properties and potentialities, and is coded with desires, hopes, anxieties, crises and pathologies. The Breadscape relies on a specific territory, that grapples with the two biblical formulations of "a land flowing with milk and honey" and "a land that devours its people".

The way that the Book of Ruth was adopted in modern secular ceremonies demonstrates that the revelatory dimension of harvesting also helped to reinforce the canonic place of the book in Israeli popular culture beyond its religious reception. On a specially decorated stage, dressed in white, with their heads crowned in leafy wreaths, kibbutzniks perform a ceremony to celebrate the fertility of the land and their arrival in their "native" place. They reenact the work of the reapers, repossessing the bountiful fields and their splendor. The symbolic interpretation of local geographies in the context of these generative themes helps to strengthen the ties between Zionism and the return to the Jewish homeland as the ultimate act of redemption (Zerubavel 1995, 217–218; Gurevitch 1997; Hirschfeld 2002).[30]

The numerous Midrash commentaries, sermons, and research on *The Book of Ruth* in the past two decades evince not only the adaptability of the narrative within a feminist, liberal context, but also its appropriation by religious leaders (including Christians) and community educators who highlight its didactic lessons of punishment and reward, love and grace. The density of the entire narrative, like a grain or seed, motivates poetic solutions to crises in the same way that Bethlehem, the House of Bread, transforms a literal granary into an ideological metaphor of the loving or benevolent body and its reproduction. More in *The Book of Ruth* than elsewhere in the Bible, a grain of wheat is a seed of prophecy in the stories told of land and nation.

Examining *The Book of Ruth* on an internal historical continuum that begins with Sodom and its destruction is critical to the understanding of the cultural paradigm of hunger and satiation within not only the Bible, but, perhaps more significantly, in the present reality of Israeli culture.

Scavengers: Separation, Exile, and Onions

In this section, I introduce works by three contemporary Israelis: *A Chronicle of Separation: On Deconstruction's Disillusioned Love* (2000), by Michal Ben-Naftali (1963–), whose work on Lot I discussed earlier; the film *Golem, the Spirit of Exile* (1992), directed by Amos Gitai (1950–); and the photograph *Ruth and Naomi – Gleaners* (2006), by Adi Nes (1966–). These works approach *The Book of Ruth* from the perspective of contemporary economies and geopolitical landscapes, insisting that issues of migration, hunger and trauma are transitional situations that despite all their mythological force, provide very little resolution: the metabread in Boaz's golden field will be reduced to onion on the dry floor of the market, and the Creolized diversified postmodern production of Gitai will take Ruth and Naomi on a conceptual journey from which they never arrive. As such, they manage to work against the hegemonic, centralized, and heroic spirit of the Zionist reading. The third part of the chapter discusses the politics of naming, "Yehuda" and "Ruth" through the poetry of Yehuda, constituting another layer in the deployment of hunger within Jewish genealogy: a thesis about the recycled, used, and secondhand aspect of Hebrew intertextuality.

For Michal Ben Naftali the story of Ruth, her own subjective narratives, and the trajectory of deconstruction as a method of textual reading and intervention are inseparable, and she writes about them through the prism of food and eating disorders especially of anorexia and bulimia. At their core, as she explains, the "profile of deconstruction" is similar to that of a woman.

[A] contrasting profile of an ambivalent woman, self-centered, while distant from herself, adopting with abandon the symbolic order, and yet, closed and detached almost, at times, to the point of psychosis; she is desperately dependent on her mother, on mothers, but repudiates and prevents this instinctual connection, preventing it from flourishing.

(Ben-Naftali 2000, 133)

Ben-Naftali sets an analogy between the main motive of bodily practices and the inner drive of deconstruction as they both seek desperately and ceaselessly to reach or test a limit and to get to the core of that which is unattainable.

Amos Gitai's work on biblical narratives intends to revamp the ambiguity of the sanctified, mythical narratives, highlighting the everyday dimension of the great epics and myths, and creating a modern myth within heterogeneous, transnational frameworks of representation. Gitai's film *Golem, the Spirit of Exile* (1992) is the third in a trilogy on exile and utopia, after *Esther* (1986), and *Berlin-Jerusalem* (1989). Filmed in France, it approaches the narrative of *Ruth* as a story about migration, displacement, and colonization.

For Gitai, the challenge is how to take mythological narratives such as *The Book of Ruth* and negotiate between their grand, epic value and their contemporary relevancy. The Parisian urban landscapes of rusty cranes expand the cinematic language, introducing a whole global scope to the phenomenon of exile and foreignness that further diversifies the allegorical possibilities of the narrative beyond Jewish, Hebrew, and biblical cultures. In fact, Gitai seeks to narrate the missing, ignored "process of transition" (Levin 1991, 103) in the biblical voyage of Ruth and Naomi, turning it into a conceptual, dynamic, never-ending journey of coming home. Gitai's use of a multiracial and multicultural cast contributes to the climate of transnationalism: Boaz is played by Sotigui Kouyaté, 1936–2010, a native of Bamako, Mali; Orpah by the French actress, Fabienne Babe; Naomi by the Israeli Ophrah Shemesh, a nonactress; and Ruth by the French Mireille Perrier.

Adi Nes whose work "Abraham and Isaac" I discuss in Chapter 1, has devoted two artworks to *The Book of Ruth* in his *Bible Series*, one of them being *Ruth and Naomi - Gleaners* (2006), where he redefines the biblical landscape of gleaning and gathering. The work is inspired by Jean-François Millet's oil painting, *Des Glaneuses* (The Gleaners) of 1857. Nes's focus on the gleaners is a dark commentary on the current socio-political economy, where the biblical fields of golden grain are replaced as dry land, at the closing of the produce market. In comparison to the biblical narrative, Nes further excludes the women from any community, including Boaz's. In their solitude, in the deserted market, late in the day, both Ruth and Naomi appear grief- and poverty-stricken. If

Figure 3.1 Adi Nes's Ruth and Naomi.[a]

a Modified title "Untitled (Ruth and Naomi Gleaning), 2006" c-print © Adi Nes. Courtesy of the artist and Jack Shainman Gallery, New York.

they ever were to make it to any home, they would remain, nonetheless, homeless. In Israeli society these gleaners can refer to the poorest Jews, Arabs, and foreigners, although the ethnic identity of the women is not obvious (Figure 3.1).

Nes's aesthetic of hunger and scarcity is revealing; it lingers on arid, bare land and bad economy; it goes beyond any romantic hunger of the Bible, shifting unambiguously from its promising fields of golden barley to the dry soil of the market ground. The ground is littered with trashy, empty white plastic bags, torn boxes, empty produce cartons of white yellowish rotting fruits, and the scattered onions. I will return to the onions.

In cheap sandals, wearing a few layers of earth-colored summery clothes, they bend at the waist. The bodily gesture obeys the reality of the scattered food. It accompanies the engaged, observing bodies of the gatherers, adding to their generally lowly posture and appearance. The box and the hands replace the folded skirts in which Millet's women gather barley. Many have commented on the silence of his gleaners. It speaks through the body, where the long gleaning hand is the agent of salvaging.

In the critical economy of body and mind, the onion is Nes's ultimate signifier of poverty. As the Arabic proverb, commonly used by Israelis, tells us, *"yom asal, yom basal"* ("a day of honey [is followed by] a day of onion") reminding us of the temporality of fortune and adversity, as sweetness and tears rule the cycle of life.[31] Together with bread, onion forms a basic meal for the poorest peasants. In Nes's dictionary of poverty, the onion replaces any possible "bread" of poverty. Within the discourse of hunger, the field of Bethlehem (literally "the House of Bread") has drawn the potential horizons of growth and harvest in all aspects. The super food that is bread has become part of the ontology of the fields and the land, of law and ritual; it has constituted a cultural metaphoric potentiality of well-being and satiation, an allegory of all food and nourishment.[32] Nes subverts the hierarchy of poverty food, placing the onion as the symbol of ultimate and utter scarcity. It replaces not only the metabread of *The Book of Ruth*, the utopian, desired bread of Brenner and Agnon, but also the very intimation of provision on Alterman's "Silver Platter" of the sacrificed body of nation, along with the milk and honey and sacrificial knife, and all other appetizers and gifts in the Jewish-Israeli imagination. Nes does not seek to feed his reader, or to "saturate" further symbols and images; on the contrary, he strips meaning and layers of feeding as a critique of the mythological density of culture. What is more, the bare environment of the market evacuates any sense of love, grace, and maternal potential.

Against the attempts to deny the magnitude of poverty and hunger in Israeli culture, Nes launches a pessimistic commentary on the extent and depth of the destitution of both the women and the land, as he strips the bread of its utopian value, tying it to new intertexts that will reflect its reality of consumption. Far from the land flowing with the seeds of bread, men, stories, and histories, a land scattered with onions articulates a "tearful" critique of the land and its prospective feeding. To glean for onions is to be reminded of the aridity of the soil, a testimony of an unrealized dream, and as Nes concludes in Kogan's interview, a dire depiction of "the end of the world in my eyes" (Kogan, Ibid.)

The Knowledge of Emptiness

Yehuda Amichai presents us with a key poetic interpretation of the biblical Story of Ruth in his series of poems, "The Bible and You, the Bible and You, and Other Midrashim". Amichai grounds the historical narrative of the Bible in the critical dialectic of knowing and knowledge, as if asking, what is the core of this knowledge that was needed to mobilize narrative and history? Critical, though, is the fact that he represents both Ruth the Moabite and Naomi through a totality of knowledge: "Ruth ... *Yad'ah ha-kol*" (Ibid. 34) and "Naomi... *Yad'ah ha-kol*"[33] (Ibid. 35): [both women] were all-knowing. And to know all is, for Amichai, to take an absolute epistemological position; I will show how Amichai, Ruth, and Naomi's *epistēmē* relies on a specific logic of return and reproduction pertaining to nature, the land, kinship and the female body. "*Yado ba-kol*, his hand is in all (in everything and everywhere," lyrically echoes "*yad'ah ha-kol*", (she) knew everything, suggesting the linguistic and semantic proximity between *yad* and *yada*,' hand and knowledge, back in Chapter 2, when "knowing" is transmitted through touch. As important, the construction of knowledge as is graspable, sexual congress as an act of "knowing". Here Amichai deepens the ethos of Zionist reading that is based on the prophetic value of the word: a drive to transform the hollow space of emptiness into a melodic space of reproduction.

> Ruth the Moabite knew all about wheat and wheat fields,
> about eyes big with love
> and golden stubble after the harvest.
> And Naomi, who said, I went out full
> And the Lord hath brought me home again empty –
> she knew all about the physics of the empty and the full,
> About her sons who died, about the stifled cry
> of a womb emptying like an accordion
> which makes music out of the full and the empty.
> (Amichai, trans. Bloch and Kronfeld 2000, 23)[34]

The concept of the total (*ha-kol*) is familiar to us from the story of Ishmael and the *kolbo*. And it is exactly the potential dialectical meaning between *kalah* and *kol*, or between the inherent totality of the act of annihilation and its sweeping breadth, that we encountered again in *The Book of Ruth*. It takes us back to the first verses of *The Book of Ruth* (*Ruth* 1:2), where we are introduced to Naomi's sons, Machlon and Kilyon, whose very names condition their short life spans (see also Bal 1988a). The name "Machlon" derives from either or both *halah*, sick, or *machah*, to wipe. The name "Kilyon" derives from the root *kalah*, "to annihilate or consume", exposing the inherent connection of the verb to the noun *(kol)* which means all, whole, each and every, similar to the *kol-bo* (all in it).

From Naomi and Ruth's perspectives, this totality of knowledge is respectively an *a priori* wisdom of their experience of death, destruction, and hunger on the one hand, and life, restoration, and satiation on the other. Their omniscience is underscored by Amichai's use of the verb *ya'da*, "to know", which effectively opens a discursive space that encompasses mental, sexual and emotional knowledge. For Ruth, it is knowledge of wheat and love that encapsulates the entirety of her sensual and intellectual experience. It is a knowledge that will culminate in her seduction of Boaz, in her magical satiation (*va-tisba'*), and in her motherhood. For Naomi, it is embodied knowledge of the extremes of life and death and the possibility of change that she sees in them. Amichai's accordion is their Breadscape. But Amichai does not seek to romanticize the biblical Ruth and Naomi. Rather, he invokes their lucidity and mettle in the face of enduring trauma, revealing a sheer void at the heart of displaced identity, which belies the possibility of integrated, embodied knowledge and change.[35] To the extent that Naomi's body is a metaphor for Israeli history and its Zionist narrative, it is easy to accept that its music, the historical narrative, is composed of similarly stifled cries and barren wombs.

Amichai articulates this knowledge as the position of radical difference: a point of change and narrative departure. This knowledge of life in its fullness sets a model of imagined potential and real possibility. The knowledge of the wheat, the land, the gift, the food and feeding, of sharing and having enough, is so whole and perfect that it can generate a paradigmatic change, transitioning one from life in its utter doomed emptiness, naked, and bare condition, to its fullness. Judea and its city, *Bet Lehem* are now stacked with new meaning, drawing the contours of the Breadscape closer to the mouth. Insofar as this conception is both of body and knowledge, it is the seed of the wheat/barley that precedes, and teaches, the seed/sperm of Boaz.

Amichai expands the allegorical possibilities of empty and full as they appear in *The Book of Ruth* in relation to Naomi's body and its reproductive saga. For the story of her womb, a deep metonym of body and life, is a unique story of cries and grief within the total destruction of the female body. Naomi's knowledge of full and empty, of empty and full, becomes a singular conversion of the alternately full and empty body into knowledge: a paradigmatic template for genealogical change. In Amichai's poetic landscape, her womb is like the accordion: a musical box with historical reverberations. On the road these possibilities are strictly illogical and unfathomable: as Naomi makes clear to Ruth and Orpah, she can never bear more sons to turn them again into her daughters-in-law, recognizing the threat to her genealogy. Later, she sends Ruth to Boaz's fields. Amichai shows that in a deep metaphysical shift, Naomi is able to a grasp new physics of emptiness and fullness, and is able to create "music" out of their oscillation.[36]

Indeed, the music of inclusion is central to the Zionist project, in particular the collective tradition of sing-alongs, so unique to Israeli culture and so critical in the emergence of the vocal subject of textuality. Through years of war and endless national struggle, Israelis have developed a wide repertoire of popular songs (*Zemer* or *Pizmonim*), which had a primary role in the formative years of the pioneers' pre-statehood culture. Gradually it became the musical canon that socialized the individual into the collective, defining one's place and potential for belonging. By and large, these songs reinforce and even reproduce the master-narrative. They constitute a rich and extensive layer of public discourse, affectively shaping and crystallizing cultural imagination and aspirations. Music, especially communal singing, was perhaps one of the most effective instruments for homogenizing immigrants due to its highly seductive promise to assimilate each individual into the elitist, canonic "internal code" of Sabra culture (Almog 1997, 366; Reshef 2004). And as Batya Roded and Oren Yiftachel further emphasize, this music had a major role in "making Jewish" both its singers and Zionism as a whole, to the extent of excluding and making invisible Palestinians and other Others (Yiftachel and Roded 2003).

Hebrew songs scripted Israelis' approach to every aspect of everyday life, supplying standards and models for emotions and actions in practices pertaining to feeling pain, intimacy, love, heroism, and death. Through singing one could mourn the dead, pray, fall in love, walk the land, or affirm one's commitment to both the language and the nation. The collectivizing speech acts not only reinforced the idea of the melting pot and *kibbutz galuyot*, the ingathering of traditions, but also promised the touch of the pantheistic magical symbolism of the sung reality. Along with other collective practices such as the Israeli Sabra folk dancing, or the *hora*, communal singing provided illusory membership amidst ideological exaltation. Hebrew popular songs and the ritual of singing provided outlets for pathos and ecstasy. They codified a seamless hierarchical system of accent, class, gender, ethnicity, and official Zionist history, brimming with patriotism and heroism. Ultimately, it reasserted an ideological scale of national attachment, belonging, and collectivity, highlighting the selective mechanism of its memory. Only recently have scholars begun to explore in depth the immense cultural capital of these songs, and how they have fashioned Israel into a romantic and nostalgic country whose citizens still sing together to the homeland around campfires and in large public concert halls, often accompanied by projected slides of the lyrics. Such scholarship focuses on the role of music in the construction of subjectivity, motivation in collectivizing society in the army, or homogenization of immigrant cultures (Almog 1997, 362–368; Hirschfeld 2002, 1054–1058).

Amichai's ambivalence towards the singing tradition appears in many of his earlier poems, and the lines from such Israeli songs are interwoven in his poetry as an additional intertextual conversation. In general, he mocks this tradition, suggesting that this national ritual promotes a false togetherness, symptomatically keeping the singers in a collective amnesia. Here, he juxtaposes Naomi's womb and body with the accordion, a musical instrument that often led these songs. Like biblical narratives, and personal names, they have become fetishistic objects of identification. Together, they are recycled fragments of an ideological narrative that blurs the distinctions between signifier and signified, between the singing "I" and the collective "we", or the songs and the ones who sings them.[37]

Amichai's critical stance on Hebrew songs is more strongly articulated in his poem, "'*Im Mizvadah Be-yadi Be-'eretz Zarah*", "With a Suitcase in My Hand in a Foreign Land":

> I remember my father's prophecy, "When you grow up,
> you'll be able to travel alone," and I fulfill it.
> I remember, in my childhood in a foreign land
> my mother and I were knocked down by a bicycle.
> Since then, I've grown up and learned to sing the proud song,
> "Tough we were knocked down, we were not dismayed," I
>   sang with them all, for I was them-alled, very them-alled,
>   with them all.
> And now I am alone in a foreign land. And what's happened to
>   them all?
> Some were dismayed, some were knocked down and got up,
>   and some remained fallen. My mother is dead. The
>   witnesses are gone.
> I remember only one wheel of the bike still spinning a little,
>   spinning freed from the hard earth.
>
> (Amichai in Alter 2015, 392)

Singing with everyone the "proud song", "if we were knocked down, we did not fear" results in a change that Amichai articulates through his invented verbal construct *kulamti*, or "I everyoned", which does not exist otherwise in Hebrew. Amichai's innovative language illustrates the homogenizing power of singing. *Kulamti*, in the first person and past tense, derives from the noun *kulam*, meaning all, whole, each and every one, or everybody, and recalls the root *kol* (all, entire, as in *kolbo*) and *kalah* (to wipe out or erase). *Kulamti* is phonetically close to the verb, *nikhlam*, and the noun *klimah*, from the same roots, which means being ashamed and humiliated, accentuates the discomfort of such immersion. However, in *kulamti*, Amichai conveys not only the total assimilation of the self in that homogenized collectivity, but the power of singing to assert a presencing voice, a ritual which is coded with intimate promise of becoming a "mouthful fellowship". The "proud song", the Zionist song of the movement, leaves no space for individuality. Now, feeling like his land is foreign, and with his suitcase full of memories and songs, he is able to account for the fact that *kulam*, the collective of everyone, has been ruptured; some got scared, or knocked down and got up, or are still down (a reference to the fallen).

In another poem, "*Ha-Yehudim*" ("The Jews"), Amichai conveys his representation of Yehuda (the name and the person) in a collective chorus of his people and culture. The poem ends with the similar ironic

tone, even when sacred, religious orality is at stake. Here Amichai returns to the religious *piyyut*, the traditional refrain, "There is no God
like our God" in the daily dawn prayer, (1989, 132–133).

> And what about God? We once sang
> "There is no God like our God" now we are singing
> "There is no God"
> But we are singing. We are still singing.

Whereas in "Names, Names, in Other Days and in Our Time", Amichai
blends the identities of the two Ruths and their names, his poems "The
Bible and You, the Bible and You, and Other Midrashim", present us
with an explicit poetic interpretation of the biblical Ruth.

The Book of Ruth is paradigmatic of the way in which Jewish history
has been construed, as it provided the very basis for its construction.
Israeli Jewish history and consciousness have been mobilized by a seemingly endless series of crises that bind together bodies and resources,
home and exile, scarcity and surplus, and death and survival. Amichai
rearranges all the used, recycled, second- (and third- and fourth-) hand
names and other objects that are stored in the warehouse of culture.
To the extent that these local and domesticated objects help us claim
ownership, they also permit us to rob and to colonize subjectivity as the
assumed object of culture.

Amichai writes about how he became one with everyone (*kulam'ti
im kulam*). Already the exiles of Babylon scripted their iconic collective return through their nostalgic tears, songs, harps, and memory
(Psalms 137), asking the question that occasioned the return, "How
shall we sing the LORD'S song in a foreign land?" (Ibid. 4). Singing
in Israel, in Hebrew, is an intensified textual act of return. It enables
through lyrics, melodies, the Hebrew language and its intertextual layers
and gushing sentiments, to relegate further old distances, heightening
the Zionist, Hebrew identity. When Israelis sing together, they always
re-turn a bit closer, always become; they are always more present.

The Armadillos, a group that sings comedic folk music, also invokes
the collectiveness but around the "speaking bread"; The comic song
of the Armadillos tells about encountering a loaf of bread, that reveals
to them: "We are all slightly bread / on the shelf of life / waiting for
someone to spread on us jam, jam, jam".[38] The opening lines of the
song state "*Ze shir 'al lekhem / lo shir 'alekhem*" "this is a song about
bread / not a song about you (pl.)", deemphasizing individual and collective subjectivity in favor of the national agricultural enterprise—
bread—that reduces its subjects to larder goods awaiting consumption
(devouring its people). Later the refrain shifts to "We are all slightly
pita", tying the narrative more closely to specifically Israeli modes of

production and consumption. The fetishistic quality of the song and its subject matter speak to a widespread cultural preoccupation with bread and its discourse.

Recycled, Used, and Secondhand Names

> Every time a person increases their good deeds, they earn themselves a new name. There are three names by which a person is called: one which their parents call them, one which people call them, and one which they earn for themselves. The last is the best one of all.
>
> Midrash Tanhuma, *Parashat Vayakhel* 1[39]

My work has shown that Ruth's story is a generative story; it provides her with metabread, a resource that optimistically transforms the consciousness of trauma and hunger into a sustainable site of impregnation. *Ibaneh*, the desire to be built or to become, works not only on the level of seeding fields and bread, not only as a sight of impregnation of male and female bodies, but in the very construction of narratives. We will find it resurfacing in national narratives of names, poems, and songs. This works on a textual level, but to what extent is it realizable in real life? How does *Ruth* help a reader who is him- or herself a survivor of insidious trauma?

Proper nouns have been theorized in the social sciences as cultural artifacts. In *The Book of Ruth*, however, proper nouns are a source of material substance. The naming of Obed is a community event; the women name him in an act that expands the collective gaze of the community, making clear that the gift of the child is inextricable from the gift of naming in a moment of exchange between outsiders and insiders, the newcomers and oldtimers. Names are attached to new life and the trajectory of their meanings. Like the bread, the name forms a metalanguage of provision that eventually manifests as substance. It might explain that "name" in Hebrew, *shem*, carries the spark of the divine; with the definite article (*hashem*), it is a reference to God, initially a euphemism that intended to circumvent the possibility of taking the name of God in vain. As a discursive event, a name not only speaks to the inherent force of the meaning of language and letters, of uttering, or of what is breathed in the name: it is packed with potentiality and intertextual force. We can think about Amichai's approach to names as a thesis about intertextuality and citationality.

Names in the Bible, as Mieke Bal writes, "have a specific meaning that integrates the character into its life, and that can also imprison it" (1988a, 73). They are iconic rather than symbolic. Names are themselves narratives, they "predict one's life" (Ibid.). Bal examines proper nouns in the construction of character and representational devices in

The Book of Ruth in the interest of elucidating the idea of chronology. The proper noun and its narrative function both demonstrate that analogy can operate only within the concept of chronology and history. Names are emblematic of the dialectics of analogy and chronology; analogy is a biblical metatextuality. The narrative order articulates and models destiny (Ibid.).

Biblical names, as well as other historical Jewish names, reproduce narratives as they are read back into the long-animated genealogy of men and women, family relatives and historical heroes. They contextualize a massive grid of references that inform *a priori* one's psychological development and narrative of self. In their augmented representation they produce, interiorize, and intimate collective memory and cultural consciousness.

The problem of the tension between chronology and analogy is central in the contemporary relationship of Israelis to the Bible, and raises perennial questions about Israeli native identity and the wider philosophical question of historical change. Some of these questions include: to what extent does history repeat itself in the form of exodus or persecution? Or, how much significance should be attributed to historical developments and their chronology? Within the wider Israeli discourse, *The Book of Ruth*, like other biblical narratives, is an institutionalized metatext in which names are fragments of historical narratives and encode layers of evolving meaning and performance. My aim is to unpack the layers of such tightly sedimented meanings. In the narrative of return, names play an important role as they codify cultural and national norms and values, systematically articulating a broad, horizontal system of identitarian belonging. The system of names celebrates the tradition and its selected heroes even if at times the person behind the name is not a subject for celebration or mimicry (Zerubavel 1995, 19). Overall, such a system of naming weaves a tight, metonymic net of historical, dialogic relationships between kinships, genealogies, places and events.

Here I refer again to Amichai's poetry. As I mentioned in the previous chapter, more than in his other work, Amichai articulates most clearly in his last collection *Open Closed Open* (1998) his philosophical thesis and poetics about life as a Jew in Israel at the turn of the second millennium. In this section, I focus more closely on his approach to names, including his own name, Yehuda, and names like Ruth, as they embody his critical discussion of selfhood and otherness both in a personal, autobiographical sense, and in a collective Jewish sense. The role of the Bible in this project is irrefutably enormous.

Deconstructing historical names and identities means both to learn them as much as to unlearn their fixity and certainties (English 2003). Language (including poetry) affords the possibility of describing subjectivity through one's multiple experiences. In Amichai's biblical context, identity comprises an already established cultural convention, such as naming practice, that is externally imposed. Amichai attempts to destabilize the frozen identity of his name through the multiple poetic names that he invokes. His first and last names are culturally loaded. In addition to Yehuda, to which I turn below, his last name that he chose, means *'ami chai* (my nation or my people are alive), an expression that builds on the symbol of *chai* as an icon of eternal Jewish existence.

Amichai teases out the semiotic overtones of Hebrew names, including his own and that of Ruth. The name *Yehuda*, for example, juxtaposes place of origin with acquired identity; the personal name alludes to the ancient region of Yehuda/Judea, where the tribe of Judah that descended from one of Jacob's twelve sons dwelled. But looking back on the name, Yehuda is also root of the adjective *Yehudi*, Judean, an Israelite, and later comes to mean a Jew, Jewish, or Judaic (*Yehudim*, in plural). As a personal name, "Yehuda" makes it impossible to determine the boundaries between private and collective identity. The unbearable existential weight of such a name in Jewish hermeneutics and epistemology is evident in the enormous space that it occupies between the personal and the national, the ethnic and the religious, leaving little room to differentiate between the fictive and the real, the personal and the allegorical. The inevitable question is one that Yehuda Amichai introduces: himself or his name? What in his name "belongs" to him? What is in the sound and rhythm of such a name and what is at its core? In the following poems (the first three of a series of sixteen), Amichai cunningly deploys the wide cultural space that the name, its morphemes (*ye – hu – da*), and the nouns that rhyme with it (e.g. *tehuda*, meaning resonance and reverberation), hold:

1

My name is Yehuda. The stress on the *hu*,[40]
Yehu, yoo-hoo – a mother's voice calling her little boy in
     from play,
who who, a voice that crieth from the wilderness, who who,
A voice that crieth unto the wilderness. A surprising *yoo*
     and a surprised *hoo*,
A long-drawn-out who of the lovers of my life.

My name is Yehuda, the stress on the *da*,
Yehuda like "thank you" in Hebrew, *todah*, a Yehudean pride,
relic of the heroics of Judah the Maccabee,
Yehuda like a resounding oud – a dull echo
like a string wrapped around a pack of letters,
or a sharp echo like an elastic band snapping
at a woman's waist. *Da da*, no Yehu, no Yahweh,

but a daring plunge with a wide-open parachute
    into a wedding,
down through the atmospheric layers of my life.

2
My name is Yehuda, but those who love me call me Yuda
As old Jews used to be called, like Grandpa's brother.
Yuda. *Yoo-yoo* a child calls out from his hiding place,
Yoo of longing, *yoo-yoo* a ship's foghorn,
Yoo yowling or *hoo* hailing Hallelujah, *yoo-yah* Hallelujah.
Yoo from the depths and *hoo* from the heights,
You and who together in the chambers of love.

3
My name is Yehuda, and its taken
from the names warehouse. The organ is mine,
The erection is mine. But the sperm is from the sperm bank
That is infinite and returns through my children
to the big sea.
                    (Amichai, trans. Bloch and Kronfeld 2000, 127)[41]

As Amichai's elaboration on the name Yehuda reveals, meaning is inscribed in every sound and syllable. Meaning is situated and contextualized in a wide range of sounds, rhythms, and evocations from the
popular to the sacred: from children at play to the desert wind, from the
elastic band snapped against a woman's waist to a ship's lonely foghorn.
Amichai's ironic, subversive position becomes apparent with the realization that the poetic dispersion of his name Yehuda also obliterates
its meaning. His poetic deconstruction of names makes a maximal use
of the semiotic space of each name in a nonlinear, associative order. He
explores the phonetics and semantics of his name and the morphemes
thereof in terms of their etymological connections: *hed* (echo), *tehudah*
(resonance/reverberation), and *todah* (thanks). Names are also modified
by age, sex, and gender, and convey autobiographical stations, transitions and anecdotes. They both expose and hide bodies and identities.
In "Names Names, in Other Days and in Our Time", Amichai amplifies the space that resonates with his name, combining the root of the
name, *hodah* (to thank) with its very *hed* (echo) as an echo that is always
already there, reverberating on its essence and performance. Layers of
such representation are embedded in the depth of roots and meaning
in the signifying process of one's life. The names that one calls oneself, one's nicknames, the name that one's mother uses, the name that
lovers use, one's official name, and one's vernacular and legal names
comprise a life-historical commentary on naming practices as systems
of communication. Amichai describes Yehudah as a "dull echo", a name

that resonates throughout Jewish history. He animates the palimpsest of the name Yehudah: the biblical Yehudah, son of Jacob; Yehudah the Maccabee; Yehuda Halevi, the medieval poet; and Amichai's great uncle, Yuda, "as old Jews used to be called;" and all the other Yehudas, young and old, "down through the atmospheric layers of my life".[42]

In the same way, "hoo", "yoo-yoo", and "yoo-ha", are both plaintive and joyful sounds of travel in Amichai's desert, valley, or mountain, exposing the enigmatic name of God in between the syllables *ye* and *hu*, which reach a crescendo in "Hallelujah", thereby cunningly invoking the name of God that should not be mentioned explicitly. The intertextuality of names and their syllables forms a lingering thread of memory around a packet of letters from the past. Echoes and their memories, memories and their echoes—the dull and sharp sounds of the plucked string of history. The long memory-string coiled in Amichai's "warehouse of names" has become an essential aspect of Jewish ontology no different from the organ, penis, an erection, or sperm; it constitutes the core of phallocentric patriarchy. Through body and its potency, names tell their story of memory-making, stretching back to the covenant of Avraham, Yitzchak and Yaakov, and to the promise of infinity. In Amichai's grand scheme of all things Jewish, not just names, but sperm and bodies, are all metonyms of identity.

The question is not only to what extent Amichai embodies who he is named after, but how much he is who he names himself by expanding the imaginary semantics and semiotics around Yehudah. In part, his nominal playfulness is directed against the essentialization of names and identities, as evident in the problematics of bearing a singularly Jewish name like Yehudah. Obviously, names are reused and recycled. What kind of a naming system would we have if names were novel, always new, never reused? Names with their historical accumulation become a category, a classification of identity, and for Amichai, as I suggest, a rhetorical device in the service of ideology. The question is, can one fully inhabit a name such as Yehudah or Ruth without being colonized? Is it possible to feel "at home" with names without suffering the limitation and the burden of names' historical meaning, or as English suggests, without becoming claustrophobic? (2003).

In Jewish history, names and their morphemes become testimony of the fragments and ruins of different moments and locations as they are read back into a long genealogy of used objects. The renowned poet Zelda[43] tells us that "Every one of us has a Name" (1974) also the title of what has become a staple in memorial ceremonies and national Holocaust events and sites, such as Yad Vashem. Our names were given to us by every aspect of our existence, our God and parents, our geography, history, and blindness. It is our relationship to every aspect of our existence that names and identifies us. Here, somehow more critically, Amichai approaches names as a microcosm of Jewish history and identity.

But the critical position is a poignant one, for he argues that they are lonely fragments of Jewish gravestones. Alas, like the epitaphs on those grave-stones, names and parts of names evoke the untold, forgotten subtexts of their experience. Can they be compared to Agnon's appetizers? How?

In Hebrew, the verb *kara'* means both to read or recite and to call or summon, as in the second line of Amichai's poem, *'em kor't li-vnah*, "a mother is calling her son". Insofar as one can call or address their fellow Israelis, they doubly become members of a "readership". Linguistically, the idea of naming is transformed into a calling; a name, thus, interpolates its bearer into a historical, preordained Jewish subjectivity. Thus, names and naming are embodied by the authority of the covenant and the overdetermined nature of Jewish intertextual practices. Poetry too is read or recited in the same way that names designate the space of *kara'*.

As the title of Amichai's poem suggests, what he calls "recycled names", "used names" and "secondhand names" are the inherited stuff of culture. Their bearers can easily become imprisoned in the biographies of their names. Layers of Jewish history reveal that names hide biographies, un-folding a subject within a subject—a name within a name—concealing the blood and the wounds of the past, and transforming eulogy and lament, or, as in the case of the prayer "Hosh'ana", into a singing hymn (Amichai 1998, 132–133). In the historical travels of Jewish narrative— "names without people, people without names" (Ibid. 138)—mutilated and injured beings produce incomplete, distorted and confused nar-ratives within a framework that draws the lines between "speakable names" and "unspeakable" ones (Ibid. 139). Constructed through these fragments of collective diction, Amichai's inventive paradoxes lead to the discovery that God has long left the country, asserting that names play such a critical role in Zionist, secular culture by attempting to fill a cer-tain void created by God's departure. In another series of twenty-seven poems, "Gods Change, Prayers are here to Stay", he expands on how the dark emptiness of the "warehouse of names" overshadows the once promised people who, now, fifty years after Auschwitz, conclude that God has not yet decided who will be his chosen people (Amichai 1998, 1–19; Bloch and Kronfeld 2000, 37–48). As long as names testify to the ruins of Jewish culture, they themselves embody its ruins.

Ruth's Return as Otherness

> Ruth Ruth Ruth, the girl of my youth –
> Now she's a stand-in for Otherness.
> Otherness is death, death is Otherness.
>   (Amichai in Bloch and Kronfeld 2000, 131)[44]

In Amichai's poetic inventory of names, titled *Names, Names, in Other Days and in Our Time*, Ruth is the ultimate representative of otherness ('*acherut*), the subject of the fourteenth and fifteenth poems.[45] Moreover, he knowingly invokes Ruth in every mention of *'acherut*, for the connection between the two is clinched by language and sound: *Rut rut rut, ha-yaldah min ha-yaldut 'akhshav hi netsigat ha-'acherut* (Ruth Ruth Ruth, the girl of my youth, now she's a stand-in for Otherness). In Hebrew, Ruth (*Rut*) and *'acherut* (otherness) rhyme. In order to create the rhyme, Amichai invokes the "*ut*" sound, also present in *yaldut* (childhood), as a suffix that forms the abstract noun. Semantically, it is impossible to separate *rut* from *'acherut*, Ruth from otherness, as phonetically, "otherness" is superimposed on *Rut*. Ruth's otherness is also evident in the following lines, where Amichai deploys the verbs *shav*, to return, and *yashav*, to sit, settle, or dwell, accentuating the themes of return and settlement as the main tropes that motivate *The Book of Ruth*. One nominal form of the root of both verbs is *tshuvah*, which means to repent and, metaphorically, to restore.[46] The next four lines repeat the verb *la-shuv* (to return) four times, underscoring Amichai's reliance on this verb in his approach to *The Book of Ruth* as a narrative of mobility and return. Although Ruth may have been a newcomer to Bethlehem, she is represented as a returnee, a status that juxtaposes her return (*shivah*) with her moral repentance (*tshuvah*).[47] Her return is an ultimate act of choice, denoted by the verbal adjective *shava* (Ruth 1, 22), a condition that defines her in perpetuity. This is the case even though her return was made possible by virtue of Naomi's act, for Ruth is *shava 'im*, returning *with* (Naomi) and not merely returning.

In fact, the space that the term *shav* occupies in Israeli/Jewish discourse is boundless. The Jewish Law of Return (*chok ha-shivah*, or more commonly, *chok ha-shvut*), is a central tenet of Zionism and a pivotal condition for identity and identification in the modern Israeli state. A brief digression on the Law of Return is useful at this juncture.

The Israeli Law of Return was promulgated on July 5, 1950 by the Israeli Knesset, stating that any Jew had the right to return to Israel, as well as the right to live there and, upon arrival, to gain citizenship. This was later amended to include people of Jewish ancestry as well as their spouses. Initially, a Jew was defined as any person who is born to a Jewish mother, or converted to Judaism, and is not of another religion. This definition sparked a contentious debate over the notion of who, and what, is a Jew, and what conversion to Judaism entailed. In 2005, the Israeli Supreme Court ruled that conversions conducted by reform and conservative rabbis were legitimate. As I discuss in the introduction, since the inception of the state, civil and halakhic laws were entangled. The main, pressing question, formulated more than a century ago in the first Zionist Congress, remains unresolved: Is Israel a Jewish state? Is it the state of the Jews? (Kimmerling 2004).

This ideology of return is at the roots of the complicated tension between Israelis and their land and their Book. Within the secular and religious mindset alike, informed by biblical narratives and their accumulated history, "the choice of Palestine as a choice of the new Jewish settlement was a choice not only of rescue and revolution of the diasporic state, but a choice of return" (Gurevitch 1997, 204).[48] Amichai builds on the wider metaphysical meaning of *la-shuv*, to return, adding the possibility of non-return as a category of otherness that Ruth's otherness ambiguously embodies.

Amichai extends the theme or issue of non-return through the figure of another Ruth, "the girl of [his] youth" who perished in a concentration camp (Amichai, trans. Bloch and Kronfeld 2000, 181).[49] It becomes impossible to distinguish between the two Ruths: the superimposition of the biblical name "Ruth" on the "girl of my youth" incorporates the latter into the genealogy of the former. The narrative of the two Ruths thereby becomes one: Ruth the Moabite and Ruth of the Holocaust are here mutually constitutive and merge together in a representation of otherness.[50] Ruth is always already assimilated in the very word that proclaims otherness, including her own. Does the Hebrew connection between *Ruth* (*rut*) and *'acherut* virtually decree that Ruth will always be colonized by otherness?

To the extent that the "Law of Return" discriminates between those who can return and those who cannot, Amichai introduces the critical Law of Return based on his experience. The non-return as a metaphysical condition is manifested not in the biblical intertext of Ruth or the law of return, but in the discriminatory law that marked Jewishness in Auschwitz.

It is possible that Auschwitz is made responsible for the law that is strictly discriminating between those who can return (Jews) and those who cannot (non-Jews), unless they convert halakhically. Otherness—Ruth's otherness—as defined by Amichai, is premised on a critical law of return based on his experience; he exaggerates the irony of non-return as a metaphysical condition manifested both in the biblical intertext of Ruth, the returnee, and in the Law of Return. The vexing question Amichai poses in his poem is how Ruth can remain completely other even though she was so thoroughly and consciously assimilated. Despite being the ultimate assimilated foreigner and the maternal ancestor of King David, Ruth remains outside of the Judean community; it is not hers to return to because she never belonged to it in the first place. Her assimilation—conversion—is a moot point.

Amichai explores the gist of otherness not only through Ruth. In his equations of meaning ("Ruth is otherness", "otherness is death, death is otherness"), nouns are substantiated in a construct that does not necessitate a verb, thus fixing their meaning in an eternal axiom. Amichai is well aware of the fact that names are informative codes that can reveal the deep, tangible meaning of abstract concepts such as death, change, otherness and God. And in his account of definitive poetic knowledge they are nothing but interchangeable components of the land to which there is no return. In these equations, he concludes that otherness is God. Otherness operates on the principle of violence and remains fixed and dead, like a text without context. As Amichai proclaims:

> Otherness is God. Otherness killed Him. The truth is,
> Otherness killed Ruth.
>
> (Amichai in Bloch and Kronfeld 2000, 31)[51]

Amichai's journey traverses the mountains and valleys of Jewish wandering in an attempt to reconcile the paradoxes and ironies of history and religion, language and prayer, and otherness and belonging. Only in the final, fiftieth poem of his long Jewish trek, "Jewish Travel: Change is God and Death is His Prophet", does Amichai arrive at this realization. Change, as the ability to shift positions, places, contexts, or paradigms, he suggests, must be attributed to God for humans are incapable of generating such a powerful shift:

> Once I said, Death is God, and change
> is His prophet.
> Now I have calmed down, and I say:
> Change is God and death is His prophet.
>
> (Amichai in Bloch and Kronfeld 2000, 124)[52]

In part, the force of the poem is the proximity between the two utterances "once I said" and "now I have calmed down, and I say…" (Ibid.), which signal a realization created by the possibility of simply reversing the truth.

Children and the Burden of Storytelling

> And Momik holds Grandfather's hand and feels the warm currents of the Grandfather's story flow into his own hand and up to his head, and he draws strength from Grandfather, unbeknownst to him, and squeezes the strength out for himself till finally Grandfather lets out a kind of howl and pulls his hand away and looks at Momik as if he understands something.
>
> (Grossman 1989, 71)[53]

Life in Citations tells the stories of the crowding of the reference, whether as a knife, milk, a *kolbo* a hand, or a name. In the previous chapters, I trace them and begin to account for them in Israeli Hebrew reality. My questions are, therefore, laced with what has long compensated for the nothingness with which Adam began. I interrogated the ideology and aesthetics of the density of the reference. How is the debt to the story negotiated, and what amounts to a commensurate reparation of the debt? What is the performance of overflowing memory, the texture of loaded, saturated pasts? And to what kind of anxieties have they given and do they continue to give birth? One way to address the question of language is to attend to the economic space of metaphoric and figurative language as an attempt to move against the abyss of meaning that metaphors and the subsequent distortion of narrative entail.

Agnon's feast of Chasidic oral tradition of the *akedah* is interrupted. Hebrew literature seeks to mend this rupture of narration, whereby much of the responsibility of telling is placed on the younger generation. I will conclude this section with two exemplary narratives. Yotam and Momik, protagonists of Benny Barbash's *My First Sony*,[54] and David Grossman's *See Under Love*. They are respectively, both young, and seek to reconstruct the story that has been ruptured. They are both obsessed ethnographers of the hyperreal, transcribing life into texts. This obsession is in direct relation to the weight of the burden of history coupled with the fact that they know that their inability to produce the story means death: death of the narrative as much as the death of its people.

The fixation on childhood and young adulthood as a site where trauma takes place competes with nostalgic narratives that aim to flavor Israeli childhood with "milk and honey". Childhood narratives are seductively compelling; they claim to present an authentic joy and pain, a pure, vulnerable, and innocent voice against the manipulation of adult culture. It appears non- or pre-ideological. The socio-historical silence of the first generation on the one hand, and the overwhelming ideological production of national narratives on the other, contributed to the dependency on both the story that was told and the one that was still unuttered. They were dependent on multiple traumas and silences. The Holocaust was a major contributor, but other traumas such as the War of Independence, the Nakba, immigration and scarcity of national and individual resources were critically effective.

Hebrew literature represents its children as those who, if not starving, are at least ready to gorge themselves. Literature that speaks in a child's voice opens a wide range of literal possibilities; for the author has the freedom to unload the page with what seems the raw material of culture, in a child's register: noncommitted syntax, long sentences and paragraphs, stream of consciousness, and endless relative clauses that presumably follow the mysterious maze of the child's wandering mind. More than that, the breathless style of narration highlights the passionate act of storytelling and the urgency of delivering as a critical moment between life and death.[55]

In *See Under Love* (1986) David Grossman attempts to write in measured, economic prose a new dictionary of horror, carefully contextualized and subjectively situated in the biographic experience of Grandpa Anshel and several Auschwitz survivors in his life. The first part of the book, "Momik", concerns the eponymous protagonist, starving for the full story of the Holocaust. He is enacting the experience as the struggle against the Nazi Beast. Momik also documented his parents' survival story, taking down secret notes, dreams, mutterings, and tattooed numbers, as he collects them into his notebook which he keeps under his pillow. The child's imagination codifies new signs into a secretive language. The raw material of communication is slowly crystallized into the second-generation narrative of both mystification and demystification of the story and discourse of "the land over there" ("*eretz sham*"). Alas, as the epigraph tells us, language cannot contain the horror of this narrative, and it is through the hand that Momik gains access. Momik is so totally committed to deciphering the codes of the narrative that he can receive the current of the story not through words, but by squeezing it out through touch. His is an all-consuming, psychic enterprise. He knows that:

> in the land over there they are all covered since with a thin glass that does not allow them to move, and it is impossible to touch them, and as if they live but they are not, and only one person in the entire world can save them, and it is Momik.
>
> (Grossman 1989, 47)

Grossman's semiotic operation breaks through the thin glass to create this full system of reference for the untold story while cushioning its effect on the reader. The narrator also highly identifies with Momik. The result is that Grossman manages to turn the misanthropic caricature of Momik into an archetype of the nation. He creates an ultra-empathic second-generation child to the extent that one critic wrote that "we are all Momik" (Dar 2006). The reader's identification is absolute.[56]

Works that are based on ethnography comprise an esteemed genre on the Hebrew bookshelf. They oscillate between journalism, ethnography, and fiction. Amos Oz's, *In the Land of Israel* (*Po ve-Sham be-'Eretz Israel*, 1983), and David Grossman's *Yellow Wind* (*Ha-Zman ha-Tsahov*, 1987), both feature the author as investigative author-figure, although the texts differ greatly in their style and political commitment. Oz conducts interviews in different locations across Israel, such as a *Kibbutz*, settlements, the West Bank, Orthodox communities, and *Beit Shemesh*, a Mizrahi community near Jerusalem. Grossman focuses exclusively on bringing the concerns of Palestinians to the fore of Israeli consciousness. The premise of documentation is so enticing that the fictional aspect of these texts has been muted, and with it, the political-ideological dimension has gone largely unaddressed. The ethnographic attempts to "write culture" both purported to deliver a larger cultural "truth" about the other, and, thanks to their trustworthy (read: canonic) authorship, were understood as legitimate in this regard.

To the extent that Oz and Grossman fail to understand that representation is always a political undertaking, the premise of the hyperreal and the legitimacy that they brandish speaks to the desire to correct existing mythologies. Oz goes to the different sites with his recorder as the highly inclusive, fair, "good guy", who knows how to engage socially and comes back with a cultural map of Israel. He nevertheless advances a text in which the secular Ashkenazi subject-position continuously reproduces itself. Grossman, meanwhile, goes to the Palestinian refugee camps, speaks with its people in Arabic, and translates to his ravenous readers children's dreams, and the lives of older people.

Benny Barbash's *My First Sony* (1994) tells the story of the collapse of the Israeli family from the perspective of the nine-year-old Yotam Lazar, a third generation Holocaust survivor, who records his family's narrative with the eponymous child's Sony tape recorder. The novel is about the end of the story and the inability to replace the story. The burden of the first generation can be lifted not through narrative or storytelling, but through documentation. Yotam's father Asaf, a writer, is suffering a debilitating writer's block where he has no more stories to tell, and it is perhaps for this reason that he deploys the Sony tape recorder, a simplified colorful toy, which he gives to Yotam. Barbash's book has been widely lauded, translated in to many languages and adapted to stage productions and teleplays in Israel as well as in Europe.[57] The play is presented by critics as a prototypically Israeli work depicting a typical Israeli family. A recent discussion raised the question not of why Barbash's work is so easily adaptable to stage and screen, but why other successful works by authors such as Meir Shalev are not.

Yotam is not an author, he becomes an author so he can bear witness and save his father.[58] As an omniscient ethnographer, he carries the tape recorder with him everywhere, to every crisis; he learns how to engage with and learn from the stories. He records daily speech, storytelling, and gossip, the substance of his narrative, which he reproduces/duplicates as absolute truth. The recorded material gradually increases in value: not only does Yotam slowly develop a small-scale market of his stories; he "sells" sensational, obscene stories to other kids for one Israeli shekel. They devour these tapes, listening to them repeatedly until the cassette tapes wear out. At other times, his material becomes an archive of sorts, used by his grandfather to prepare his lectures for Passover.

Yotam painstakingly creates his own timeline devoid of its historicized and situated context. That Yotam is always present with his tape in the most unusual situations tells us about his internalized responsibility to make himself available to the story, and even more so, his miraculous good fortune to be in the right place at the right time, unable to afford to miss it. Documentation has become a life mission, a strategy against the death of the body, against the death of the story. Mobilized by the ethos of Jewish victimhood, Yotam's strategy is one of indiscriminate absorption. Archivism is both his ideology and his ontology. Indeed, technology has introduced an accelerated mode of production, but it is the insistence on the reliance of the narrative upon said technology that makes this reproduction so critical to this discussion. The most trivial, even the ellipses of silence—presenting literature as an abstract distillation according to which each moment in life acquires narrative significance: it can be "duplicated", "rewound" and "played back". In this mimetic archive, reality is the best story, not only "stranger than fiction", but ostensibly more faithful. We live in a story, in the midst of its production.[59]

Much of the narrative of *My First Sony* evolves therefore around the production of the story, moving from Yotam's life story—keeping the child's perspective—to its recorded reality. The name Yotam is also symbolic, alluding to innocence, naiveté and the youth who insists on seeing and telling the truth. It refers to the biblical Yotam, but etymologically, "tam" means innocent and truth seeker. Through this child's voice, the humor and pain—the intensity of grotesque moments or emotionally charged situations—are transcribed into the literal, sometimes objective manners of the distant child who seems bound to the rules of language and transcription of words more than to their meaning.

Eventually, Yotam's need to document reality becomes a mental fixation, whereby the tape recorder is his condition for life, which he refers to as a transfusion of blood (1994, 26). This metaphor highlights narratives as the oxygen of life, for as long as one still has stories, one is surely alive. Indeed, early in the book Yotam reveals his father's sufferings because "he had finished having stories" (Barbash 1994, 7). As a temporary solution, and in order to quiet his wife, Asaf accepts a freelance job at Yad Vashem as a ghost writer of memorial books for Holocaust survivors who reveal to him their nightmarish stories, along with the objects, photographs, and dreams that they have kept throughout the years. It is Yotam, his son, who discovers on his father's computer screen an urgent call for help: "SOS" (save our souls) repeated across ten full pages. Once able to read, the child's role reverses. He must now rescue his father. Asaf's inability to write is both an existential and an ontological problem, resulting in a diminished salary, ridicule from his wife (emasculation), bodily failure, and depression, ending in his suicide. Having no stories means chronically feeling stifled. His suicide is symbolic; he strangles himself. When the body-text system that has mobilized the core of his identity collapses, it becomes impossible to carry on.

Performing Hunger

Barbash's hunger in *My First Sony* is symptomatic of how Israeli writers continuously produce hunger through their narratives. In that sense, hunger for food and hunger for narratives always coincide. In what follows I focus on an episode in which hunger is fully realized as a narrative performance, in the first encounter between Yotam's grandparents, in the Partisans' forest back in Poland. The circumstances of both the encounter in Poland and its narration in Tel Aviv amplify the volume of hunger, loss, separation, and love with layered meaning. It is told by Grandpa—an enthusiastic member of the revisionist Zionist movement Betar, who comes to Europe to help rescue Jews. Now, drunk and jolly in Tel Aviv, on Grandma's seventieth birthday, he finally tells the story to his children and grandchildren for the first time. Fluids like coffee and alcohol add to the fluidity of narrative and further saturate the transitions between the two realities. Here is Yotam's account of the events, based on the recording.

> On the way back, next to Sanuk, their Jeep broke down in the middle of the night, and they stopped to fix it. Suddenly, shadows emerged from the trees and advanced towards them, and at first, Grandpa and his friends were alarmed and cocked their guns and fired into the air; because at that time there were a lot of cases of hungry people looking for food who were so desperate that they even attacked soldiers, but cries immediately arose telling them not to shoot, not to shoot, in all kinds of languages, and Grandpa stopped shooting and asked who they were, and grandma took a few steps forward into the light from the headlamp of the jeep, and here Grandpa stopped his story and looked at Grandma, who looked at him crossly but said nothing, and everybody asked him to go on with his story, because to that day Grandma had never told us what had happened to her in the Holocaust, and how she succeeded in escaping from the Trawniki camp, and all we knew was from friends who had known her during that period, and Grandpa asked her if he could go on, and she said, now you are asking? And Grandpa said, if you tell me to stop I'll stop, and Grandma said, you are completely drunk, do what you like, I'm going to put water on for coffee, and she left the living room, and Grandpa took another sip and thought for a minute, and said that Grandma entered the beam of light, thin, with hair like a hedgehog, wrapped in an old blanket, and told Grandpa that she and her friends were the Columbus Flying Circus, and they were prepared to put on their show for him, and Grandpa asked what their show was, and Grandma said it depended on what they paid, and Grandpa asked how do you want to be paid? And Grandma said that *the best payment was food*, and then Grandpa said all right, they would give them food....
>
> (Barbash 1994, 45–46) [iv]

What kind of performance can hunger perform? Can it testify fully? A story within a story within a long recorded narrative, it sets a stage within a stage, all to reveal that beneath one layer of hunger lies a deeper one, in such a way that hunger resets the limits of language, body, and silence, while mobilizing plot and actions. To start with, to what extent can aestheticized hunger ever articulate the depth of the catastrophic hunger and starvation of its actors? Framed as an exchange for food, it already changes its meaning, augmenting it with a cunning moral of gift exchange.

> and then Grandma called one of the children, who began to do a pan-tomime in the light from the headlamps, and next to him stood a girl who explained his movements in a recitation, and it was a quarrel in a family in the ghetto about how to divide a piece of bread, with everyone explaining why he deserved to get the biggest piece. The father said that he worked in the Resort, which is a workshop that the Nazis had set up in the ghetto, and so he deserved it; and the mother pointed to her belly, which had another baby in it; and the little boy said that he was a child and needed to grow; and the little girl didn't say anything, she only cried without a sound. And the little boy doing pantomime was once the father and once the mother and once the daughter and once the son, and in the end also a bird who flew past and snatched the crumb of bread they were squabbling over, and Grandpa said a number of times during the act, stop it, please stop it, we'll give you food without the show, it's too horrible, but the boy went on, and Grandpa and his friends lowered their eyes because they couldn't bear to watch, and when it was over, and the other children sitting and watching laughed and clapped, Grandpa repeated that they would give them food without seeing the rest of the show, but Grandma refused to accept any favors, because anyone who received a favor owed a favor and they didn't want to owe any-one anything, and she announced the second number in the show, which was imitations of owls and forest animals and the screams of a person in a schlage, which is an instrument of torture... ...
>
> (Barbash Ibid.)[60]

Hunger performs fully from within the condition of total physical hun-ger for both food and stories. Paradoxically, the space between food and narrative, between the body and language, is materialized within the lacuna of hunger as a contagious, autoreferential affect. Ironically, the story feeds the bird while the audience devours the story. Barbash's multilayered performance turns the hungry mouth into the spectacle of consumption through its visual, acoustic, and figurative representations. Pantomime—controlled, mimetic, and silent—deepens the ironic abyss of hunger, for it wears on its face that one does not perform bread but has to snatch it. Indeed, the performance is embedded within several frames of reference and groups of addressees, enacting hunger again on its stretched continuum from the most literal to the most metaphoric.

Surely, hunger performs well; it is perhaps one of the most effec-tive ideological tropes. The plot, that is always aware of its mode of production, is highly generative of both food and lack thereof. The Holocaust has produced its unique tormenting traumatic hunger. Historically, this same hunger has played a central role in shaping Israeli and Jewish consciousness and its collective memory. The experience of starvation and abuse that characterized the daily experience in the concentration camps as part of the general destruction of the Jewish body continues to hover over our deepest nightmares. Such a horror has had immense impact on the textual representation of hunger within a Jewish/Israeli contextual framework of ideology and nationalism, and its transformation into a cultural trope that underscores the subtext of narratives and their conception. The stratification and translation of hunger within the continuum of daily survival becomes a loaded, saturated code of existence.[v]

Seventy years after the Holocaust, its specifically Jewish body has become a timeless signifier, an eternal ruin and wound in crumbling desolation. Insofar as the Muselmann, with his striped uniform, empty eyes, distended stomach, and pallid skin, is able to witness, it is his impoverishment that he communicates. If the idea of such a hungry body is somehow possible to grasp, the idea of the "hungry story" and the hunger for stories are much less accessible. Barbash's tape recorder produces narratives that, while feeding us, also constantly remind us of the starvation for the story. It asks for narratives. As much as his story becomes the stage of performance it dialectically reproduces the anxiety of nothingness. In other words, while the story slowly erases the distinction between the hungry subject/actor and the audience/listener, another desire for a good family story triggers an old mythological hunger of its own.

The aftermath of the Holocaust keeps the imaginary fields of combat alive, asking for the story, any story, the story that can be told and retold. Since Auschwitz we have learned to live on stories as *menot krav*, rations. But rather than simply a strategy, the story itself has become a form of rescue: the ration of the battlefields, a zone of war and survival that defers death. To think about the place of the story in Israeli culture as a ration is different from Agnon's and Kurzwiel's feast, the *se'udah*; it is a tragic commodity of life, and like blood transfusion is part of a rescue operation. Insofar as Jabes' nothingness produces anxiety, the danger of it—is that in order to compensate for the void, we will anxiously construct fullness (and everythingness) as life. Nothingness in effect creates a hunger that feeds a bottomless, infinite desire for more, which in turn creates a greater hunger and an inability to satiate it. In the shadow of Adam's nothingness, the plate is empty, always imagined empty, and as a result, it is piled high with everything edible and inedible. These are two extreme situations that paradoxically feed each other, fight each other and acknowledge each other. This dynamic is, I argue, at the heart of Jewish textual tradition. It orders us to fill the plate, the *kolbo*, and join the meal.

A ration highlights the isolation of the fighter, an eternal survivalist who paves the way through words, citations, and divergences of voices, echoes, and ramifications. The story as *menat krav* is a metaphor of living on the edge, with a consciousness of loss and constant trauma. Moving from appetizers to *menat krav* through Boaz's slice of sacred metabread defines the contours of the Hebrew Breadscape.

Hunger generates narratives, just as narratives seek to feed certain hungers. But more radically, food and hunger are transformative events; they can build and unbuild the subject. Ruth's bread brings her home, turning her into the quintessential native; through the link to the story of Lot and his daughters, Ruth is reinvested with the blissful ability to cross several boundaries—something her foremother, Lot's wife, would never have been able to do. She becomes, in the ontological sense of becoming, the cultural daughter of Naomi. Indeed, Zionist reading has highlighted Ruth's journey to Bethlehem as an act of return. Her return is loaded with endless possibilities of renewal and transformation. For *The Book of Ruth*, it is the homecoming act of the transformed, satiated Ruth, and for the Jew of the twentieth century it is the homecoming journey of the new Jew, now interpolated with the redemptive nationalism of the nation-state. At its heart is the process of making native the population of newcomers; accelerating the transformative mechanism of the Jewish immigrants into Israeli Hebrews. Catalyzed by the effects of European anti-Semitism and the Holocaust, the homecoming ethos gains more validity with the broad articulation vacancy, of "a land without a people for a people without a land", the vacant land in Israel awaiting for the return of its Jewish people, as much as for the return of the story, advocating directly and indirectly the de-nativization of Palestinians.

Notes

1 Literally, a small, petite famine.
2 When Jacob, for example, sends his sons to Egypt it is clearly evident that "there is still corn (grain) in Egypt" (Genesis 42: 1).
3 *Lelaket* means to collect through gleaning. It is part of an established Jewish Halachic practice whereby the farmer does not harvest the crops that the plow is unable to collect, instead leaving them to be gleaned by the poor, orphans, and widows. It is one of the few "gifts to the poor" established in Leviticus, as a system to protect the disenfranchised. According to Jewish Halakah it is limited to two stocks of barley. If three are taken, the landlord can return to collect them.
4 Recent studies have praised *The Book of Ruth* for preserving a unique authentic female voice, or as a celebration of female bonding and solidarity, or even as the storytelling of a female scribe that is based on women's oral tradition. B.M. Vellas, for example, contests the idea that the book was written against the prohibition of marrying foreign women, writing, "a book which was written in those troubled times of Ezra and Nehemiah as a protest against those men could not possess that beautiful atmosphere and those idyllic surroundings which, so skillfully, the author of *Ruth* creates, nor could it be possible to possess an unforced, serene and calm tone of

style" (1954, 7). More recently, Ilana Pardes assumes that *The Book of Ruth* is of an idyllic revisionist character, as it provides us clues to understand the story of Rachel and Leah. For Pardes, alluding to these matriarchs in the last chapter of *The Book of Ruth* serves to harmonize the relationship between Rachel and Leah in the same way that Ruth's infinite estrangement is transformed into rootedness (1992, 113). Julia Kristeva's work attempts to explore how foreignness is inscribed in the lineages of sacred texts. Mieke Bal's positions *Ruth* as an "institutional metatext", in which analogy and chronology interact to create a *mise en abyme*, reflected in Ruth's naming system.

5 In the Bible, *The Book of Ruth* is the second of the Five Scrolls (the *Megillot*), following the *Song of Songs*. In the Septuagint, *Ruth* is placed after *Judges*, in an order that has been preserved in English translations ever since. As such, *Ruth* is a functional postexilic text, reconstructing the period circa 968 BCE, when it is assumed that Ruth married the Judge Ivtizan (also in Kristeva 1991, 70).

6 According to certain Rabbinic scholars, the period of Judges dates from the death of Joshua, lasting 365 years, which places Ruth either during the period of Shamgar and Ehud, or of Debora, Barak, and Yael. See Ruth Rabba (1); and the BT Baba Batra (91a).

7 Another kind of dialogue or intertext in *Ruth* is created through allusions to other biblical figures such as Rachel and Leah (*Ruth* 4: 11), or Tamar and Yehuda (Ibid. 4: 12). See also Ilana Pardes (1992).

8 Babylonian Talmud (Sotah 42b).

9 Rogoff's concept, which initially refers to modern Israeli society, is equally relevant to (and indeed, derives from) the biblical narrative.

10 In English too, "hunger" refers to the desire, need, physical sensation, or craving for food while "famine" emphasizes extreme scarcity or a shortage of food.

11 Works on trauma in the Bible have only recently begun to surface. See, for example Meira Polliack's study, "Joseph's Journey: From Trauma to Resolution", where she examines Joseph's traumatic abandonment by his brothers and his recovery through the framework of recovery provided by the psychiatrist Judith Lewis Herman: safe environment, remembrance, mourning and reconnection (Polliack 2010, 147–174).

12 According to Derrida, the tradition and practice of hospitality help to explain ethical and political situations whereby the stranger or foreigner encounters "the limits of power, norms, rights and duties" (2000, 77).

13 In Pamela Levi's painting, "Lot and His Daughters" (1994), a faceless Lot is pictured lying stark naked on a bed in a room that replaces the cave in the Bible. According to Orly Lubin, male nudity signifies the anonymous pornographic gaze, and thus, in the painting, highlights Levi's subversive attempt to unframe and fragment the biblical narrative (Lubin 2003, 262–275).

14 Whereas Lot was slow to rise and greet the angels, Abraham *ran* to welcome them (cf. Genesis 18:1–2 and 19:1–2).

15 The Midrash contends that Lot's daughters did not accept the yoke of the Law, the Torah (*Sefer Ha-aggadah, Matan Torah* 59).

16 See also Kristeva (1991, 74–75). Recently, other feminists have addressed this connection: Frymer-Kensky, for example, introduces a more tolerant view of the incest (2002, 258–263).

17 A different approach was introduced by the Sages who rationalized the incestuous act as Lot's punishment for offering his daughters to the lascivious men of Sodom (*Midrash Tanhuma, Va-yera'* 12).

18 https://almogbehar.wordpress.com/2008/04/18/על-שירתה-של-ברכה-סרי/)

19 In admonishing Ruth and Orpah to return to their people, Naomi further acknowledges their foreignness, and in articulating her concern for them, she marks their ethnic difference as a critical factor defining their problematic chances of belonging.

20 According to Ruth Rabba (2: 21) you are required to reject the convert three times, and if s/he insists after the third time, s/he is accepted.

21 Sodom features prominently in contemporary Israeli culture among numerous critical venues. One of the recent Israeli blockbusters, *This is Sodom* (2012), by Segev and Anderson and the cast of *Eretz Nehederet*, is a comedic satire of the last three days of Sodom, an allegorical critique of contemporary life in Tel Aviv, the city of sins, its harsh economy, and its approach to Arabs and Palestinians. Lea Aini's *Sdom'el* is a feminist novella on incest and sacrifice, a flaming indictment of the Sodomite God who sends his children to the sacrifice (Aini 2001). Earlier, Binyamin Galai's play *Sdom Sity* (Sodom City) was produced by Haifa Theater in 1968. Ehud Azrieli Meir's play, *Ben Sdom ve-Yafo* (Between Sodom and Jaffa), tells a homoerotic story between two ultra orthodox men and was directed by Sara Harari. On *Sodom* Bad as an allegory of the Apartheid and the Israeli-Palestinian conflict, see Uri Avneri, "Mitat Sdom" (Sodom Bad), *Haaretz* 4.22.2007.

22 The Semitic verb *sava'* implies not only eating one's fill, but also the ultimate sense of satisfaction and contentment, as in metaphorical expressions such as *sva' 'ayin* (lit., "one with a satiated eye" or visually content) or *sva' ratzon* (lit., "one with a satiated desire" or emotionally content). In the Bible, Abraham died satiated, at a ripe old age (*zaken ve-savea'*) (Genesis 25: 8).

23 Although the verb *le-hatkin okhel* is more common in Agnon's language, I find the use of "*okhel metukan*" more evocative in the story framed by the idea of *pat shlema* (perfect bread). "I rejoiced imagining how I would sit around a full table with a clean tablecloth, and waiters and waitresses would serve me *ma'akhal metukan* (prepared/repaired food) over which I wouldn't have to sweat, for I was already sick of the tasteless meals I had prepared at home (*she-hayiti matkin-li*)"(Ibid. 143).

24 Kurzweil (1970).

25 Adorno (2005).

26 Kurzweil also uses Adorno's aphorism in German as an epigram to this section of his essay. Although Kurzweil does not evoke the reference of barbarism, it might be implicated in his essay as he begins the essay with the reference to Adorno. But his assertion keeps in line with Agnon's metaphor and imagery in the "Apology."

27 The Yiddish, Hebrew writer Mendele Mocher Sfarim (1835–1917) and his fictional shtetl, Kabziel, an allegorical, satirical Jewish town of lazy, unproductive baggers, and the poet Haym Nachman Bialik and his renowned poem, responding to the Russian pogroms of Jews in Kishinev, in the 1903 pogrom, as published first before being changed to "*Be-'ir Ha-haregah*", In the City of Slaughter (1904).

28 "Ve-'im tomar, ma nuchal?" Or also, "Where our food will come from in the seventh year of the sabbatical year of the land" (Leviticus 25; 20). The expression often appears in the writing of Shalom Aleichem and Mendele Mocher Sfarim.

29 That words are even more satiating than bread is articulated in Judeo-Iberian culture. Tamar Alexander-Frizer's voluminous collection of Judeo-Spanish proverbs is entitled, after one such proverb, "Words are Better than Bread" (*Milim Masbi'ot Mi-lechem*, literally, words are more satiating than bread, (Jerusalem: Ben Zvi and Ben Gurion University of the Negev Press, 2004).

30 Zerubavel (1995), and especially Gurevitch (1997), highlight the emplotment of the national narrative around the Bible in more general concepts,

such as the "people of the book", or Jewish collective memory and its detailed semiotic manifestations.

31 Hebrew literature built on this proverb a whole parody, bringing to mind
Bialik's articulation of *Aluf batzlut, aluf shum*, Knight of Onion-ness and
Knight of Garlic. *shum* (garlic) also means "nothing" in Hebrew.
   www.fluentcollab.org/mbg/index.php/reviews/review/112/97

32 Symbolically, the Jewish bread of poverty and affliction is the Passover
matzah: the quick, "fast food" with a unique place in the Jewish narrative,
calendar and palate. But in Israeli ontology, matzah is used only on Passover.
It is not the actual food of poor people.

33 This has lyrical echoes of "yado ba-kol"—his hand is in all (in everything
and everywhere)—from Ishmael, recalling the intimate relationship and
power dynamic around knowledge, sexuality, and touch.

34 In Hebrew, Amichai (1998, 34–35).

35 Scholars debate the degree of Amichai's critical position, with some locating
him within the conscious mainstream while others situate him as sociopolit-
ically subversive (see for example, Kronfeld 1996).

36 In Hebrew *tahalikh* means a process, which Bloch and Kronfeld translate as
"physics".

37 For a critical approach to Hebrew singing that argues that Hebrew singing
not only developed a national Israeli identity, avoiding mention of Arabs,
Palestinians, and occupation made the singer more Jewish. A Jewish state
as such does not permit entrance to non-Jews, increasing the technocratic
identity of Israel. See Yiftachel and Roded, (2003).

38 Armadillos, "*Zeh shir 'al lekhem*" ("This is a Song about Bread") by Maor
Goldstein and Ido Frankel, Domino Gross (2009)·

39 www.on1foot.org/text/midrash-tanhuma-parshat-vayakhel-1
   Translation by Hillel ben Panim.

40 Or, if translated more literally, "on the second syllable."

41 In Hebrew in Amichai (1998, 130–131). Bloch and Kronfeld translated only
twelve of the sixteen poems in "Names, Names, in Other Days and in Our
time" (Bloch and Kronfeld 2000, 125–127). The translation of this third
poem is mine.

42 Yehuda Halevi also seems to evoke the palimpsest-like depth of names in his
own name, Yehuda. See for example, his poem, "*Le-kha nafshi betuchah*"
and the line, '*ve-eck yishckach yehuda et yehuda?*' (and how would Yehuda forget Yehuda?) Thanks for Karyn Berger for this reference. https://
benyehuda.org/rihal/travel_no_nikkud.html

43 Zelda Schneersohn Mishkovsky.

44 In Hebrew, Amichai (1998, 138), "*Shamot, Shamot, Shamot, Shamot, ba-
Yamim ha-Hem, ba-Zman ha-Zeh.*" Although the Hebrew title repeats
"Names" four times, Bloch and Kronfeld stop at two.

45 The discrepancy in the numeration of the poems in English and Hebrew is
due to the omission of several poems in the English translation.

46 Amichai repeats the verb *lashuv* thirteen times in different tenses. Interesting
here is the noun *ha-shava*, meaning "the returnee" in feminine, (Ruth 1: 22).

47 Surprisingly, Naomi, in a passive voice, describes herself as the one who
has been brought back to Bethlehem, saying, *ve-reikam heshivani yohovah*
("God brought me empty") (Ruth 1: 21), in reference to both her losses and
her return. The verb, *heshivani* in *hif'il* (*shuv* in the causative and transitive
verb form) emphasizes that Naomi's return is an act of God—she is the
object of the sentence. Still, the symbolic concepts of *meshiv* and *meshiv
nefesh*, (Ruth 4:15) are strongly associated with the idea of restoring the
spirit, as a reference to God.

48 Recent political and demographic concerns have focused on the recent influx of immigrants from Russia whose Jewishness is questioned along with the legal status of their Israeli nationality.

49 Amichai's earlier poem, "Little Ruth", addresses the girl of his childhood saying: "If were alive now, you would be a woman of sixty-five years" (Amichai 1989, 70, my translation).

50 My articulation of Ruth is informed by my own name; as the first girl born in Israel of a newly immigrated Iraqi family who was initiated into Sabrahood, I belong to this genealogy of names. My name was recommended to my parents by a nurse at the hospital where my mother gave birth. It was a very popular name for girls of the baby boom generation of the 1950s.

51 In Hebrew, Amichai (1998, 20).

52 In Hebrew, Amichai (1998, 125). It is still unclear whether the word *nevi'o* (his prophet), with the pronoun suffix, modifies "God" or "change"; more likely it refers to both, since one is the other: death is the prophet of God and of change.

53 Grossman (1986). All quotes are from Betsy Rosenberg's English translation, Grossman (1989).
   Momik: short, concluding style.

54 Benny (1951–) has published five novels, numerous press articles, written scripts and TV episodes, directed and produced feature films, documentaries, and short films, often working with his brother Uri Barbash. He co-wrote the award-winning and Oscar-nominated *Beyond the Walls*, which was directed by his brother (1984).

55 Barabash's young hero juxtaposes air and time: (83–84) "But oxygen is breathing. The substance of survival."

56 Twenty years after the publication of Grossman's *See Under Love*, the story of Momik was published in a separate novella as *Momik* (2005, Hakibbutz Hameuchad) in paperback, and was also produced for the stage for the Gesher Theater by Yevgeny Arye with Elena Laskin in 2006.

57 In 2002, he adapted the book into a twelve-part miniseries for primetime Israeli TV. The book was also adapted for the stage as both a monodrama by Roi Horowitz for the Teatronto Festival in Tel Aviv, and in German for the Mousontrum Theater in Frankfurt, directed by Stefen Bitton, in 2008. Both productions built on the technological dimension of recording. In Horowitz's show, all the characters except for Yotam participate in the show through their recorded voices. Bitton, on the other hand, introduces a stage with two big trampolines, actors on skates, and motorized armchairs that move like bumper cars. In 2008, at the Salon du Livre du Paris, the book won the Public's Favorite Prize.

58 See Agamben's discussion of Primo Levi. For Agamben, the desire to become a witness is the very impetus of survival (Agamben 2002, 15–39).

59 As the Hebrew expression says, we live in a film, "*haim be-seret*", which is also the name of a website that produces personalized documentaries based on people's lives. (http://haimbeseret.co.il/events.html).

60 In Hebrew (1994, 38–39).

In Lieu of an Epilogue
Ruptured and Departure: Palestinian Breadscape

> What would you say to a novel-writing project? I know you'll tell
> me I don't know how to write novels. I agree, and I'd add that no one
> knows how to write because anything you say comes apart when you
> write it down, and turns into symbols and signs, cold and bereft of life.
>
> Elias Khoury, *Bab al-Shams*[1]

> That way we can compose our story from the beginning without leav-
> ing a single gap for death to enter through.
>
> Elias Khoury, *Bab al-Shams*[2]

Reading from an ideologically saturated position demands full identification with the narrative, as it implicates the reader of the story within
the textual matrix and its genealogy as the eternally surviving offspring
of Jewish culture. It frames reading in the domain of the debt economy,
for victimhood has become a demand of the text; as it is circulated and
imagined, there is an imperative to internalize and identify with its message of obedience and to read the text "as if" we have become either
Abraham or his son. In its extreme economy, and due to the privileged
position of texts in the culture, *tsatetet*, citationality, helped us ask what
invisible charge the long, historical relationship with the texts have generated, and what we owe to the texts. The critical question now to undo
textuality, the *chov*, is what one is "*chayav*", as I mentioned before,
meaning committed to, obliged to, but also what one owes, to the point
of being indebted and bound.

My reading of biblical narratives, artwork, poetry, film, and fiction
asks us to shift the focus back toward the texts by subaltern authors
with which I close out the previous chapters: Elkayam, Shababo, Bachar,
Chetrit, Nes, Suisa. Their work points to the problematics of Israeli intertextuality, the exhausting demands of the Hebrew-Jewish bookshelf,
and the taken-for-granted privilege of their power, first with Elkayam's
interrogative mouth and disputed covenant, then Chetrit's explicit admission of its destructive potential, and later with Suisa's self-conscious

appropriation of these tropes for broad cultural critique, and finally to Eli Bachar and his request for "exact food", an economic measure in quantified time to trim all the extra "doing" of reading. Will these authors offer some redemptive potential to liberate the reading subject from the overburdened network of referentiality, or at least allow the subject to suspend it?

By now we better understand the drama of the overflowing body of references and the dialectic of submission and resistance to the reference. Michal Naaman was able to write her critique, nicely contained between the lines and still produce a line. Other artists represent such a pathological reality with a much more chaotic sense. Almog Behar contrasts Hebrew to Arabic, his mother tongue, in a language of pathology. His Arabic—"mute, throat-suffocated, cursing itself with no words…hiding behind the curtains of Hebrew"—is mute; his Hebrew —"gushing, running between rooms, and neighbors' balconies, one moment naked and another dressed"—is deaf. Behar provides an Arabic translation of this Hebrew poem as a way to treat the muteness of Arabic.[3]

It will thus be appropriate at this stage to stay a little longer with Ishmael, the child of the Kolbo, who as we saw, is more and more culturally included and not in striking opposition to Isaac.[4] I will add to the small sample of Palestinians writers, an initial comparison between the Hebrew-Jewish Breadscape and the Palestinian one through works that address politics of be/longing at the intersection of nations, war, poverty, memory, and textual production. Through the tropes of food, specifically bread and pita, I examine the way several Palestinian authors, Mahmoud Sayf al-Irani, Anton Shammas, and Elias Khoury, position attempts to construct the Palestinian Breadscape at the place where the story has lost its mouth, like its body, memory, and consciousness. I conclude by conflating the story of Jewish return and the story of Palestinian departure, and the way they have mobilized, transformed, and uplifted (from *'aliyah*, ascending) newcomers into natives, while they alternately have paralyzed, made invisible, and starved the Palestinian natives. Bread signals cultural and national difference.

Mahmoud Saif Al-Din Al-Irani's short story provides an excellent starting point from which to launch an investigation into what might constitute the Palestinian Breadscape and its own sites of hunger. Al-Irani (1914–1974) was a prominent intellectual and public figure, and a contemporary of Agnon, active during the same years and in the same city, Jerusalem.[5] Al-Irani published his story *"Rrif el-khubz"* (A Loaf of Bread) in Arabic in 1937, five years after Agnon published his story, *"Pat shlemah"*, in Hebrew.[6] Al Irani's "A Loaf of Bread", is an account of hunger as crisis: it opens with the straightforward description of the sad departure of Sharifa and her two children, from the loving father, Ibrahim, due to abject poverty, going from Jaffa to Jerusalem, during World War I. The institute where Ibrahim teaches, which was unable to pay him his last five monthly salaries, has offered to provide them some support while in Jerusalem, the institute's headquarters, which will help see the family through this time of adversity. In the meantime, Ibrahim will remain in Jaffa where he will continue his teaching job. Without his family, quite like Agnon's narrator, the man is at a total loss, anguished. Al-Irani describes him at the moment of separation:

> The cart left quickly, leaving behind a ruined man, confused and dull-minded, who stood waving his white kerchief intensely like a madman. For a moment he felt like running after the cart, screaming with all his voice, but a mighty force held him in his place, and from the depth of his tortured soul he envisioned the shape of a loaf of bread. Slowly the cart disappeared in the darkness, but the clattering of the four horses continued to knock in his ears a painful chatter for a long time. His body shivered as if he had a fever.
>
> (Al-Irani 1970 [1937], 54, my translation)

Al-Irani's Breadscape brings several competing hungers to their moral edge; with no medication the baby dies and Ibrahim is forced to join his family in Jerusalem and do all kind of lowly jobs. The situation worsens before it improves. When Ibrahim's young son runs back from the bakery with warm bread in his hand—the daily payment for Ibrahim's work in the bakery—he encounters a starving soldier, a beggar, crying "hungry, hungry..." (Ibid. 57). Like in Brenner's story, nature further accentuates the circumstances with a dark, windy, snowy night. Brenner's protagonist, who stands for the diasporic condition of hunger, remains hungry, even though he pilfers the bread, for he drops it in the filthy road. Al-Irani's son also remains hungry, albeit differently; he fully hears the soldier's cry. "His shattered voice reverberated in the stormy soul of the son, causing him lifelessness and emotional confusion. Engulfed with mercy he hardly noticed, he found himself handing the soldier the loaf of bread..." (Ibid. 57).

The expression "he found himself handing ..." suggests that the son's benevolent act was the only humane option available to him. Years later, the son will become a resourceful, self-sufficient young man, the author of an intimate diary, where he writes his short impressions and inner thoughts. Al-Irani concludes with six short accounts, where the young man expresses his desire to resist the old generation's burden, and to rebel against the tyranny of his own fear.

The bread keeps occupying a wide space of desire, for the concrete struggle for food turns it from an open signifier of the utmost manifestation of provision into a biting image of its absence. As the gift of the poor it has inscribed an infinite chain of narratives. In this enigmatic moment, one loaf of bread, a cultural "given", becomes the generative epicenter of food and stories to come. Al-Irani's story advocates an "unconditional gifting", even in a poverty that draws heavily on the reality of time. The diaries that were written between 1915 and 1916 by Muhammad-Adil al-Salih, from Jerusalem—presumably a pseudonym of Ihsan Tourjman—provide us with a bleak picture of this historical moment (Jacobson 2008).[7] His world is also permeated by a reality of war and the collapse of daily order: his disrupted studies, scenes of disease and hunger in the streets, the shortage of tobacco, and the love for his missed family:

> I have never seen such a day in my life … All [supply] of flour and bread stopped. When I walked to the headquarters [*manzil*] this morning, I saw many men, women, and children in Bab al—Amud [looking] for some flour... . I see that the enemy gets stronger than the fellahin (farmers) … How poor these people are … but all of us are miserable these days … Two days ago we ran out of flour. My father gave my brother –Arif, one dirham to buy us bread. He left the house and looked for bread but could not find any. In the end he received some bread for our relatives …
>
> (Jacobson Ibid. 35)

And yet, al-Irani's starving soldier introduces a different abyss of hunger; fighting on several fronts, he survives one battle only to be confronted by another. If bread is first introduced as the food of scarcity, now, when life is reduced to the bare minimum, his hunger is injected with an additional layer of paucity, stretching the limits of the body's tolerance and asking for bread as an immediate answer. One unconditionally gives the little he has. Al Irani's hunger explicitly mobilizes narratives and literature from within the void of its human condition. They reference a specific reality as they hover between the literal, written testimony and its symbolic manifestation. The story ends with several short accounts in the style of diary entries that describe social isolation and restlessness, overwhelmed by inner desires. The final account shifts in tone, reviving the narrator's memory of giving.

> I was walking on my way. It was night and the wind was blowing. The cold air pierced the body, like needles. I came upon a thin child, wearing rags and shivering from the cold. "Hungry", he said, pleading. I've already heard this voice. Where? When? I could not recall. I instructed him to come with me. He followed like a trained animal. We sat at a table and ate. I gave him my clothes and put some money in his pocket.
>
> (pp. 58–59)

Al-Irani's *ars poetica* intersects bread and writing, explicitly telling us that the ability to produce stories like loaves of bread arises from the generative condition of ultimate hunger. It is only through the *act* of giving, more than the actual bread, clothes, and money, that the subject constitutes himself. The last line of the last account reads,

> This encounter was fuel to my fire... I am the happiest I've ever been. I found someone crazy like me. And now we are two, we are three, four... they come to us. Our will is one, our desires are identical. I am happy.
>
> (59)

The narrator's unconditional hospitality becomes the rewarding production of a community where giving and being given are the rules that, in Al-Irani's case, go against the cultural conventions of giving to the poor; it transforms poor individuals into a part of the giving economy. "A Loaf of Bread," both a question and an answer, illustrates the need to radicalize and diversify the economy of hunger, and to approach it as if one were a madman.

The Breadscape of Palestinian narratives after 1948 and the Nakba introduces a new economy and density of hunger. Bread, as we see, is never symbolic, for the regenerative narrative of Al-Irani's "A Loaf of Bread", relies heavily on the generosity of the bread that the impoverished soldier gives the hungry man and on its allegorical possibilities. We move now to the post 1948 bread and pita, and their far more restricted economy.

The Torn Pita of Occupation

Elias Khoury (1948–) is a prolific Lebanese author who is deeply committed to Palestinian Liberation.[8] This engagement is most visible in his novel, *Bab al-Shams* (1998). The story of the pita bread that has been sewed together, told in *Bab al-Shams*, testifies to a harrowing reality of Palestinian departure. A counter-narrative to that of return, it puts forth a thesis about the inseparability of the pita from the telling of the story, as both manifest hunger and utter silence.

Khoury's story is recounted at the site of ultimate destruction, in the Shatila refugee camp, south of Beirut.[9] Khalil tells the story to Yunes Ibrahim al-Asri, the Palestinian hero who lies comatose in The Galilee Hospital in Shatila, as if the story—beginning when all other things and places collapse—were able to awaken him. In this way Khalil is like Scheherazade: he tells the story to defer his terminal acceptance of Yunes's "fragmented" condition (Shammas 1998). Shammas articulates it well: "In Bab al-Shams, Khoury gives the margins the right of return to the center, the refugees the right of return to the story, and the Galilee the right of return to the map of Palestine" (Ibid.). By situating his narration in Shatila, Khoury turns the contested massacre into an open grave/wound of narration.[10] The narrative, open and begging resolution, is still unfinished, not *finally* dead, still conjurable; the grave is unsealed, unfixed, like the meaning around the massacre. But even more so, within its history, Khalil's challenge is not just to narrate, but to resolve the mechanics of narration and piece together a narrative that has been "torn to shreds".

> Whenever I ask you what happened, you start mixing events up, jumping from month to month and from village to village, as though time had melted away among the stones of the demolished villages. My grandmother used to tell me stories as though she were tearing them into shreds; instead of gathering them together, she'd rip them apart, and I understood nothing. I never was able to understand why our village fell or how.
>
> (Khoury 2006, 173)

In Khoury's dismantled world, narrators weep stories. As Umm Sa'ad Radi, a village elder, testifies, "real tears" were gushing "even from my mouth" (185). This is where the narrative mouth and the consuming mouth are also the mouth that cries. The story of the pita bread sheds chilling light on the journey of displacement and the making of the unhomely Palestinian refugee. There are several versions of the story of the pita, one of many departure stories during the Nakba from 1948; thirty-odd years later, the narrative is unfixed but multiplied, and thus, as the narrator suggests, even its validity is in question. It takes place on the way to Beit-Jaan, an Arab village in northern Israel. Amidst a convoy of refugees, the hungry boy is walking at night with his mother as Khalil's grandmother (who relates the story to Khalil) walks nearby. At one point, the boy starts crying. Since his sobbing runs the risk of exposing the convoy, an old man threateningly offers to kill him if he does not stop, so the grandmother removes a pita—her only sustenance—from her inner pocket and gives it to the mother, who tears the bread in half, giving one half to the boy and the other back to the grandmother. But the boy keeps crying, insisting on the whole pita (*pita shlemah*). The grandmother rushes to give him her half, but again, he wants the whole pita, not two halves. So the boy's mother takes out a needle and thread and sews the two halves together. This initially quiets the boy, until he realizes that the pita is in fact two pieces sewn together, and he cries even louder. Alas, the pita has been devoured by the old man, who was hungrier than the boy.

Once he is carried in his mother's arms and wrapped inside the blanket, it is unclear exactly how the child dies. Is it the force of his mother's embrace against her collarbone? Is it the old man who walks behind them, pressing the child against his mother's shoulder? Khoury leaves us with several options, not knowing which story is the reliable one and whom should the reader believe? On the Palestinian road of departure, the homely bread is transformed into a scream: the uncanny bread of refugees. Khoury tells a story of fraught, interwoven complicities and potentialities, leaving the story's ending deliberately unresolved. Whereas Shammas suggests that this is a sympathetic gesture to soften the shocking impact of the narrative, Khoury elaborates, in an interview:

> That's the style of the book. Multiple endings were not written to soften the end. It's part of the format of the novel. It's a story told by people, by *the* people, and the repetition is the main literary device...I think that the style fits the very experience embedded in recollection, which had not been yet manifested...Memory cannot express itself in one narrative... Literature exposes the richness of the human condition, which has no one narrative. And when you have only one narrative, it means to be imprisoned by ideology. If literature is looking for human depth, it cannot say one coherent thing to convey one ending. The story of the pita is a very cruel story, and it doesn't matter which ending we will choose. The child died. The baby died. Who killed him? The man? His mother? It doesn't matter. In both cases, the ending is terrible.
>
> (Khoury, in Shammas 2002, 58)

Khoury's story, then, needs to be able to make the difference, a story that has to voice different imagined narrative possibilities, for its witnessing has collapsed, seeking to construct one narrative out of the catastrophic collapse of narration. Like the pita bread—torn, sewn, yet unmendable— the story and its resolution are deferred indefinitely. Indeed, the layers of vacant mind and drained consciousness are far-reaching and extremely complex; Yunes, whose consciousness is beyond our reach, is present in body but absent in mind, where mind, in fact, has been a place for assumptions, wonders, and conversation. A sealed reference system, the body gives signs but it is also dead.

And yet, Ariana Melamed suggests, for Ariana Melamed, Khoury manages to tell us, "what is at the heart of the refugee's experience." Comparing the Nakba to the Jewish experience,[11] she answers that it is done through the "[p]reserving of memory his and others, sometimes a pathetic attempt to hang the hope for better days on minute symbols, objects, rituals,... " (Melamed 2002). These shreds of memory communicate the horror to the reader. Ammiel Alcalay elaborates:

> "Writers are strange. Don't they know that the real stories aren't told since everyone knows them?" Here, and throughout the novel, Khoury masterfully uses the intimate relationship he has created

between Dr. Khalil and the reader to comment on the art of story-telling, to create an aesthetic that the stories themselves enact.

(Alcalay 2002)

The excerpt Alcalay chooses to highlight is downright prescient in its multivalence, simultaneously critiquing the abundance of representation given to tired, hegemonic images while also drawing attention to the culture of silence that surrounds narratives of "humiliation and interior defeat" (Khoury in Shammas interview), which Khoury distinguishes from the over-familiar images of Palestinians as heroic martyrs.

The temporal dimension of war and occupation is a critical image introduced through bread as part of the condition of hunger. Anton Shammas's magnum opus, *Arabesques* (1986) introduces this temporality not through bread but through dough. In general, Shammas laboriously constructs a hospitable Palestinian site—the arabesques—as a meticulously crafted home through which he navigates the story of the *nakba*, in Hebrew, the language of the occupier. He is nonetheless keen on answering the question of "how to describe a home to someone you love…?" (Shammas 2001, 149). Shammas' storytelling is a magical maze of hospitality that leads from the deepest interiority of being to the surface, a description that touches "from within the skin outside" (Shammas 1986, 133).

This same description that "touches you from inside" is a literary strategy that works on several structural levels, from within the body, the homes, the land, and the arabesques, to the form of the novel itself. In the description of the occupation of the village, we enter into Em Shacker's kitchen, but here time is measured not through clock time, but through an inner system with its own pulse of signification. "Em Shacker came home and saw that the dough she had kneaded hastily that morning had risen and was threatening to overflow the basin" (Shammas 2001, 122).

The time of occupation relies on intimate, internal parameters, for it is measured from within the gendered space of the kitchen, by the dough and the extent of its fermentation. In this ancillary site of domesticity, the rising of the dough becomes a temporal signal of emergency. Shammas's "bread clock" calls to mind the story of Exodus, where the baking of the matzah is the ultimate articulation of hastiness, fast food for those who are rushing to depart. In contrast, the rising dough highlights the temporal aspect of those who remain, a position that intensifies its presence within the physical home and the village, and within the literary home in which Shammas plays host. The narrative return to the kitchen is loaded with the signifying meaning of the banality of the occupation and its affect in the domestication of body and mind.

Insideness in *Arabesques* is a reading methodology to draw the reader into relationships with the Arabesques, a cultural grid that will teach her to engage in the culture of the occupied other, while still reading in

Hebrew. The intimate tone of love, the incredible gesture of Shammas's hospitality, seeks to enable the reader to unlearn national Zionist reading strategies in favor of acquiring alternative ones, although the novel is written in Hebrew. Bread in this grid has a critical role in the intersection of home and love. So rather than simply "un-Jewing the Hebrew language" as Hochberg suggests, (2007, 94), Shammas is reclaiming the Hebrew language by bringing us into the interiority of the Arabic culture and its unique Breadscape.

The history of the Nakba distinguishes between two groups of Palestinians, those who escaped or were exiled in 1948, and later came to form the Palestinian diaspora; and those who remained in Palestine. These trajectories are at the heart of the political tragedy around the Nakba and the Palestinian right of return.[12] Shammas's dough and Khoury's pita, in their own way, make the same distinction around the trope of hunger and food. Whereas Shammas's dough spirits one home, introducing its own capricious (or is it divine?) leavening, that when sour, can sour mind and history—Khoury's pita ruptures the possibility of any shelter. Unable to establish the coherent document of witnessing, Khoury's halved pita opens an unfinished new Breadscape of cultural cuts and tears, which fragments space, time, land, and mind, and breaks apart the very story and its ability to be told.

The Breadscape is able to articulate the singularity of the cultural condition. Benjamin talks about the distinction between *brot* and *pain*, and between the associations and allusions they convey, speaking to the wealth of symbolic meanings invested in as culturally variable a concept as "bread" (1968). Short narratives in these three major contributions have such significance not only in the narratives, but in the broader experience of the Nakba. Bread holds a huge space in the imagination of the Palestinian trauma as both the most concrete daily staple and the reference for life. It is through bread and pita that the depth of violence is articulated at the intersection of collapsed realities and emerging new ones, when one mouth replaces the other, generating rather than narratives, the threat of their silence.

In each work, the bread is tightly connected to the strategy of the narrative: dough in the homeliness of the home brings its people further inside, and shreds of pita on the road of exile are part of the fragmented reality of a story that cannot yet be brought home. In both cases, the authors are not intending to feed their readers. The longing for the story lies in the deeper remorse for memory. The burden to write the silence has replaced memory.

Notes

1 Khoury (2006), 214.
2 Khoury (2006), 517. The book was published in Arabic in 1998 and later translated to English by Humphrey Davies.

3 "Ha-'Aravit sheli 'Ilemet", in *Tsim'on Be'erot*, 2008, Tel Aviv: 'Am 'Oved. pp. 15–16.

4 See for example Shimon Adaf's science fiction short story, "Ishmael" in www.shortstoryproject.com/he/story/ישמעאל/

5 Al-Irani was first active during the early 1930s in Jaffa, where he was born, and after a few years in Jerusalem moved in 1942 to Amman, Jordan where he settled. In 1935–1936, still in Jaffa, he founded the magazine *al-Tahreer* ("the Liberation"), with Iskandar al-Ḥalabi. Al-Irani's short stories were first published in Arabic journals, and later in several collections, including his first collection *The Beginning of the Race* in 1937, *Among People*, which was published in 1953, and *Fingers in the Dark* in 1971.

6 The story appeared in the collection *The Beginning of the Race*, published in Jaffa, 1937. It was published in Hebrew in the collection *Palestinian Stories* (1970) that were edited and translated by Shimon Ballas, pp. 52–59.

7 Ihsan Tourjman, the author, did not live to see his twenty-fifth birthday; he survived the adversities of famine, cholera, locust attack, and the wholesale forced movement of population, but subsequently, in 1917, he was fatally shot by an officer of the withdrawing Ottoman army (Jacobson 2008, 34).

8 Khoury, a Lebanese novelist, playwright, critic, and prominent public intellectual, divides his time between Beirut and New York, where he teaches at NYU.

9 Shatila refugee camp is a camp in southern Beirut, originally established in 1949 by Palestinian refugees. It was also the site, on September 16–18 1982, of the Sabra and Shatila massacre, whereby the Christian Lebanese party Kataeb (Phalange), under orders from the IDF, killed between 762 and 3500 civilians. (www.unrwa.org/where-we-work/lebanon/camp-profiles?field= 15&qt-view__camps__camp_profiles_block=2#qt-view__camps__camp_ profiles_block)

10 This reminds us of Yehudit Katzir's narrative in Schlaffstunde, telling her story in front of the open grave. See Chapter 3.

11 Ariana Melamed Ynet, 20.2. 2002. www.ynet.co.il/articles/1,7340,L-168 2808,00.html

12 Emil Habibi, the foremost Palestinian author, intellectual and public figure, ensured before his death that his grave would bear the inscription "Emile Habibi – Remained in Haifa". This is also the title of Dalia Karpel's documentary on Habibi (1997).

Bibliography

Abdo, Nahla and Ronit Lentin, editors. 2002. *Women and the Politics of Military Confrontation: Palestinian and Israeli Gendered Narratives of Dislocation*. New York: Berghahn Books.

Abraham, Nicolas and Torok Maria. 1994. *The Shell and the Kernel*. Edited and translated by Nicholas T. Rand. Chicago: University of Chicago Press.

Adorno, Theodor W. 2005. *Critical Models: Interventions and Catchwords*. Translated by Henry W. Pickford. New York: Columbia University Press.

Adorno, Theodor W. 2006. *History and Freedom: Lectures 1964–1965*, edited by Rolf Tiedemann, trans. R. Livingston, Cambridge: Polity Press.

Agamben, Giorgio. 2002. *The Remnants of Auschwitz: The Witness and the Archive*. Translated by Daniel Heller-Roazen. New York: Zone Books.

Agnon, S.Y. 1960 [1932]. "'Pat Shlemah' (Perfect Bread)". In *Sefer Hama' asim (The Book of Deeds)*, 143–55. Jerusalem and Tel Aviv: Schocken.

Agnon, S.Y. 1966. *Sippurim ve-'Agadot (Stories and Tales)*. Jerusalem: Schocken.

Agnon, S.Y. 1998 [1962]. *Ha-Esh Veha-'Etsim (The Fire and the Woods)*. Jerusalem and Tel Aviv: Schocken.

Ahmed, Sara. 2004. "Affective Economies," *Social Text* 22, no. 2: 117–39. https://muse.jhu.edu/article/55780/summary

Aini, Lea. 2001. *Sdom'el (Sdommel)*. Tel Aviv: Hakibbutz Hameuchad.

Alcalay, Ammiel. 1993. *After Jews and Arabs: Remaking Levantine Culture*. Minneapolis: University of Minnesota Press.

Alcalay, Ammiel, editor. 1996. *Keys to the Garden: Israeli Writers in the Middle East*. San Francisco, CA: City Lights Books.

Alcalay, Ammiel. 2002. "1001 Palestinian Nights." In *The Village Voice*, March 19, 2002. www.villagevoice.com/arts/1001-palestinian-nights-7142446.

Alexander-Frizer, Tamar. 2004. *Milim Mashi'ot mi-Lechem (Words are Better than Bread)*. Jerusalem: Ben Zvi and Ben Gurion University of the Negev Press.

Al-Irani, Mahmoud Saif Al-Din. 1970 [1937]. "Kikar Lehem." In *Sipurim Palestinyim (Palestinian Short Stories)*, edited and translated by Shimon Ballas, 52–59. Tel Aviv: Eked.

Almog, Oz. 1997. *Ha-Tsabar – Profil (The Sabra – A Profile)*. Tel Aviv: Am Oved.

Almog, Oz. 1999. *Predah mi-Srulik, (Farewell to 'Srulik', Changing Values Among the Israeli Elite)*. Haifa: Haifa University Press.

Almog, Ruth. 1966. "A Good Spot." In *New Women's Writing From Israel*, edited by Risa Domb, 21–33. Elstree: Vallentine Mitchell.

Alter, Robert. 2004. *The Five Books of Moses: A Translation with Commentary*. New York: W. W. Norton & Company.

Alterman, Nathan. 1947. "*Magash ha-Kesef*" ("The Silver Platter"). *Davar*, "Hatur ha-Shvi'i". 19 December, 1947. Translated by Ami Isseroff, in *Historical Source Documents: Zionism, Israel and Palestine*. http://zionism-israel. com/hdoc/Silver_Platter.htm

Alterman, Nathan. 1962. "Al ha-Yeled Avram" ("About the Child Avram"). In *Ha-Tur ha-Shvi'i (The Seventh Column)*, vol. 2. Tel Aviv: Hakibbutz Hameuchad.

Althusser, Louis. 1994. "Ideology and Ideological State Apparatuses (Note Towards an Investigation)." In *Mapping Ideology*, edited by Slavoj Žižek, 100–40. New York: Verso.

Amichai, Yehuda. 1963. *Shirim 1948–1962 (Poems 1948–62)*. Jerusalem and Tel Aviv: Schocken.

Amichai, Yehuda. 1989. *Gam Ha-'Egrof Hayah Pa'am Yad Ptuchah ve-'Etsba'ot, (Even a Fist Was Once an Open Palm With Fingers)*. Jerusalem: Schocken.

Amichai, Yehuda. 1998. *Patuach Sagur Patuach: Shirim (Open Closed Open: Poems)*. Jerusalem and Tel Aviv: Schocken.

Amichai, Yehuda. 2000. *Open Closed Open: Poems*. Translated by Chana Bloch and Chana Kronfeld. New York: Harcourt, Inc.

Amichai, Yehuda. 2005. "Now, When the Waters Are Pressing Mightily." Translated by Leon Wieseltier. *The New Yorker*, January 10, 2005.

Anderson, Benedict. 1991. *Imagined Communities: Reflections on the Origin and Spread of Nationalism*. London: Verso.

Anidjar, Gil. 1996. "Jewish Mysticism Alterable and Unalterable: On Orienting Kabbalah Studies and 'the Zohar of Christian Spain.'" *Jewish Social Studies* 3 (Fall): 89–157.

Anidjar, Gil. 1997. "On the (Under)Cutting Edge: Does Jewish Memory Need Sharpening?" In *Jews and Other Differences*, edited by Jonathan Boyarin and Daniel Boyarin, 360–96. Minneapolis: University of Minnesota Press.

Anidjar, Gil. 2003a. *The Jew, The Arab: A History of the Enemy*. Stanford, CA: Stanford University Press.

Anidjar, Gil. 2003b. "The Jew, the Arab: An Interview with Gil Anidjar." Interviewed by Nermeen Shaikh. The Asia Society. http://asiasociety.org/ jew-arab-interview-gil-anidjar

Arens, William. 1998. "Rethinking Anthropophagy." In *Cannibalism and the Colonial World*, edited by Francis Barker, Peter Hulme and Margaret Iverson, 39–62. Cambridge: Cambridge University Press.

Asad, Talal. 2003. *Formation of the Secular: Christianity, Islam, Modernity*. Stanford, CA: Stanford University Press.

Austin, J.L. 1962. *How to Do Things with Words*. Oxford: Oxford University Press.

Avidan, David. 1978. "Tyutah" (A Draft). In *Shirim 'Ekroniyim (Axiomatic Poems)*, 48. Jerusalem: 'Achshav.

Avneri, Uri. 2007. "*Mitat Sdom*" ("Sodom Bad"). *Haaretz*, April 22, 2007.

Azoulay, Ariella. 2008. *Alimut Mechonenet: 1947–1950 Constituent Violence, 1947–1950*. Tel Aviv: Resling.

Azoulay, Ariella and Adi Ophir. 2002. *Yamim Ra'im: Ben Ason le-Utopia* (Bad Days: Between Disaster and Utopia). Tel Aviv: Fetish, Resling.

Bachar, Eli. 1982. *Tor La-'Ahavah (Appointment for Love)*. Tel-Aviv: Stavit ('Akhshav).

Baklash, Rivka. 2007. "*Dimuy ha-Meraglim: Transformatsyah me-'Eretz Za-vat Chalav u-Dvash' le-'Eretz 'Ochelet Yoshvehah'*" The Image of the Spies: Transformation from 'a Land of Milk and Honey' to 'a Land that Devours its People,'" nes Mutar, Tel Aviv. www.mofet.macam.ac.il/amitim/hashiva/Documents/תרומתאומנויות-נספח-4תשע.pdf

Bal, Mieke. 1988a. *Lethal Love*. Bloomington: Indiana University Press.

Bal, Mieke. 1988b. "The Rape of Narrative and the Narrative of Rape: Speech Acts and Body Language in Judges." In *Literature and the Body*, edited by Elaine Scarry. Baltimore, MD: Johns Hopkins University Press.

Ballas, Shimon. 2003. *Tel Aviv Mizrach: Trilogiah (Tel Aviv East: Trilogy)*. Tel Aviv: Hakibbitz Hameuchad.

Barbash, Benny. 1994. *Mai First Sony (My First Sony)*. Tel Aviv: Hakibbutz Hameuchad.

Barbash, Benny. 2005. *My First Sony*. Translated by Dalya Bilu. London: Review.

Bartov, Omen. 2005. *The "Jew" in Cinema: From the Golem to Don't Touch My Holocaust*. Bloomington: Indiana University Press.

Bashir, Abu-Manneh. 2014. "Palestinian Trajectories: Novel and Politics since 1948." *Modern Language Quarterly* 75, no. 4: 511–39. doi: 10.1215/00267929-2796886

Bat-Zion, Ella (Gavriella Elisha). 1993. "Meh Chalamti?" ("What did I Dream?"). High Holiday Supplement, *Ha-Me'asef*, 7.

Behar, Almog. 2008. "'*Al Shiratah shel Bracha Seri*" "On the Poetry of Bracha Serri." *Almog Behar* April 18, 2008. https://almogbehar.wordpress.com/2008/04/18/על-שירתה-של-ברכה-סרי/

bell, hooks. 2001. "Eating the Other: Desire and Resistance." In *Media and Cultural Studies, Keyworks*, edited by Meenakshi Gigi Durham and Douglas M. Kellner, 426–38. Oxford: Blackwell.

Bellei, S.L.P. 1998. "Brazilian Anthropophagy Revisited." In *Cannibalism and the Colonial World*, edited by Francis Barker, Peter Hulme and Margaret Iverson, 87–109. Cambridge: Cambridge University Press.

Ben-Ari, Eyal and Yoram Bilu, editors. 1997. *Grasping Land: Space and Place in Contemporary Israeli Discourse and Experience*. Albany, NY: State University of New York Press.

Benjamin, Jessica. 1988. *The Bonds of Love: Psychoanalysis, Feminism, and the Problem of Domination*. New York: Pantheon Books.

Benjamin, Walter. 1968. *Illuminations: Essays and Reflections*. Translated by Henry Zohn. Edited by Hannah Arendt. Tel Aviv: Schocken Books.

Benjamin, Walter. 1996. "On Language as Such and on the Language of Man." In *Selected Writings, Volume 1, 1913–1926*, translated by Edmund Jephcott, 62–74. Cambridge, MA: Harvard University Press.

Ben-Naftali, Michal. 2000. *Khronikah shel Predah, A Chronicle of Separation: On Deconstruction's Disillusioned Love*. Tel Aviv: Resling.

Ben-Naftali, Michal. 2006. *Sefer Yaldut (Childhood, a Book)*. Tel Aviv: Resling.

Ben-Yehuda, Eliezer. 1959. *Milon ha-Lashon ha-'Ivrit ha-Yeshanah veha-Chadashah (Complete Dictionary of Ancient and Modern Hebrew)*. Jerusalem: Thomas Yosseloff.

Ben-Zvi, Tai and Yael Lerer, editors. 2001. *Self Portrait: Palestinian Women's Art*. Tel Aviv: Andalus.

Berg, Nancy. 1996. *Exile from Exile: Israeli Writers from Iraq*. Albany, NY: State University of New York Press.

Berger, Tamar. 1998. *Dionisos be-Dizingof Senter (Dionysus at Dizengof Center)*. Tel Aviv: Hakibbutz Hameuchad.

Berkovitch, Nitza. 1997. "Motherhood as a National Mission: The Construction of Womanhood in the Legal Discourse in Israel." *Women's Studies International Forum* 20, no. 5: 605–19. doi: 10.1016/S0277-5395(97)00055-1

Berkovitch, Nitza. 2001. "Ezrachut ve-'Imahut: Ma'amadan shel ha-Nashim be-Yisra'el" (Citizenship and Motherhood: Women's Status in Israel). In *Yisra'el: me-Chevrah Meguyeset le-Chevrah 'Ezrachit (Israel: From a Recruited Society to a Civil Society)*, edited by Yoav Peled and Adi Ofir, 206–43. Tel Aviv: Hakibbutz Hameuchad.

Berlovitz, Yaffah. 1996. *Lehamtsi 'Eretz Lehamtsi 'Am (Inventing a Land, Inventing a People)*. Tel Aviv: Hakibbutz Hameuchad.

Berlovitz, Yaffah. 2009. "Prose Writing in the Yishuv: 1882–1948." *Jewish Women: A Comprehensive Historical Encyclopedia*, March 1. http://jwa.org/encyclopedia/article/prose-writing-in-yishuv-1882–1948

Bhabha, Homi K. 1994. *The Location of Culture*. London: Routledge.

Biale, David. 1992. *Eros and the Jews: From Biblical Israel to Contemporary America*. Berkeley: University of California Press.

Biale, David, editor. 2002. *Cultures of the Jews: A New History*. New York: Schocken Books.

Bialik, Hayim Nahman. 1904. "'Al ha-Shchitah," ("City of Slaughter"). In *Shirim (Poetry)*. Warsaw: Dvir.

Blumental, Yisrael. 1947. *'Agadot Rut (Ruth in the Midrash)*. Jerusalem: Spero Publishing Co.

Borges, Jorge Luis. 1962. *Ficciones*. Translated by Anthony Kerrigan. New York: Grove Press.

Boullata, K. 2001. "'Asim Abu Shaqra: The Artist's Eye and the Cactus Tree." *Journal of Palestine Studies* 30, no. 4: 68–82. doi: 10.1525/jps.2001.30.4.68

Bourdieu, Pierre. 1990. *The Logic of Practice*. Translated by Richard Nice. Stanford, CA: Stanford University Press.

Bourdieu, Pierre. 1991. *Language & Symbolic Power*. Cambridge, MA: Harvard University Press.

Bourdieu, Pierre. 1994. "Doxa and Common Life: An Interview with Terry Eagleton." In *Mapping Ideology*, edited by Slavoj Žižek, 265–77. New York: Verso.

Bourdieu, Pierre. 1995. "Physical Space, Social Space and Habitus." *Lecture*, Institutt for sosiologi og samfunnsgeografi, Universitetet i Oslo.

Boyarin, Daniel. 1997. "Colonial Drag: Zionism, Gender, and Mimicry." *Te'oryah u-Vikoret* 11: 123–44.

Brenner, Yosef Haim. 1900. "Pat-Lechem" ("A loaf of bread"). *The Ben Yehuda Project*. http://benyehuda.org/brenner/pat.html

Brinker, Menachem. 1989. *Ha-'im Torat-ha-Sifrut 'Efsharit? (Is Literary Theory Possible?)*. Tel Aviv: Sifriyat Po'alim.

Butler, Judith. 1988. "Performative Acts and Gender Constitution: An Essay in Phenomenology and Feminist Theory." *Theatre Journal* 40, no. 4 (December): 519–31.

Butler, Judith. 1999. *Gender Trouble*. 2nd ed., New York: Routledge.

Butler, Judith. 1993. *Bodies that Matter*. New York: Routledge.

Caruth, Cathy. 1995. *Trauma: Explorations in Memory*. Baltimore, MD and London: The John Hopkins University Press.

Cernea, Ruth Fredman. 1981. *Passover Seder: An Anthropological Perspective on Jewish Culture*. Lanham, MD: University Press of America.

Chen, Nancy. 1992. "'Speaking Nearby:' A Conversation with Trinh Minh-Ha." *Visual Anthropology Review* 8 no. 1: 82–91.

Chetrit, Sami Shalom. 1996. "On the Way to Ein Harod." In *Keys to the Garden: Israeli Writers in the Middle East*, translated by Ammiel Alcalay, 358. San Francisco, CA: City Lights Books.

Chetrit, Sami Shalom. 1997. "The Dream and the Nightmare: Some Remarks on the New Discourse in Mizrahi Politics in Israel, 1980–1996." *News from Within* 13: 49–59.

Chetrit, Sami Shalom. 2003. *"Ba-Derekh le-'Ein Charod"* ("On the Way to Ein Harod"). In *Shirim Be-Ashdodit*, 30. Tel Aviv: Andalus.

Chetrit, Sami Shalom. 2010. "Revisiting Bialik: A Radical Mizrahi Reading of the Jewish National Poet." *Comparative Literature* 62, no. 1: 1–21.

Cixous, Hélène. 1976. "The Laugh of the Medusa." Translated by Keith Cohen and Paula Cohen. *Signs* 1, no. 4 (Summer): 875–93.

Cixous, Hélène. 1986. *Inside*. Translated by Carol Barko. New York: Schocken.

Cixous, Hélène. 1991. *Coming to Writing and Other Essays*. Edited by Deborah Jenson, translated by Sarah Cornell, Deborah Jenson, Ann Liddle and Susan Sellers. Cambridge, MA: Harvard University Press.

Cixous, Hélène and Catherine Clément. 1986. *The Newly Born Woman*. Translated by Betsy Wing. Minneapolis: University of Minnesota Press.

Clifford, James. 1986. "Introduction: Partial Truth." In *Writing Culture: The Poetics and Politics of Ethnography*, edited by James Clifford and George Marcus, 1–26. Berkeley: University of California Press.

Cohen, Yisrael. 2015. *"Ha'azinu: Yitschak Navon Meshachzer 'et Pgishat Ben-Gurion veha-Chazon 'Ish of Blessed Memory"* ("Listen: Yitzhak Navon Recalls the Meeting Between Ben Gurion and the Chazon Ish"). *Kikar Hashabat*, November 7, 2015. www.kikar.co.il/abroad/184900.html

Cole, Tim. 2004. "Nativization and Nationalization: A Comparative Landscape Study of Holocaust Museums in Israel, the US and the UK." *Journal of Israeli History* 23, no. 1 (Spring): 130–45. doi: 10.1080/1353104042000241965

Culler, Jonathan. 1997. *Literary Theory: A Very Short Introduction*. Oxford: Oxford University Press.

Dahan-Kalev, Henriette. "Henriette, You're So Pretty–You Don't Look Moroccan." *Israel Studies* 6, no. 1: 1–14. doi: 10.1353/is.2001.0002

Danon, Efrat. 2004. *Dag ba-Beten (Bellyfish)*. Tel Aviv: Hakibbutz Hameuchad.

Darr, Yael. 2006. *Umi-Safsal ha-Limudim Lukachnu (Called Away from Our School-Desk)*. Jerusalem: Magnes and Hebrew University Press.

Darwish, Mahmoud. 2013. *Unfortunately It was Paradise: Selected Poems*. Translated by Munir Akash and Carolyn Forché. Berkeley: University of California Press.

de Lange, N.R.M. 1997. *Midrash Tanhuma*. Translated into English with Indexes and Brief Notes. (S. Buber Recension.) Volume II. *Exodus and Leviticus*. John T. Townsend. Hoboken, NJ: Ktav.

Deleuze, Gilles and Félix Guattari. 1986. *Kafka: Towards a Minor Literature*. Translated by Dana Polan. Minnesota: University of Minnesota Press.

de Man, Paul. 1979. *Allegories of Reading*. New Haven, CT and London: Yale University Press.

Derrida Jacques. 1974. *Of Grammatology*. Baltimore, MD: Johns Hopkins University Press.

Derrida, Jacques. 1982. *Positions*. Translated by Alan Bass. Chicago, IL: University of Chicago Press.

Derrida, Jacques. 1987. *"Geschlecht* II: Heidegger's Hand." In *Deconstruction and Philosophy: The Texts of Jacques Derrida*, edited by John Sallis, translated by John Leavey Jr., 161–96. Chicago: The University of Chicago Press.

Derrida, Jacques. 1988. *Limited Inc*. Evanston, IL: Northwestern University Press.

Derrida, Jacques. 1998. *Monolingualism of the Other; or, The Prosthesis of Origin*. Translated by Patrick Mensah. Stanford, CA: Stanford University Press.

Derrida, Jacques. 2000. *Of Hospitality: Anne Dufourmantelle Invites Jacques Derrida to Respond*. Translated by Rachel Bowlby. Stanford, CA: Stanford University Press.

Derrida, Jacques. 2002. *Acts of Religion*. Edited and with an introduction by Gil Anidjar. New York and London: Routledge.

Deutsch, Helene. 1965. "Some Forms of Emotional Disturbance and their Relationship to Schizophrenia." In *Neuroses and Character Types: Clinical Psychoanalytic Studies*, edited by John D Sutherland and M. Masud R. Khan, 262–81. New York: International Universities Press.

Disch, Lisa and Mary Hawkesworth. 2016. "Agency as Resistance." In *The Oxford Handbook of Feminist Theory*, edited by Lisa Disch and Mary Hawkesworth, 44–46. Oxford: Oxford University Press.

Dominguez, Virginia. 1989. *People as Subject, People as Object: Selfhood and Peoplehood in Contemporary Israel*. Madison: University of Wisconsin Press.

Dundes, Alan. 1977. "Seeing is Believing." *Natural History* 81, no. 5: 8, 10–12, 86–87.

Durkheim, Emile. 1915. *The Elementary Forms of the Religious Life*. Translated by Joseph Swain. Oxford: Pantianos Classics.

Durkheim, Emile. 1995. *The Elementary Forms of Religious Life*. Translated by Karen Fields. New York: The Free Press.

Elkana, Yehuda. 1988. *"bi-Zkhut ha-Shikhechah"* ("The Need to Forget"). *Haaretz*, March 2, 1988.

Elkayam, Shelley. 1983. *Nitsat Ha-Limon (The Lemon-Bud's Light)*. Jerusalem: 'Ekhut.

Elkayam, Shelley. 1987. *Shirat Ha-'Architekt (The Poetry [or Singing] of the Architect)*. Tel Aviv: Zamorah Biton.

Elkayam, Shelley. 1993. *"Le'an 'Ata 'Ohev 'Oti?"* ("Whereto Do You Love Me?"). Holiday Supplement in *Ha-Me'asaf*, 8.

English, Hugh. 2003. "Learning and Unlearning Historical Sexual Identities." *Radical Teacher* 66 (Spring): 5–10.

Ensler, Eve. 1998. *The Vagina Monologues*. New York: Villard Books.

Erlikh, Zur. 2010. *"Ha-machsan shel Ke-illu"* ("The Storehouse of Keillu"). *Makor Rishon Bainternet*. www.makorrishon.co.il/show.asp?id=16902

Even-Zohar, Itamar. 1980. *"ha-Tzmichah veha-Hitgabshut shel Tarbut 'Ivrit Mekomit ve-yelidit be-'Eretz Yisr'ael 1882–1948"* ("The Emergence of a Native Hebrew Culture in Palestine 1882–1948"). *Cathedra* 16: 165–89.

Exum, Cheryl. 1993. *Fragmented Women: Feminist (Sub)version of Biblical Narratives*. Sheffield: Sheffield Academic Press.

Ezrahi, Sidra Dekoven. 1999. "Back to the Future: The Jewish Bookshelf as Contraband." *Judaism* 48 (Fall): 397–406.

Fanon, Frantz. 1967. *Black Skin, White Masks*. Translated by Charles L. Markmann. New York: Grove Press.

Felman, Shoshana. 1992. "Education and Crisis, or the Vicissitudes of Teaching." In *Testimony: Crises of Witnessing in Literature, Psychoanalysis, and History*, edited by Shoshana Felman, and Dori Laub, 1–57. New York: Routledge.

Felman, Shoshana and Dori Laub. 1992. "Foreword." In *Testimony: Crises of Witnessing in Literature, Psychoanalysis, and History*, edited by Shoshana Felman, and Dori Laub, xiii–xx. New York: Routledge.

Fenster, Tovi. 2013. "Moving Between Addresses: Home and Belonging for Israeli Migrant and Palestinian Indigenous Women over 70." *Home Cultures* 10, no. 2: 159–88.

Fiener, Shmuel. 2010. *Shorshei ha-Chilun: Matiranut ve-Safkanutbe-Yahadut ha-Me'ah ha-18 (The Roots of Secularisation: Permissiveness and Skepticism in 18th century Judaism)*. Jerusalem: Merkaz Zalman Shazar Letoldot Ysrael.

Fogel, Yehezkel, editor. 1995. *Sefer Mikra'ot Temimot 'al Rut (The Complete Bible Commentary on Ruth)*. Jerusalem: Yachdav.

Foucault, Michel. 1982. *The Archaeology of Knowledge*. Translated by Sheridan Smith. New York: Pantheon Books.

Fox, Everett. 1997. *The Five Books of Moses*. The Schocken Bible, Volume 1. New York: Schocken Books.

Frankenberg, Ruth. 1997. "Introduction: Local Whitenesses, Localizing Whiteness." In *Displacing Whiteness: Essays in Social and Cultural Criticism*, edited by Ruth Frankenberg. Durham, NC: Duke University Press.

Freedman, H., Maurice Simon and Judah J. Slotki. 1939. *Midrash Rabbah*. London: Soncino Press.

Freud, Sigmund. 1958. *Basic Writings*. Translated by A.A. Brill. New York: The Modern Library.

Frymer-Kensky, Tikva. 2002. *Reading the Women of the Bible*. New York: Schocken Books.

Funkenstein, Amos. 1993. *Tadmit Ve-Toda'ah Historit Ba-Yahadut Ubi-Svivatah Ha-Tarbutit (Perceptions of Jewish History from Antiquity to the Present)*. Tel-Aviv: Am Oved.

Galai, Binyamin. 1959. "*Sdom Sity*" ("Sodom City"). In *Machazot (Plays)*. Tel Aviv: Dvir.

Gan, Alon. 2014. *Korbanutam Umanutam: mi-Siach Korbani le-Siah Riboni (From Victimhood to Sovereignty: An Analysis of the Victimization Discourse in Israel)*. Yerushalayim: The Israel Democracy Institute.

Gardi Tamar and U al-Ghubari, Noga Kadman, editors. 2012. *'Omrim Yeshnah 'Eretz (Once Upon a Land)*. Tel Aviv: Sedek, Zochrot/Pardes.

Gell, Alfred. 1999. *The Art of Anthropology: Essays and Diagrams*. London: Athlone Press.

Gershon, Shafir, Yoav Peled and Micael Feige. 2004. *Settling in the Hearts*. Detroit, MI: Wayne State University Press.

Giesen, Bernhard. 2004a. "Noncontemporaneity, Asynchronicity and Divided Memories." *Time & Society* 131: 27–40. doi: 10.1177/0961463X04040741

Giesen, Bernhard. 2004b. *Triumph and Trauma*. Boulder, CO: Paradigm.

Ginsburg, Shai.2010. "Introduction." In *Ha-Hitnagdut le-Te'oria (Resistance to Theory)* edited by Paul de Man, translated by Shai Ginsburg, 7–31. Tel Aviv: Resling.

Gizbar, Yehuda. 2014. *"Li-Zkor 'et 'Asher Shakhachnu"* ("To Remember that Which We Forgot"). *Ha-Krikhah Ha-'Achorit: She-Tihyi li- ha-Sakin (Be My Knife)*. https://gizbar.wordpress.com/tag/%D7%A9%D7%AA%D7%94%D7%99%D7%99-%D7%9C%D7%99-%D7%94%D7%A1%D7%9B%D7%99%D7%9F/

Gluzman, Michael 1997. "Longing for Heterosexuality: Zionism and Sexuality in Herzl's Altneuland." *Te'oryah u-Vikoret* 11: 145–62.

Goldberg, Amos. 2006. "Hakdamah" ("Introduction"). In *Li-Khtov Historia, li-khtov Traumah (Writing History, Writing Trauma)*, translated by Yaniv Farkas, 7–27. Tel Aviv: Resling.

Gouri, Haim. 1960. "Yerushah" ("Inheritance"). In *Shoshanat ha-Ruchot: Shirim (Compass Rose: Poems)*, 28. Tel Aviv: Hakibbutz Hameuchad.

Grossman, David. 1986. *Ayen 'Erekh ''Aahavah'*. Tel Aviv: Siman Kri'ah, Hakibutz Hameuchad.

Grossman, David. 1987. *Ha-Zman ha-Tsahov (Yellow Wind)*. Tel Aviv: Siman Kri'ah, Hakibbutz Hameuchad.

Grossman, David. 1989. *See Under Love*. Translated by Betsy Rosenberg. New York: Picador.

Grossman, David. 1998. *She-tihyi li Ha-sakin (Be My Knife)*. Tel Aviv: Hakibutz Hameuchad.

Grossman, David. 2001. *Be My Knife*. Translated by Vered Almog and Maya Gurantz. New York: Picador.

Grossman, David. 2008. *'Isha Borachat Mi-Besora (A Woman Escapes a Message)*. Tel Aviv: Hasifriyah Hachadashah.

Grossman, David. 2011. *To the End of the World*. Translated by Jessica Cohen. New York: Knopf.

Gur, Batyah. 2002. *Eini yodea mah yomru `alai ha-hem she-`od yavo'u* (I have no idea what those who come next will say about me), *Haaretz*, October 31, 2002.

Gurevitch, Zali. 1997. "The Double Site of Israel." In *Grasping Land*, edited by Eyal Ben-Ari and Yoram Bilu, 203–16. Albany, NY: State University of New York Press.

Gur-Ze'ev, Ilan. 2004. *Likrat Chinukh la-Galutiyut (Towards a Diasporic Education)*. Fetish series. Tel Aviv: Resling.

Halevi, Yossef. 1996. *Bat ha-Mizrach ha-Chadashah: 'al Yetsiratah shel Shoshana Shababo (The New Daughter of the East: On the Work of Shoshana Shababo)*. Ramat Gan: Bar Ilan University Press.

Hall, Stuart. 1998. "The Local and the Global: Globalization and Ethnicity." In *Dangerous Liaisons*, edited by McClintock, Mufti & Shohat, 173–87. Minneapolis: University of Minnesota Press.

Harries, Martin. 2007. *Forgetting Lot's Wife: On Destructive Spectatorship*. New York: Fordham University Press.

Harshav, Benjamin. 1993. *Language in Time of Revolution*. Stanford, CA: Stanford University Press.

Hassan, Riffat. 2006. "Islamic Hagar and Her Family." In *Hagar, Sarah and their Children*, edited by Phyllis Trible and Letty M. Russell, 149–67. Louisville, KY: Westminster Knox Press.

Hatuka, Tali. 2008. *Regei Tikun: 'Alimut Politit, Arkhitekturah veha-Merchav ha-'Ironi be-Tel Aviv (Revisionist Moments: Political Violence and Urban Space in Tel Aviv)*. Tel Aviv: Resling.

Hefling, Stephen. 2000. *Mahler: Das Lied von der Erde (The Song of the Earth)*. Cambridge: Cambridge University Press.

Heidegger, Martin. 1968. *What is Called Thinking?* Translated by Glenn Gray. New York: Harper & Row.

Heilbronner Oded and Michael Levin, editors. 2007. *Ben Sderot le-Sderot Rotshild (Between Sderot and Tel Aviv)*. Tel Aviv: Resling.

Herz Imber, Naftali. "Hatikvah." 1877. Iaşi: Publisher unknown.

Herzl, Theodor. 1896. *The Jewish State*. Translated by Sylvie D'Avigdor. MidEastWeb. www.mideastweb.org/jewishstate.pdf

Hess, Amira. 1993. "Hirhurim Be-'ikvot Mot Vivi" ("Reflections Following Vivi's Death"), High Holiday Supplement, *Ha-Me'asef*, 7.

Hever, Hannan. 2002. "Mappah shel Chol: Mi-Sifrut 'Ivrit le-Sifrut Yisra'elit" ("A Map of Sand: From Hebrew, to Israeli Literature"). *Te'oryah u-Vikoret* 20: 165–90.

Hever, Hannan, Shenhav Yehouda and Pnina Motzafi-Haller, editors. 2002. *Mizrahim be-Yisra'l: 'Iyun Bikorti Mechudash (Mizrahim in Israel: A Critical Observation into Israel's Ethnicity)*. Jerusalem: Makhon Van Lear, Hakibbutz Hameuchad.

Higgins, Lynn and Brenda Silver. 1991. *Rape and Representation*. New York: Columbia University Press.

Hill, Tom, JW. 2005. *Historicity and the Nakba Commemorations of 1998*. Florence: European University Institute Working Papers.

Hillis Miller, J. 2008. "Touching Derrida Touching Nancy: The Main Traits of Derrida's Hand." *Derrida Today* 1, no. 2 (November): 145–66.

Hirschfeld, Ariel. 2002. "Locus and Language: Hebrew Culture in Israel, 1890–1990." In *Cultures of the Jews*, edited by David Biale, 1011–60. New York: Schocken.

Hochberg, Gil. 2007. *In Spite of Partition: Jews, Arabs, and the Limits of Separatist Imagination*. Princeton, NJ: Princeton University Press.

Hollander, Aaron. 2007. "Impossible Ethics: A Response to the Sacrifice of Isaac." *Swarthmore Writing Associates Program*. www.swarthmore.edu/writing/impossible-ethics-a-response-to-sacrifice-isaac

Hollywood, Amy. 2002. "Performativity, Citationality, Ritualization." *History of Religions* 42, no. 2 (November): 93–115. www.jstor.org/stable/3176407

Horowitz, Amy. 1996. "Overcoming Music Ghettos: An Interview with Avihu Medina, Mizrahi Musician in Israel," *Cultural Survival Quarterly*, edited by Anthony Seeger 20, no. 4: 55–59.

Horowitz, Amy. 1999. "Israeli Mediterranean Music: Straddling Disputed Territories." *Journal of American Folklore* 112, no. 445 (Summer 1999): 450–63.

Hulme, Peter. 1998. "Introduction: The Cannibal Scene." In *Cannibalism and the Colonial World*, edited by F. Barker, P. Hulme and M. Iverson, 1–38. Cambridge: Cambridge University Press.

Illouz, Eva. 2014. "*Ve-hineh ha-Torah Shelanu: Sheshet ha-Dibrot la-Chiloni ha-Ge'eh*" ("And Here is our Torah"). *Haaretz*, June 5, 2014. www.haaretz. co.il/magazine/the-edge/.premium-1.2340449

Irigaray, Luce. 1977. *This Sex Which Is Not One.* Translated by Catherine Porter with Carolyn Burke. Ithaca, NY: Cornell University Press.

Irigaray, Luce. 1985. "The Mechanics of Fluids." In *This Sex Which is Not One*, translated by Catherine Porter and Carolyn Burke, 106–18. Ithaca, NY: Cornell University Press.

Izraeli, Dafna. 1997. "Gendering Military Service in Israel Defense Forces." *Israel Social Science Research* 12, no. 1: 129–66.

Jabès, Edmond. 1989. "Adam or the Birth of Anxiety." In *The Book of Shares*, translated by Rosmarie Waldrop, 25–28. Chicago, IL: University of Chicago Press.

Jacobson, Abigail. 2008. "Negotiating Ottomanism in Times of War: Jerusalem during World War I through the Eyes of a Local Muslim Resident." *International Journal of Middle East Studies* 40, no. 1: 69–88. www.jstor.org/stable/30069652

Jamal, Amal. 2003. "Palestinian Dynamics of Self-Representation: Identity and Difference in Palestinian Nationalism." *Hagar: Studies in Cultures, Polity & Identities* 4, no. 1–2: 123–43.

Jameson, Fredric. 1991. *Postmodernism, or, the Cultural Logic of Late Capitalism.* Durham, NC: Duke University Press.

Jayyusi, Salma Khadra, editor. 1995. *Anthology of Modern Palestinian Literature.* New York: Columbia University Press.

Kadman, Nogah. 2008. *Be-Tsidei ha-Derech uve-Shulei ha-Toda'ah (On the Sides of the Road and on the Margins of Consciousness).* Jerusalem: Sifre November.

Kafka, Franz. 1995 [1953]. *Letters to Milena.* Translated by Philip Boehm. New York: Schocken Books.

Kahn, Susan. 2000. *Reproducing Jews: A Cultural Account of Assisted Conception in Israel.* Durham, NC: Duke University Press.

Kanafani, Ghassan. 2000. *Palestine's Children: Return to Haifa and Other Stories.* Boulder, CO: Lynne Rienner Publisher.

Karpel, Dalia. 1999. "*Mah 'Ani 'Omeret 'al ha-'Intelektu'aliyut Sheli*" (What am I Saying about My Intellectualism"). *Haaretz*, February 12, 1999.

Kartun-Blum, Ruth. 1996. "*Pachad Yitshak: Mitos Aa-'Akedah'ke-Mikreh-Bochen ba-Shirah ha-'Ivrit ha-Chadashah*" ("The Fear of Isaac: The Myth of the Sacrifice as a Test-case in Modern Hebrew Poetry"). In *Mitos Ve-Zikaron (Myth and Memory)*, edited by David Ohana and Robert Wistrich, 231–47. Jerusalem: Van Lear Institute.

Kartun-Blum, Ruth. 1999. *Profane Scripture: Reflections on the Dialogue with the Bible in Modern Hebrew Poetry.* Cincinnati, OH: Hebrew Union College.

Katriel, Tamar. 1987. *Communal Webs.* Albany, NY: State University of New York Press.

Katz, Sheila Hannah. 1996. "Adam and Adama, 'Ird and Ard: En-gendering Political Conflict and Identity in Early Jewish and Palestinian Nationalisms." In *Gendering the Middle East: Emerging Perspectives*, edited by Deniz Kandiyoti, 85–105. London: I. B. Tauris.

Katzir, Yehudit. 1990. *Sogrim 'et ha-Yam* (*Closing the Sea*). Tel Aviv: Siman Kri'ah, Hakibbutz Hameuchad.

Katzir, Yehudit. 2006. *Closing the Sea*. Translated by Barbara Harshav. New York and London: Toby Press.

Kemp, Adriana, David Newman, Uri Ram and Oren Yiftachel, editors. 2004. *Israelis in Conflict: Hegemonies, Identities, and Challenges*. Portland, OR: Sussex Academic Press.

Kenan, Amos. 1984. *Ha-Derech le-Ein Harod* (*The Road to Ein Harod*). Tel Aviv: Am Oved.

Keynar, Gad. 1998. "The Holocaust Experience through Theatrical Profanation." In *Staging the Holocaust: The Shoah in Drama and Performance*, edited by Claude Schumacher, 53–69. New York: Columbia University Press.

Khoury, Elias. 1998. *Bab al-Shams* (*Gates of the Sun*). Tel Aviv: Andalus.

Khoury, Elias. 2006. *Gates of the Sun*. Translated by Humphrey Davies. New York: Picador.

Kilgour, Maggie. 1998. "The Function of Cannibalism at the Present Time." In *Cannibalism and the Colonial World*, edited by Francis Barker, Peter Hulme and Margaret Iverson, 238–59. Cambridge: Cambridge University Press.

Kimhi, David (RaDaK). 1842. *Perush Radak 'al ha-Torah: Sefer Bereshit* (*Commentary of Radak on the Bible: Genesis*). Presburg: Gedrukt Bay A. Fon Shmid.

Kimmerling, Baruch. 2001. *Ketz Shilton Ha-'Achusalim* (*The End of Ashkenazi Hegemony*). Jerusalem: Keter.

Kimmerling, Baruch. 2004. *Mehagrim, Mityashvim, Yelidim* (*Immigrants, Settlers, Natives*). Tel Aviv: Am Oved.

Kogan, Simona. 2007. "Photographer Adi Nes Connects Ancient and Modern Israel." *ISRAEL21c*. www.israel21c.org/photographer-adi-nes-connects-ancient-and-modern-israel/

Kristal, Merav. 2015. "*Mankal Shtraus: Mekhirat Tnuva le-Chevra Zarah-'Iyum 'Estrategi*" ("Straus's CEO: Selling Tnuva to a Foreign Company–a Strategic Threat"). *Ynet Economy*, June 15, 2015, www.ynet.co.il/articles/0,7340,L-4668794,00.html

Kristeva, Julia. 1980. "Word, Dialogue, and Novel." In *Desire in Language: A Semiotic Approach to Literature and Art*, edited by Léon Roudiez, translated by Alice Jardine, Thomas Gora and Léon Roudiez, 64–91. New York: Columbia University Press.

Kristeva, Julia. 1991. *Strangers to Ourselves*. Translated by Leon Roudiez. New York: Columbia University Press.

Kristeva, Julia. 1995. "Reading the Bible." In *New Maladies of the Soul*, translated by Ross Guberman, 115–26. New York: Columbia University Press.

Kronfeld, Chana. 1996. *On the Margins of Modernism*. Berkeley: University of California Press.

Kurzweil, Baruch. 1966. "An Analysis of the Story 'Pat Shlemah' ('Perfect Bread'), as a Model for Deciphering the Stories in the *Book of Deeds*." In *Essays on S.Y. Agnon's Stories*, 86–94. Jerusalem and Tel Aviv: Schocken.

Kurzweil, Baruch. 1970. *Mason 'al Sipure Agnon* (*Essays on Agnon's Stories*). Jerusalem: Schocken.

La Capra, Dominick. 2006. *Li-Khtov Historia, li-khtov Traumah* (*Writing History, Writing Trauma*). Translated by Yaniv Farkas. Tel Aviv: Resling.

Lacoue-Labarthe, Philippe and Jean-Luc Nancy. 1990. "The Nazi Myth." Translated by Brian Holmes. *Critical Inquiry* 16, no. 2 (Winter): 291–312.

Lacoue-Labarthe, Philippe and Jean-Luc Nancy. 2004. "*Ha-Mitos ha-Natsi*" ("*Le Mythe Nazi*"). Translated by Jonathan Goor. Tel Aviv: Resling.

Lamdan, Yizhak. 1982. "*Al ha-Mizbeiach*" ("Upon the Altar"). In *Kol Shirei Yitzchak Lamdan* (*Collected Poems*). Tel Aviv: Mosad Bialik.

Laor, Yitzhak. 1995. '*Anu Kotvim'Otakh Moledet* (*Narratives with No Natives: Essays*). Tel Aviv: Hakibbutz Hameuchad.

Laor, Yitzhak. 1999. *Ke-'Ayin* (*As if Nothing*). Tel Aviv: Hakibbutz Hameuchad.

Laub, Dori. 1992. "Bearing Witness or the Vicissitudes of Listening." In *Testimony: Crises of Witnessing in Literature, Psychoanalysis, and History*, edited by Shoshana Felman, 59–63. New York: Routledge.

Levi, Tikva. 1996. "Tikva Levi." In *Keys to the Garden: Israeli Writers in the Middle East*, edited by Ammiel Alcalay, 334–56. San Francisco, CA: City Lights Books.

Levin, Hanoch. 1987. *Mah 'Ikhpat la-Tsipor: Satirot, Ma'arkhonim, Pizmonim* (*What Does the Bird Care: Songs, Sketches and Satires*). Tel Aviv: Sifre Siman Kri'ah.

Levin, Hanoch. 1993. "The Sorrows of Job." In *Modern Israeli Drama in Translation*, edited by Michael Taub, 1–44. Portsmouth: Heinemann Press.

Levine, Mark. 2005. *Overthrowing Geography: Jaffa, Tel Aviv and the Struggle for Palestine, 1880–1948*. Berkeley: University of California Press.

Levine, Rabbi Aaron. *Kol Bo Le-Yahrzeit* (*The Complete Yizkor Handbook*). 2 vols. (no city): Zichron Meir Publications.

Levine, Stephan. 1991. "The Spirit of Exile: Interviews with Amos Gitai and Henry Alekan." *Framework* 38/39: 95–116.

Liebes, Tamar. 1997. "'*Tovah ha'Aretz Me'od Me'od': ha-Makor ha-Tanachi le-Be'ayat ha-'Obyektiviyut be-Divuach*" ("'Good is the Land Exceedingly, Exceedingly': The Biblical Origin for the Problem of Objectivity in Reporting"). *Dvarim Achadim* 2: 120–33. https://lib.cet.ac.il/pages/item.asp?item=21896

Liebman, Charles S. and Eliezer Don Yehia. 1983. *Civil Religion in Israel: Traditional Judaism and Political Culture in the Jewish State*. Berkeley: University of California Press.

Liebman, Charles S. and Yaacov Yadgar. 2009. "Secular-Jewish Identity and the Condition of Secular Judaism in Israel." In *Religion or Ethnicity? Jewish Identities in Evolution*, edited by Zvi Gitelman, 149–70. New Brunswick, NJ: Rutgers University Press.

Lubin, Orly. 1999. "Body and Territory: Women in Israeli Cinema." *Israel Studies* 4, no. 1: 175–87.

Lubin, Orly. 2002. "Israeli Cinema in its Socio-political Context: Resistance of the Popular." *Israel Studies Forum: An Interdisciplinary Journal* 17, no. 2: 61–85.

Lubin, Orly. 2003. '*Ishah Koret 'Ishah* (*Women Reading Women*). Zmorah, Bitan & Haifa: Haifa University Press.

The Marker. 2008. "*Ha-Sipur she-Me'akhrei Giv'at 'Amal B*" ("The Story behind Givat Amal Bet"). *The Marker Digital*, July 29, 2008. www.themarker.com/realestate/1.500282

Maimonides. 1999. *Rambam: Shemonah Perakim: A Treatise on the Soul.* Translated by Leonard Kravtiz and Kerry M. Olitzky. New York: UAHC Press.

Malkki, Liisa. 1992. "National Geographic: The Rooting of People and the Territorialization of National Identity among Scholars and Refugees." *Cultural Anthropology* 17, no. 1: 24–44. www.jstor.org/stable/656519

Margalit, Avishai. 2002. *The Ethics of Memory.* Cambridge, MA: Harvard University Press.

Martin, Elaine. 2006. "Re-reading Adorno: The 'After-Auschwitz' Aporia." *Forum* 2: 1–13.

Maschler, Yael. 2001. *"ve-Ke'ilu Haragláyim Sh'xa Nitka'ot bifním Kaze* ('and *like* your feet get stuck inside *like*'): Hebrew kaze ('like'), ke'ilu ('like'), and the Decline of Israeli *dugri* ('direct') Speech." *Discourse Studies* 3, no. 3: 295–326.

Massey, Doreen. 2005. *For Space.* London: Sage.

Mauss, Marcel. 1967. *The Gift: Forms and Functions of Exchange in Archaic Societies.* Translated by E. E. Evans-Pritchard. New York: Norton.

Melamed, Ariana. 2002. "Geography of Words: Ariana Melamed on *Bab El-Shams.*" *Ynet,* February 20, 2002.

Melamed, Ariana. 2008. *"Lo Agadah, Re'ai?"* ("It's not a Tale (Legend) my Friends"). *Haaretz,* February, 29, 2008.

Melamed, David. 2013. "'Eizo 'Agalah Mele'ah Yoter: Ha-Chilonit 'o ha-Charedit?" *NRG, Makor Rishon,* August 26, 2013. www.makorrishon.co.il/nrg/online/11/ART2/502/494.html

Melamed, Shmuel Moshe. 1945. *"Ha-Filosofyah shel -ha-Sifrut ha-'Ivrit"* ("The Philosophy of Hebrew Literature"). In *Mivchar ha-Masah ha-'Ivrit, me- Reshit ha-Haśkalah ve-'ad Yamenu (Selection of Hebrew Essays),* edited by Yaakov Becker and Shlomo Shpan, 556–62. Tel Aviv: Gazit.

Minh-ha, Trinh. 2011. "Far Away, From Home (The Comma Between)." In *Elsewhere within Here: Immigration, Refugeeism, and the Boundary Event,* 11–25. New York and London: Routledge.

Miron, Dan. 1984. "Modern Hebrew Literature: Zionist Perspectives and Israeli Realities." *Prooftexts* 4, no. 1: 49–69. www.jstor.org/stable/27815370

Mishani, Dror. 2003. "Riches from the East." *Haaretz,* December 26, 2003. www.haaretz.com/life/2.205/riches-from-the-east-1.109859

Montaigne, Michel de. 1928 (c. 1686). "Of Cannibals," *Essays of Montaigne, in 10 vols.* Translated by Charles Cotton. New York: Digireads.com. https://en.wikisource.org/wiki/The_Essays_of_Montaigne/Book_I/Chapter_XXX

Morris Benny. 2004. *The Birth of the Palestinian Refugee Problem Revisited.* New York: Cambridge University Press.

Mossinson, Yigal. 1949–1994. *Hasambah.* Series of 44 books. Tel Aviv: Yediot Ahronot.

Mulvey, Laura. 1999. "Visual Pleasure and Narrative Cinema." In *Film Theory and Criticism: Introductory Readings,* edited by Leo Braudy and Marshall Cohen, 833–44. New York: Oxford University Press.

Naficy, Hamid. 1999. "Framing Exile." In *Home, Exile, Homeland,* 1–13. Edited by Hamid Naficy, New York: Routledge.

Nakassis, Constantine V. 2013. "Citation and Citationality." *Signs and Society* 1, no. 1 (Spring): 51–78. doi: 10.1086/670165

Naqqash, Samir. 1996. "Signs in the Great Disorder: An Interview with Samir Naqqash by Ammiel Alcalay." In *Keys to the Garden: Israeli Writers in the Middle East*, edited by Ammiel Alcalay, 101–110. San Francisco, CA: City Lights Books.

Nes, Adi. 2008. "An Interview with Adi Nes." Interview by Jess Dugan. *Big, Red & Shiney*, April 27, 2008. https://web.archive.org/web/20090814190053/http://www.bigredandshiny.com/cgi-bin/retrieve.pl?issue=issue81&section=article&article=INTERVIEW_WITH_ADI_2574332

Neumann, Boaz. 2009. *Tshukat ha-Chalutsim* (*The Pioneers' Passion*). Tel Aviv: Am Oved.

Neumann, Boaz. 2011. *Land and Desire in Early Zionism*. Translated by Haim Watzman. Waltham, MA: Brandeis University Press.

Ofrat, Gideon. 2010. "*Birkat ha'Adamah u-Klalatah*" (The Blessing of the Land and its Curse"). http://gideonofrat.wordpress.com/2010/12/23/ברכת-האדמה-וקללתה

Ofrat, Gideon. 2014. "Ha-Meraglim she-Chazru min ha-Chom" (The Spies that Returned From the Heat). In *Ha-Machsan shel Gideon Ofrat* (*Gideon Ofret's Storage*). https://gideonofrat.wordpress.com/2014/06/13/המרגלים-שחזרו-מן-החום/

Ohana, David. 2017. *Nationalizing Judaism: Zionism as a Theological Ideology*. Lanham, MD: Lexington Books.

Ong, Aihwa. 1999. *Flexible Citizenship: The Cultural Logics of Transnationality*. Durham, NC: Duke University Press.

Ophir, Adi. 2000. "The Identity of the Victims and the Victims of Identity: A Critique of Zionist Ideology for a Post-Zionist Age." In *Mapping Jewish Identities*, edited by Laurence Jay Silberstein, 174–200. New York: NYU Press.

Ornan, Uzzi. 1999. "*Tsipornav shel Ashmadai: Shmonah Prakim be-Chiloniyut*" (*The Claws of Asmodai: Eight Chapters in Secularism*). Kiryat Tiv'on: 'Einam.

Oz, Amos. 1983. *Poh ve-Sham Be-'Eretz Yisra'el* (*Here and There in the Land of Israel*). Tel Aviv: Am Oved.

Pagis, Dan. 1991. *Kol Kitve* (*Collected Poems*). Jerusalem: Hakibbutz Hameuchad.

Pappe, Ilan. 2004. *A History of Modern Palestine*. New York: Cambridge University Press.

Pardes, Ilana. 1992. *Countertraditions in the Bible: A Feminist Approach*. Cambridge, MA: Harvard University Press.

Pardes, Ilana. 1994. "*Ledamyen 'et ha-Aretz ha-Muvtachat: Shneim 'Asar ha-Meraglim be-'Eretz ha-Nfilim*" ("Imagine the Promised Land: The Twelve Spies in the Land of the Giants"). *Te'oryah u-Vikoret* 5: 105–15.

Pardes, Ilana. 2000. *The Biography of Israel: National Narratives in the Bible*. Berkeley: University of California Press.

Pedaya, Haviva. 2006. "*Higi'a ha-Zman Lomar 'Ani''Acheret ba-Shirah ha-'Ivrit*" ("It's about Time to Say "I" Differently in Hebrew Poetry). *Haaretz*, May 8, 2006.

Peled, Rina. 2002. "*Ha-'Adam Ha-chadash'*" *shel Ha-mahpekhah Ha-tsiyonit* ("*The New Man' of the Zionist Revolution*"). Tel Aviv: Am Oved.

Perry, Menachem. 2008. "Bikoret borachat mi-Sefer: o"'al Chashivutam shel ha-Pratim ha-'Meyutarim,' o: be-Shevach ha-'Spoilerim'" ("A Review Escapes a Book"). *The New Library*, May 26, 2008.

Polliack, Meira. 2010. "Joseph's Journey: From Trauma to Resolution." In *Genesis, Texts @ Contexts*, edited by Athalya Brenner, Archi Chi-Chung Lee and Gale A. Yee, 147–75. Minneapolis, MN: Fortress Press.

Rabinowitz, Dan. 1997. *Overlooking Nazareth: The Ethnography of Exclusion in a Mixed Town in Galilee*. Cambridge: Cambridge University Press.

Ram, Uri. 2006. *Ha-Zman shel ha- 'Post':Le'umiyut veha-Politikah shel ha-Yeda' he-Yisra'el* (*The Time of the 'Post': Nationalism and the Politics of Knowledge in Israel*). Tel Aviv: Resling.

Ram, Uri. 2009. "Ways of Forgetting: Israel and the Obliterated Memory of the Palestinian Nakba." *Journal of Historical Sociology* 22, no. 3 (November): 366–95. doi: 10.1111/j.1467-6443.2009.01354.x

Ram, Uri. 2014. *Israeli Nationalism*. New York and London: Routledge.

Raz-Krakotzkin, Amnon. 1998. "*Orientalism, Mada'ei ha-Yahadut veha-Chevrah has-Yesra'elit: Mispar he'arot*" ("A Few Comments on Orientalism, Jewish Studies and Israeli Society"). *Jama'a* 3: 34–61.

Raz-Krakotzkin, Amnon. 1999. "A National Colonial Theology." *Tikkun* 14, no. 3: 11–16.

Regev, Motti. 2000. "To Have a Culture of Your Own: On Israeliness and Its Variants." *Ethnic and Racial Studies* 23, no. 2: 223–47. doi: 10.1080/014198700329033

Reshef, Yael. 2004. *Ha-Zemer ha-'Ivri be-Reshito: Perek be-Toldot ha-'Ivrit ha-Chadashah* (*The Early Hebrew Folk Song: A Chapter in the History of Modern Hebrew*). Jerusalem: The Bialik Institute.

Rogoff, Irit. 2000. *Terra Infirma: Geography's Visual Culture*. New York: Routledge.

Rokem, Freddie. 1998. "On the Fantastic in Holocaust Performances." In *Staging the Holocaust: The Shoah in Drama and Performance*, edited by Claude Schumacher, 40–52. New York: Columbia University Press.

Rosenberg-Friedman, Lilach. 2008. "The Nationalization of Motherhood and the Stretching of its Boundaries: Shelihot Aliyah and Evacuees in *Eretz* Israel (Palestine) in the 1940s." *Women's History Review* 17, no. 5: 767–85. doi: 10.1080/09612020802316249

Rosental, Ruvik. 2001. *Ha-'im Ha-shkhol Met?* (*Is Bereavement Dead?*). Jerusalem: Keter.

Rotbard, Sharon. 2005. *'Ir Levanah, 'Ir Shchorah* (*White City, Black City*). Tel Aviv: Bavel.

Rotbard, Sharon and Tsur Muki, editors. 2010. *Lo' be-Yafo ve-Lo' be-Tel Aviv: Sipurim, 'Eduyot ve-Te'udot mi-Shchunat Shapira* (*Neither in Jaffa nor in Tel Aviv: Stories, Testimonies and Documents from Shapira Neighborhood*). Tel Aviv: Bavel.

Rothberg, Michael. 1997. "After Adorno: Culture in the Wake of Catastrophe." *New German Critique* 72: 45–81. www.jstor.org/stable/488568

Rubin, Gayle. 1997. "The Traffic in Women: Notes on the 'Political Economy' of Sex." In *The Second Wave: A Reader in Feminist Theory*, edited by Linda Nicholson, 27–62. New York: Routledge.

Ruderman, David. 2010. *Early Modern Jewry: A New Cultural History*. Princeton, NJ: Princeton University Press.

Rudge, David. 2005. "Ezer Weizman Lauded as Man of Peace and Courage." *The Jerusalem Post*, April 27, 2005, www.highbeam.com/doc/1P1-108245583.html

Scarry, Elaine. 1985. *The Body in Pain: The Making and Unmaking of the World.* New York: Oxford University Press.

Schneider, Tammi. 2004. *Sarah: Mother of Nations.* New York: Continuum.

Schwartz, Regina M. 1998. *The Curse of Cain: The Violent Legacy of Monotheism.* Chicago, IL: University of Chicago Press.

Segev, Tom. 1991. *Ha-Milyon ha-Shvi'i: Ha-Yisra'elim veha-Sho'ah (The Seventh Million: The Israelis and the Holocaust).* Tel Aviv: Keter.

Semel, Nava. 2015. *Mizmor la-Tanach (Hymn to the Bible).* Raananah: Even Choshen.

Serres, Michel. 2007. *The Parasite.* Translated by Lawrence Schehr. Minneapolis: University of Minnesota Press.

Serri, Bracha. 1983. *Shiv'im Shire Shotetut (Seventy Poems of Wandering).* Jerusalem: Self published.

Serri, Bracha. 1990. *Parah 'Adumah (Red Cow).* Tel Aviv: Brerot.

Serri, Bracha. 1996. "I Am the Daughter of Lot." In *Keys to the Garden: Israeli Writers in the Middle East,* edited by Ammiel Alcalay, translated by Yonina Borvik and Ammiel Alcalay, 290–91. San Francisco, CA: City Lights Books.

Shababo, Shoshana. 2002 (1932). *Mariyah, Roman me-Chaye ha-Nezirot ba-'Aretz (Maria: A Novel on the Life of Nuns in Israel).* Tel Aviv: Mitzpeh, reprinted by Bimat Kedem.

Shababo, Shoshana. 1996. "*Yerach ha-Dvash*" ("The Honeymoon"). In *Bat ha-Mizrach ha-Chadashah: 'al Yetsiratah shel Shoshana Shababo (The New Daughter of the East: On the Work of Shoshana Shababo),* edited by Yossef Halevi, 218–28. Ramat Gan: Bar Ilan University Press.

Shafir, Gershon and Yoav Peled. 2002. *Being Israeli: The Dynamics of Multiple Citizenship.* Cambridge: Cambridge University Press.

Shahar, David. 1955. *'Al ha-Chalomot, Sippurim (Concerning Dreams: Short Stories).* Tel Aviv: Am Oved.

Shaked, Gershon. 1993. *Sifrut 'az, kan ve-'achshav (Literature Then, Here, and Now).* Tel Aviv: Zmorah Bitan.

Shaked, Gershon. 1998. *Ha-Siporet ha-'Ivrit 1880–1980,* vol. 5 (*Hebrew Narrative Fiction 1880–1980,* vol. 5). Tel Aviv: Hakibbutz Hameuchad.

Shalev, Meir. 1985. *Tanach Achshav (The Bible Now).* Jerusalem and Tel Aviv: Schocken.

Shalev, Meir. 1994. *Mabul, Nachash u-Shte Tevot: Sippure Tanach li-Yladim, (A Flood, Snake and Two Arks: Biblical Stories for Children).* Illustrated by Emanuele Luzzati. Jerusalem: Keter.

Shalev, Meir. 2015. "*Kidmah u-Masoret*" ("Progress and Tradition"). *Yediot Achronot,* Hamusaf le- Shabbat, September 1, 2015. www.yediot.co.il/articles/0,7340,L-4706013,00.html

Shalhoub-Kevorkian, Nadera. 2005. "Counter-Spaces as Resistance in Conflict Zones: Palestinian Women Recreating a Home." *Journal of Feminist Family Therapy* 17, no. 3–4: 109–41. doi: 10.1300/J086v17n03_07

Shamir, Zivah. 1990. "Sefer Chadash mishmeret chadashah" ("A New Book a New Shift"). *Iton 77,* 123, April 7, 1990.

Shammas. Anton. 1986. *'Arabeskot (Arabesques).* Tel Aviv: Am Oved.

Shammas, Anton. 1996. "Autocartography: The Case of Palestine, Michigan." In *The Geography of Identity,* edited by Patricia Yaeger, 466–75. Ann Arbor: University of Michigan Press.

Shammas, Anton. 1998. (Jacket Blurb) In *Bab al-Shams (Gates of the Sun)*, edited by Elias Khoury. Tel Aviv: Andalus.

Shammas, Anton. 2001. *Arabesques*. Translated by Vivian Eden. Berkeley: University of California Press.

Shammas, Anton. 2002. "A Fight for Life, not for Death: An Interview with Elias Khoury." *Yediot Ahronot Musaf 7 Yamim*, February 15, 2002.

Shammas, Anton. 2004. "West Jerusalem: Falafel, Cultural Cannibalism and the Poetics of Palestinian Space." Unpublished manuscript.

Sharabani, Udi. 2009. "*Mi she-Tsarikh le-Hikanes Yikanes*" ("Those Who Need to Enter, Enter"). *Ha'aretz*, April 8, 2009.

Sharoni, Simona. 1995. *Gender and the Israeli-Palestinian Conflict: The Politics of Women's Resistance*. Syracuse, NY: Syracuse University Press.

Sheleg, Yair. 2015. "*Ha-Sifrut Hafkhah le-Kolav Politi*" ("Literature Turned into a Political (Clothes) Hanger"). An Interview with Ziva Shamir, May 31, 2015. *Makor Rishon*, Shabbat, https://musaf-shabbat.com/2015/05/31/הספרות-הפכה-לקולב-פוליטי-יאיר-שלג/

Shenhav Yehuda. 2000. "*Merchav, 'Adamah, Bayit: 'al Hitnarmeluto shel 'Siach Chadash*" ("Space, Land, Home: On the Normalization of a New Discourse"). *Te'oryah u-Vikoret* (Spring): 16, 3–12.

Shenhav, Yehuda. 2003. *Ha-Yehudim-Ha-'Arvim, Le'umyut, Dat Ve-'Etniyut (The Arab-Jews: Nationalism, Religion and Ethnicity)*. Tel Aviv: Am Oved.

Sidon, Efrayim. 2003–2009. *Ha-Tanakh Ba-Charuzim (The Bible in Rhymes)*. Illustrated by David Polonski. Tel Aviv: Am Oved.

Shiffman, Smadar. 2013. "The Indelible Stamp of Reality on the Subject: David Grossman's to the End of the Land." *Hebrew Studies* 54: 359–71.

Shlonsky, Avraham. 1958. *Shirim (Poems)*. 2 vol. Tel Aviv: Sifriyat Poalim.

Shlonsky, Avraham. 1966. "Yizra'el" ("Jesrael"). In *Modern Hebrew Poetry: A Bilingual Anthology*, edited by Ruth Finer Mintz, 171–9. Berkeley: University of California Press.

Shlonsky, Avraham. 1971. *Ktavim, Shirim (Works, Poems)*. Volume 2, Jerusalem: Sifriyat Po'alim. https://bybe.benyehuda.org/read/11934

Shlonsky, Avraham. 1981. "Toil." In *The Penguin Book of Hebrew Verse*, translated by T. Carmi, 534. New York: Viking Press.

Shohat, Ella. 1988. "Sephardim in Israel: Zionism from the Standpoint of its Jewish Victims." *Social Text* 19/20: 1–35. www.jstor.org/stable/466176

Shohat, Ella. 1989. *Israeli Cinema: East/West and the Politics of Representation*. Austin: University of Texas Press.

Shohat, Ella. 1996. "Mizrahi Feminism." *News from Within* 12, no. 4 (April): 17–26.

Shohat, Ella. 2001. *Zikhronot 'Asurim (Forbidden Reminiscences)*. Tel Aviv: Sidrat Keshet Ha-Mizrah 2, Bimat Kedem Le-Sifrut.

Shohat, Ella and Robert Stam. 1994. *Unthinking Eurocentrism: Multiculturalism and the Media*. New York: Routledge.

Silberstein, Laurence J. 2000. *PostZionist Debates: Knowledge and Power in Israeli Culture*. New York: Routledge.

Silverman, Orna. 2009. "*Yitshak Kvar lo Rotseh: ha-Mecha'ah Neged Mitos ha-Hakravah ha-Le'umit*" ("Yitshak no Longer Wants: Protest Against the Myth of National Sacrifice"). Mendel Leadership Institute. http://mikranet.cet.ac.il/mikradidact/pages/printitem.asp?item=19402

Someck, Ronny. 2002. *The Fire Stays in Red: Poems*. Translated by Moshe Dor and Barbara Goldberg. Madison: University of Wisconsin Press.

Sorotzkin, David. 2014. *"Yesodoteha shel ha-Chiloniyut"* ("The Principles of Secularism"). *Te'oryah u-Vikoret* 42: 293–312.

Steiner, George. 1985. "Our Homeland, the Text." *Salmagundi* 66 (Winter–Spring): 4–25.

Stern, Ramón J. 2013. "Geographies of Escape: Diasporic Difference and Arab Ethnicity Re-examined." PhD diss., University of Michigan.

Stowasser, Barbara Freyer. 1996. *Women in the Quran, Traditions, and Interpretation*. Oxford: Oxford University Press.

Suisa, Albert. 1990. *'Akud (The Bound)*. Tel Aviv: Hakibbutz Hameuchad.

Suisa, Albert. 1992. "Escaping the Cauldron Unscathed." Translated by Marsha Weinstein. *The Melton Journal* 26 (Autumn): 14.

Suisa, Albert. 2012. "Bound Together: My (Isaac's) Longing for Ishmael." Ann Arbor, MI: Lecture, University of Michigan, March 28, 2012.

Suisa, Albert. 2013. "'Akud" ("Bound"). Translated by Ramón J. Stern. Unpublished.

Tamari, Salim and Hammami Rema. 1998. "Virtual Returns to Jaffa." *Journal of Palestine Studies* 27, no. 4 (Summer): 65–79. www.jstor.org/stable/2538131

Taylor, Mark. 1993. "Foreword." In *The Book of Margins*, edited by Edmond Jabès, ix–xvii. Chicago, IL: University of Chicago Press.

Teubal, Savina. 1984. *Sarah the Priestess: The First Matriarch of Genesis*. Athens: Ohio University Press & Swallow Press.

Tevet, Shabtai. 1997. The Burning Ground. Two Volumes. Biography of David Ben-Gurion. Tel Aviv: Schoken.

Theodor, Julius and Chanoch Albeck, editors. 1965. *Midrash Bereshit Rabba: Critical Edition with Notes and Commentary*. 5 vol. Jerusalem: Wahrmann.

Tolan, Sandy. 2007. *The Lemon Tree*. London: Transworld Publishers.

Toury, Gideon. 1998. *"Ivrut shmot mishpacha be-'Eretz Yisrael k-'tirgum tarbuti"; Targil shildi be-misgeret ha-semiotikah shel ha-Tarbut"* ("Hebraization of Family Names in (pre-1948) Israel as a "Cultural Translation": A Precursory Exercise in the Semiotics of Culture"). In *Nekudot Tatspit: Tarbut ve-Chevrah be-'Eretz Yisrael (Perspective: Culture and Society in the Land of Israel)*, edited by Nurit Gertz, Perspectives: Culture and Society in (pre-1948) Israel, 152–71. Tel Aviv: Open University.

Tsoffar, Ruth. 2006a. *The Stains of Culture: An Ethno-reading of Karaite Jewish Women*. Detroit, MI: Wayne State University Press.

Tsoffar, Ruth. 2006b. "'A Land that Devours its People:' Mizrahi Writing from the Gut." *Body & Society* 12, no. 2: 25–55.

Tsoffar, Ruth. 2007. "The Trauma of Genealogy: Ruth and Lot's Daughters." *Women in Judaism: A Multidisciplinary Journal* 5, 1: 1–13.

Tsoffar Ruth. 2009. "The Trajectory of Hunger: Appropriation and Prophecy in the Book of Ruth." In *Sacred Tropes: Tanakh, New Testament, Qur'an as Literary Works*, edited by Roberta Sabbath, 257–74. Leiden: Brill.

Tzur-Gluzman, Masha. 2013. *"Agnon Chotseh 'et ha-Kavim,"* Agnon Crosses the Lines. *Haaretz*, January 25, 2013. www.haaretz.co.il/1.1911582

Vaihinger, Hans. 1968. *The Philosophy of 'As if': A System of the Theoretical, Practical and Religious Fictions of Mankind*.

Vellas, B.M. 1954. "The Book of Ruth and Its Purpose." *Theologia* [Athens] 25: 201–10.

Weiss, Meira. 2004. *The Chosen Body.* Stanford, CA: Stanford University Press.

Weiss, Ruchama. 2010. *'Ochlim La-da'at: Tafkidan ha-Tarbuti shel ha-Se'udot be-Sifrut Chazal* (*Eating to Know: The Cultural Role of the Supper in Rabbinic Literature*). Tel Aviv: Hakibbutz Hameuchad.

Weizman, Ezer. 1996. "President Weizman Speech to Bundestag-January 16, 1996." Israel Ministry of Foreign Affairs. https://mfa.gov.il/MFA/MFA-Archive/1996/Pages/President%20Weizman%20Speech%20to%20Bundestag%20-%20Jan%2016-%2019.aspx

Wolfe, Cary. 2007. "Introduction." In *The Parasite*, edited by Michel Serres, translated by Lawrence Schehr, xi–xxviii. Minneapolis: University of Minnesota Press.

Yadgar, Yaacov. 2010. "Maintaining Ambivalence: Religious Practice and Jewish Identity Among Israeli Traditionists—A Post-Secular Perspective." *Journal of Modern Jewish Studies* 9, no. 3: 397–419. doi: 10.1080/14725886.2010.518451

Yadgar, Yaakov. 2011. "A Post-Secular Look at Tradition: Toward a Definition of 'Traditionism.'" *Tellos* 156 (Fall): 77–98. doi: 10.3817/0911156077

Yaeger, Patricia. 2002. "Consuming Trauma; or, the Pleasures of Merely Circulating." In *Extremities: Trauma, Testimony and Communities*, edited by Nancy K. Miller and Jason Daniel Tougaw, 25–51. Chicago: University of Illinois Press.

Yerushalmi, Yosef Hayim. 1989. *Zakhor: Jewish History and Jewish Memory.* New York: Schocken Books.

Yiftachel, Oren. 1995. "The Dark Side of Modernism: Planning as Control of an Ethnic Minority." In *Postmodern Cities and Spaces*, edited by Sophie Watson and Katherine Gibson, 216–39. Oxford: Blackwell.

Yiftachel, Oren. 2006. *Ethnocracy: Land and Identity Politics in Israel/Palestine.* Philadelphia: University of Pennsylvania Press.

Yiftachel, Oren and Batya Roded. 2003. "*Moledet Lelo Gvulot: Al ha-Merchavim ha-Tsiyoniyim ba-Zemer uva-Nof*" ("Homeland without Borders"). In *Moledet/Mackdonald: Magamot Be-'itzuv ha-Merchav veha-Tarbut be-Israel* (*Homeland/Mcdonald: Trajectories of Shaping Space and Culture in Israel*), 8–68. Merkaz ha-Negev le-Pituach Ezori, Beer Sheva: Ben Gurion University.

Yonatan, Zehavi and Yarin Gan El. 2015. Ma'aseh Ha-'ez," (The Tale of the Goat). You Tube video, 1:25, posted by "Yonatan Zehavi," January 4, 2005. www.youtube.com/watch?v=H2tUQhFGtU4.

Yosef, Raz. 2004. *Beyond Flesh: Queer Masculinities and Nationalism in Israeli Cinema.* New Brunswick, NJ: Rutgers University Press.

Yosef, Raz. 2011. *The Politics of Loss and Trauma in Contemporary Israeli Cinema.* New York and London: Routledge.

Yue, Gang. 1999. *The Mouth that Begs: Hunger, Cannibalism, and the Politics of Eating in Modern China.* Durham, NC: Duke University Press.

Yuval-Davis, Nina. 1985. "Front and Rear: The Sexual Division of Labor in the Israeli Army." *Feminist Studies* 11, no. 3 (Fall): 649–75. doi: 10.2307/3180123

Zakai, Orian. 2011. "Entering the Records: Difference, Suffrage and the Autobiography of the New Hebrew Woman." *Nashim* 22, no. 1 (October): 136–61.

Zakim, Eric. 2006. *To Build and Be Built: Landscape, Literature, and the Construction of Zionist Identity.* Philadelphia: University of Pennsylvania Press.

Zameret, Zvi and Moshe Tlamim. 1999. "Judaism in Israel: Ben-Gurion's Private Beliefs and Public Policy." *Israel Studies* 4, no. 2: 64–89. www.jstor.org/stable/30245511

Zelda (Schneersohn Mishkovsky). 1974. *"Le-khol 'ish Yesh Shem"* ("Each of us has a Name"). In *'Al Tirchak*. Tel Aviv: Hakibbutz Hameuchad.

Zertal, Idith. 1996. *Zehavam shell ha-Yehudim (From Catastrophe to Power: Jewish Illegal Immigration to Palestine 1945–1948)*. Tel Aviv: Am Oved.

Zertal, Idith. 2010. *Israel's Holocaust and the Politics of Nationhood*. Cambridge: Cambridge University Press.

Zerubavel, Yael. 1995. *Recovered Roots: Collective Memory and the Making of Israeli National Tradition*. Chicago, IL: University of Chicago Press.

Zerubavel, Yael. 2002. "Rachel and the Female Voice: Labor, Gender, and the Zionist Pioneer Vision." In *History and Literature: New Perspectives of Jewish Texts in Honor of Arnold J. Band*, edited by William Cutter and David Jacobson, 303–17. Providence, RI: Program in Judaic Studies, Brown University.

Zerubavel, Yael. 2004. *"Krav, Hakravah, Korban: Tmurot Be'Idi'ologyat Ha-hakravah Ha-patriyotit be-Yisra'el"* ("Battle, Self-sacrifice, Victim: Changes in the Ideology of Patriotic [Self-] Sacrifice in Israel"). In *Patriotism: 'Ohavim 'Otakh Moledet (Patriotism: Homeland Love)*, edited by Avner Ben Amos and Daniel Bar Tal, 61–99. Tel-Aviv: Hakibbutz Hameuchad.

Zerubavel, Yael. 2013. *Mirkamim: Tarbut, Sifrut, Folklore le-Galit Hasan-Rokem (Textures: Culture, Literature, Folklore for Galit Hasan-Rokem)*, edited by Hagar Solomon and Avigdor Shinan, 755–73. Jerusalem: Hebrew University Press.

Zimmerman, Moshe. 2002. *'Al Tig'u li ba-Shoah (Leave my Holocaust Alone)*. Haifa: Haifa University Press & Zmorah-Bitan.

Ziv, Effi. 2012. *"Traumah 'Ikeshet"* ("Insidious Trauma"). *Mafteach* 5: 55–74.

Zivah Shamir. 2011. *Shai 'Olamot: Ribuy Panim Bi-Ytsirat Agnon (The Multi-faceted Agnon)*. Tel Aviv: Hakibbutz Hameuchad.

Zivoni, Idan. 2015. *"Sod ve-Safah: ba-chazarah le-sifrah ha-reahon shel Amirah Hess"* ("Secret and Language: Back to Amira Hess's First Book"). *Haaretz*, Sfarim, July 3, 2015.

Žižek, Slavoj. 1994. "Introduction: The Spectre of Ideology." In *Mapping Ideology*, edited by Slavoj Žižek, 1–33. New York: Verso.

Žižek, Slavoj. 1999. *The Žižek Reader*. Edited by Elizabeth Wright and Edmond Wright. Oxford: Blackwell.

Zlotowitz, Meir. 1994. *The Book of Ruth*. Brooklyn, NY: Mesorah Publications, Ltd.

Zlotowitz, Meir and Nosson Scherman. 1994 [1976]. *The Book of Ruth, a New Translation with a Commentary Anthologized from Talmudic, Midrashic, and Rabbinic Sources*. New York: Mesorah Publication.

Zuckermann, Moshe. 2001. *Charoshet ha-Yisra'eliyut: Mytosim ve-'Idiologia be-Chevrah Mesukhsekhet, (On the Fabrication of Israelism)*. Tel Aviv: Resling.

Zur-Glozman, Masha. 2013. "Agnon Chotseh 'et ha-Kavim" ("Agnon Crosses the Lines"). *Haaretz*, January 25, 2013. www.haaretz.co.il/literature/poetry/.premium-1.2674591

Filmography

Barbash, Benny and Uri Barbash. 1984. *Me'Ever La-Soragim (Beyond the Walls)*.

Gitai, Amos. 1986. *Esther.*

Gitai, Amos. 1989. *Berlin-Jerusalem.*

Gitai, Amos. 1992. *Golem, the Spirit of Exile.*

Karpel, Dalia. 1997. *Emil Habibi: I Stayed in Haifa.*

Politi, Edna. 1982. *Anu Banu: The Daughters of Utopia.*

Shaul, Dror. 2006. *Adama Meshuga'at (Sweet Mud).*

Sivan, Eyal, writer and director. 1991. *IZKOR, Slaves of Memory.* Documentary 98 minutes.

Sivan, Eyal. 1999. *The Specialist, Portrait of a Modern Criminal.*

Tlalim, Asher, director, screenwriter & editor. 1994. *Al Tig'u li ha-Shoah (Don't Touch My Holocaust).* Documentary 150 minutes. Israel: Set Pro.

Tsabari, Doron and Amir Ben-David. 2015. *Magash ha-Kesef (The Silver Platter).* 3 part TV series, 55 min.

Veile, Andres. *Balagan.* 1994. Video. 94 minutes, Color, Hebrew, English and German. JOURNAL-FILM Klaus Volkenborn KG.

Images and Performance

Hamori, George. 1954. *"Bul ha-Meraglim"* ("The Stamps of the Spies"). Israel.

Hanson, Duane. 1970. "Supermarket Shopper." Polyester Resin and Fiberglass in Oil, with Clothing and Wig, Steel Cart, and Groceries, Life-size.

Maayan, Dudu. 1991. *Arbeit Macht Frei.* Hebrew, English and German. Acco: Acco Theater Center.

Millet, Jean-François. 1857. "The Gleaners." Oil Painting, 2′ 9″ x 3′ 8″, Paris: Musée d'Orsay.

Naaman, Michal. 1974. *"Gdi be-chalav 'Imo—'Eretz 'Okhelet Yoshveha"* ("A Kid in its Mother's Milk—A Land that Devours its People"). Pencil on paper. Petach Tikva Museum of Art. www.petachtikvamuseum.com/he/Exhibitions. aspx?eid=1247&aid=1300&wid=1392&pi1

Naaman, Michal. 1974. *"Gdi be-chalav 'Imo"* ("A Kid in Its Mother's Milk"). Tel Aviv: Hakibbutz Gallery.

Nes, Adi. 2006. *Sidrat Sipure ha-Tanakh (Biblical Stories).* Photography.

Sefer, Menashe Nechushtan. 2004. "Hagar and Ishmael." Watercolor 50×35 cm.

Segev, Muli and Adam Sanderson, directors. 2012. *Zohi Sdom (This is Sodom).* Haifa: Haifa Theater.

Music

Amiran, Emanuel. 1959. *"Eretz Zavat Chalav"* ("A Land Flowing with Milk"). *Zemereshet.* (www.zemereshet.co.il/song.asp?id=541&artist=109)

Ben-Zaken, Etty. 2013. Rajmil Fischman, "Drills in Practical Hebrew," 2003. Text by Dan Pagis in *Rishume ha-Kol (Voice Drawings)*. Steinberg, Eitan & Etty Ben-Zaken.

Goldstein, Maor & Ido Frankel. 2009. "*Zeh shir 'al lekhem*" ("This is a Song about Bread"), by Armadillos, Domino Gross. https://shironet.mako.co.il/artist?type=lyrics&lang=1&prfid=202&wrkid=2444, www.youtube.com/watch?v=oCrSLU6EFlU

Sakharof, Berry. 1998. "*'Avadim*" ("Slaves"). In *Negi'ot*, Produced by Nizan Zeira, Israel.

Index

Note: *Italic* page numbers refer to figures and page numbers followed by "n" denote endnotes.

Printed in Great Britain
by Amazon

82302167R00142